W9-CLB-483

WILD FLOWER GUIDE

Northeastern and Midland
United States

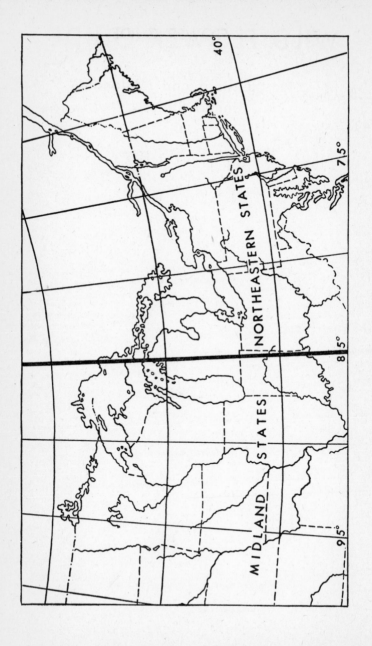

WILD FLOWER GUIDE

NORTHEASTERN AND
MIDLAND UNITED STATES

BY

Edgar T. Wherry

PROFESSOR OF BOTANY
UNIVERSITY OF PENNSYLVANIA

ILLUSTRATED BY

Tabea Hofmann

SPONSORED BY

THE WILD FLOWER

PRESERVATION SOCIETY

WASHINGTON, D.C.

1948

DOUBLEDAY & COMPANY, INC.

Garden City, New York

DEDICATED TO WILD FLOWER CONSERVATIONISTS WHO ARE

SUCCESSFULLY SAVING REMNANTS OF NATURAL

BEAUTY IN THE MIDST OF THE DRABNESS

OF THE CIVILIZED LANDSCAPE

CONTENTS

INTRODUCTION

THE STANDARD manuals of botany are so technical and cover so many species that they offer difficulty to the amateur who finds an attractive wild flower and desires to ascertain its name. There is accordingly need for field guides which will simplify the identification of the species likely to be observed; the present book represents such a guide for the most populous portion of North America.

In the United States east of longitude 100° and north of latitude 37°—that is, our Northeastern and Midland states—there grow about 400 species which are sufficiently striking to be classed as "wild flowers." Drawings of many of these, half of them in color, are here reproduced, accompanied by brief descriptive text.

Since in the interest of precision and brevity it is necessary to use in the text a number of technical terms, a glossary of these is given at the outset. Then the plants are taken up in a sequence which emphasizes their floral symmetry and its evolutionary relations. The views as to the evolution of flower features adopted are based on the principles enunciated by Bessey, Clements, and their followers. However, in order to aid students who prefer to use color as a guide for identification, a tabulation of the included species on this basis is included in an appendix.

The plants are first grouped into families, the characters of their representatives in the area covered being summarized. For each species there is given a common name, then a selected technical genus and species epithet. Next come brief statements as to distinctive features, range, and habitat. Finally, suggestions as to how the plants can be grown are added. Details as to the treatment of these topics are given on the following page.

COMMON NAME: This is a name in general use for a plant, or so descriptive that it can be appreciated by the non-specialist. When multiple names are known to be applied to individual species, the one deemed most appropriate or significant has been selected. The plans for constructing names advocated in *Standardized Plant Names* are followed, although hyphens are used more liberally than in that work.

TECHNICAL EPITHETS: To every plant there is allotted a genus and a species epithet. While these are selected on the basis of priority of publication, the views of taxonomists as to what constitutes priority change from time to time, resulting in the successive application of different epithets to the same plant. In the present book, therefore, a choice had to be made; synonyms preferred by other compilers can be found in botanical reference works. To guide in pronunciation, accents are here supplied: grave (`) indicating the long English sound of the vowel, acute (´) a shortened sound. *Trilliàceae* is pronounced, then, Trill ē ā see ē.

FEATURES: Under this heading the characters which set each species apart from others are given. While special emphasis is placed on floral structure, significant features of leaves, stems, roots, et cetera, are also mentioned. Dimensions stated represent usual or normal values, and may be exceeded by occasional individual plants.

RANGE: Here are given the regions in which each species is native. As shown in the map on page ii, the term Northeastern states is applied to those east of longitude 85° and Midland states to those between 85° and 100°.

HABITAT: The sort of place where the species normally grows is next stated, with special attention to soil features.

CULTURE: To grow a plant in an area where it does not occur naturally, its native habitat should of course be matched as closely as practicable. Supplementary notes as to the needs for cultivation of individual species are added.

INTRODUCED WILD FLOWERS: Species introduced from other countries, such as CHICORY, DAISY, DANDELION, etc., are not included with our native plants, but 100 of them are described in Appendix 3.

WILD FLOWER CONSERVATION

THE LARGE-SCALE disappearance of wild flowers is due primarily to agricultural development, the cutting of forests, the grazing of domestic livestock in grasslands, and so on. Erosion, ground fires, and general vandalism also account for considerable destruction. Fortunately there are occasional areas where, because of local conditions, agriculture is not profitable, and in these some of the natural beauty produced by wild flowers can be preserved. Even where partial destruction has occurred, attractive species can often be planted and protected against further damage, in wild-life sanctuaries, community water reserves, and other restricted areas.

In general, wild flowers will not thrive, however, when treated like cultivated plants. Many of them need specialized conditions of light, heat, moisture, soil, etc., as described for most of the individual species treated in this Guide, under the headings Habitat and Culture. The "reaction" of the soil is so important in this connection as to deserve special discussion. Soils in humid climates may be either essentially neutral or distinctly acid. The term "sour" is, however, not the same as the scientists' acid, and supposed criteria of "soil sourness" are not safe guides in wild flower culture. Whether a soil is really neutral or acid should always be established by tests with indicator dyes, such as are now on the market.

While it is simplest to plant only species adapted to the soil as it stands, a change in reaction may at times be called for. Neutralization can be effected by adding crushed limestone, manure, compost, leafmold, wood ashes, etc. To acidify a neutral soil, add acid humus materials such as peat, weathered sawdust, spent tanbark, pine, spruce, or hemlock needles; or, if the soil is already rich in humus, a light sprinkling of aluminum sulfate or powdered sulfur.

To develop and maintain a wild flower sanctuary successfully, then, plants should be set out in habitats closely similar to those in which they thrive under natural conditions. For some time thereafter they must be cared for, protected against drying out by a mulch of litter, and watered if the rainfall is scanty. Aggressive weeds, which are likely to spring up in disturbed soil, must be destroyed. The odor of freshly dug earth attracts mice, rabbits, squirrels, etc., which proceed to feed upon the newly set plants, even though they may not notice a long-established clump of the same species growing near by. To protect the tops, brush may be massed around them; and to discourage the destruction of bulbs, tubers, or fleshy roots, a handful or two of ½-in. rock chips with sharp edges should be packed around these.

From the conservation standpoint, it is desirable to propagate material to be used for planting from seeds or cuttings. In many cases, however, this is so slow and costly that digging of wild plants is resorted to. If an area is about to be cleared for agriculture, building, or other of civilization's needs, all desirable plants may as well be taken. The owners of wild land which is not to be devastated will often give permission for the digging of material; but anyone with conservation at heart will take only a third or half of the plants of any one species present, and so give nature a chance to restock the area. Wild flowers can also be purchased from dealers, some of whom pay the owners of land a fair recompense for what they remove, and are careful not to take all the plants of individual species.

The mere transplanting of a clump or colony of some desirable species from its native place to a new location does not, however, constitute wild flower conservation. When the normal life span of a plant is reached it will die; and the species will then be lost unless it has meanwhile carried out some process of reproduction, such as the forming of viable seeds or the development of offsets, runners, or other perennating structures. A given wild flower is only successfully conserved when young individuals begin to appear around the original clump, ready to take over when that passes on.

Information as to various phases of wild flower conservation can be obtained from organizations specializing in this field of activity, of which there are several in the regions covered in this book. Their work is co-ordinated by the national Wild Flower Preservation Society, Inc., the present address of which is 3740 Oliver St., Washington 15, D.C.

GLOSSARY

Acid: A chemical condition of water or moist soil capable of bringing the common indicator dyes to a red or yellow color.

Alternate: Arranged so that individual objects do not adjoin or face one another.

Anther: The enlarged tip of a stamen; in it pollen is formed.

Axis: An elongated stalk or other supporting structure.

Bilateral: Having two sides which are mirror images of one another, as the right and left hands.

Bisexual: Containing both male and female reproductive organs.

Blade: The flat terminal portion of a plant organ.

Bract: A leaf which is closely associated with a flower or a group of flowers; it may be peculiarly colored.

Bulb: A short stem closely enveloped by scales or leaf bases.

Calyx: The outermost part of a flower, comprising a group of sepals, which are often though not necessarily leaflike.

Capsule: A globular or cylindric dry multiple-seeded fruit.

Carpel: The female reproductive organ, located singly or in a group at the center of a flower (also termed pistil).

Compound: Made up of two or more parts.

Corolla: The showy part of the typical flower, situated just inside the calyx, and comprising a group of petals.

Entire: Continuous, and not interrupted by lobes or cuts.

Filament: The stalk of a stamen, which supports the anther.

Fruit: A matured carpel or group of carpels, irrespective of edibility; fruits may be either dry or fleshy.

Genus: A grouping of related species; plural, genera.

Gland: A waxy or sticky globule, often secreting fragrances.

Inflorescence: A group of flowers.

Lip: A division of a horizontally divided corolla or calyx.

Neutral: A chemical condition of water or moist soil with neither acidity nor its opposite, alkalinity, sufficiently developed to influence plant growth.

Node: The point on an axis where organs are borne.

Obsolete: Absent from a position where expected to be present.

Ovary: The hollow lower part of a carpel, containing ovules.

Palmate: Radiating, like the fingers from the palm.

Perianth: The calyx and corolla considered together.

Petal: The floral organ constituting the corolla.

Petiole: The stalk supporting a leaf blade.

Pinnate: Arranged like a feather; that is, having a central axis with organs diverging on both sides.

Pollen: Microscopic grains carrying male reproductive matter.

Radial: Diverging in various directions around a point.

Receptacle: The tip of the stalk supporting floral structures.

Salverform: Consisting of a slender tube spreading abruptly to a flat limb; applicable to a calyx or corolla.

Saprophyte: A plant obtaining all its nourishment from humus.

Sepal: The floral organ constituting the calyx.

Sessile: Attached to a support without connecting stalk.

Species: A taxonomic group comprising individual plants alike in all significant respects, but differing from all others. The singular and plural spellings are the same.

Spike: An elongate inflorescence of sessile flowers.

Stamen: The male reproductive organ, located inside the corolla; it consists of a stalk or filament supporting a hollow anther, in which pollen grains are produced.

Stigma: The tip of a carpel, to which pollen grains adhere.

Stipule: An appendage at the base of a petiole.

Style: The connecting stalk between ovary and stigma.

Symmetry: Regular repetition in a definite pattern.

Throat: The expanded upper part of a tubular calyx or corolla.

Tuber: An enlarged portion of an underground stem bearing buds.

Unisexual: Containing only one kind of sex organs.

Variety: A subdivision of a species.

Weed: A plant which tends to invade areas reserved for other kinds of plants which are deemed more desirable.

Whorl: A group of three or more objects at the same node.

FLOWER PARTS

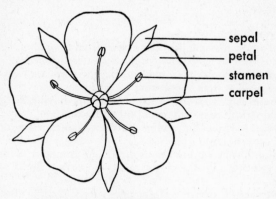

— sepal
— petal
— stamen
— carpel

RADIALLY SYMMETRIC

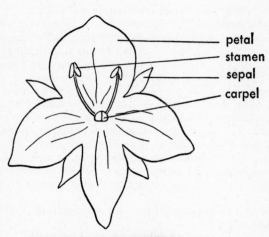

— petal
— stamen
— sepal
— carpel

BILATERALLY SYMMETRIC

CLASSIFICATION

Primitive flowers have their organs numerous, separate, and arranged in more or less spiral fashion. In the course of evolutionary advance, these organs became reduced in number, united in various ways, and changed in symmetry from spiral to radial and ultimately to bilateral. The genera are here taken up in a sequence which brings out these relationships as fully as practicable.

Divergent evolution has resulted in two main divisions of flowering plants, Monocots and Dicots. In the former, the floral symmetry is usually based on the number 3, and the chief veins of the leaves tend to be subparallel. In the Dicots, the floral symmetry is often based on the number 5, or sometimes on 4, 6, or more, while the chief veins of the leaves are divergent with strong cross connections.

The first step in the identification of an unknown plant consists, then, in observing its flower and leaf characters and allocating it to one or the other of these divisions. Next its family is to be ascertained, by the aid of a key.

A diagnostic key, as here supplied, is constructed by heading a pair of lines with a term referring to some plant part, followed by a descriptive phrase on one of the lines and a contrasted phrase on the other. Inset under one or both of these lines there may be another pair of lines; and the plan is repeated until one after another the accumulated descriptions fit a family (or other plant group).

To use a key, compare the specimen at hand with the descriptions in the outermost pair of lines, and decide which fits it the better. Under this, check the first inset pair of lines and again make a decision, repeating until at the end of a line a name is reached. Keys to genera and species are not given here, as these can be ascertained from the text data.

MONOCOTS

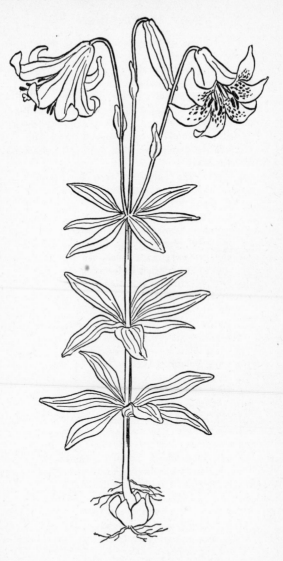

Key to Families

SEPALS markedly unlike petals in shape and color.

  TEXTURE OF SEPALS leaf-like.

    CARPELS numerous, separate . . . . **Arrowhead F.**

    CARPELS 3, more or less united.

      OVARIES united; styles separate; leaves 3 . **Trillium F.**

      OVARIES and styles united; leaves several . **Dayflower F.**

  TEXTURE OF SEPALS papery . . . . . **Yellow-eye F.**

SEPALS like petals in shape or color, or both obsolete.

  PERIANTH blue, bilateral, free from ovary . **Pickerelweed F.**

  PERIANTH otherwise.

    FLOWERS small and numerous, their hue white, greenish, bronzy, etc., only exceptionally showy.

      INFLORESCENCE cylindric or conical; perianth becoming firm and long-lasting . . . . . **Bunchlily F.**

      INFLORESCENCE a spike or dense cluster; perianth minute or obsolete, though bracts sometimes conspicuous.

        AXIS OF INFLORESCENCE thick, the flowers fused to it and to one another to form a fleshy spike **Arum F.**

        AXIS OF INFLORESCENCE slender; flowers not fused.

          DEFINITE PERIANTH present.

            COLOR white, the organs in twos . **Pipewort F.**

            COLOR brown, the organs in threes . **Rush F.**

          DEFINITE PERIANTH obsolete.

            STEM solid; leaves in 3 rows . . . **Sedge F.**

            STEM hollow; leaves set edge to edge . **Grass F.**

    FLOWERS more or less showy.

      PERIANTH TUBE nearly or quite free from the ovary.

        UNDERGROUND SYSTEM a bulb; fruit dry.

          BRACT lacking from base of inflorescence **Lily F.**

          BRACT present at base of flower cluster . . **Onion F.**

        UNDERGROUND SYSTEM a stem; fruit often fleshy.

          HABIT erect; flowers bisexual **Lily-of-the-valley F.**

          HABIT climbing; flowers unisexual . **Greenbrier F.**

      PERIANTH TUBE well united with the ovary.

        FLORAL SYMMETRY radial.

          STAMENS 6; leaves in several rows . . **Amaryllis F.**

          STAMENS 3; leaves in 2 rows . . . . . **Iris F.**

        FLORAL SYMMETRY bilateral; stamens 2 or 1, united with the carpel into a column . . . . **Orchid F.**

Arrowhead Family (*Alismàceae*)

FEATURES: Wet soil plants 1 or 2 ft. high, with delicate flowers in whorls on thick stalks. Sepals 3, green; petals 3, white, radial. Fruits small one-seeded capsules.

Broad-leaf Arrowhead (*Sagittària latifòlia*) Pl. 1

FEATURES: Flowers unisexual; stamens and carpels numerous, in spiral groups. Leaf blades arrowhead-shaped. Summer.
RANGE: Widely distributed over North America.
HABITAT: Open swamps, marshes, and shores of streams and ponds.
CULTURE: Readily cultivated; spreads rapidly by underground stems, so undesirable in small garden pools.

Eastern Water-plantain (*Alísma subcordàtum*) Pl. 1

FEATURES: Flowers numerous, small, bisexual; stamens about 6 and carpels numerous, both whorled. Leaf blades pointed at tip and rounded at base. Stalks much branched. Summer.
RANGE: Eastern half of North America.
HABITAT: Shallow water along pond and stream margins.
CULTURE: Will grow readily from seed in any wet-soil garden.

Trillium Family (*Trilliàceae*)

FEATURES: Woodland plants with tuberous underground stem; stalk 6 to 18 in. high, bearing 3 broad leaves and a large flower. Sepals 3, green; petals 3, radial; stamens 6; carpels 3, their styles separate but ovaries united. Fruit a more or less angled green or red berry.

Toad Trillium (*Tríllium séssilè*) Pl. 2

FEATURES: Flower sessile; petals small, ascending, brown or greenish; filaments short; styles spreading. Leaves sessile, mottled with brown. Spring.
RANGE: Southern, and adjacent Northeastern and Midland states.
HABITAT: Open woods, in rich neutral soils.
CULTURE: Can be cultivated in a light garden soil in partial shade, if rodents are kept from eating the tubers.
NOTES: The PRAIRIE TRILLIUM (*T. recurvàtum*) of the Midland states has down-curved sepals alternating with leaf stalks. In habitat and culture it is like the preceding.

Trillium Family, continued

Great Trillium (*Trillium grandiflòrum*)   Pl. 2

FEATURES: Flower borne on an upward-sloping stalk; petals ascending, white fading pink, broadened above middle; filaments equaling anthers; styles ascending. Leaves somewhat stalked, broadest below the middle. Spring.

RANGE: Nearly throughout our area and adjacent Canada, though chiefly in uplands.

HABITAT: Wooded slopes and hummocks in swamps, in rich neutral or moderately acid soils.

CULTURE: The most satisfactory TRILLIUM for cultivation, thriving even in ordinary garden loam.

Nodding Trillium (*T. cérnuúm*)   Pl. 1

FEATURES: Flower borne on a short stalk which curves downward; petals white or pinkish, rather narrow, curved outward; filaments slender, equaling anthers; styles thick, curved. Leaves barely stalked, broadest about middle. Spring.

RANGE: Over much of our area and adjacent Canada.

HABITAT: Moist woods and swamps, in moderately acid soil.

CULTURE: Can be grown in the moister part of a woodland garden.

Wet-dog Trillium (*T. eréctum*)   Pl. 2

FEATURES: Flower borne on an upward-sloping stalk; petals red, yellow, or white, the deeper-colored forms exhaling a rank odor to which the common name refers; filaments short; styles thick, curved. Leaves sessile, broadest above middle. Spring.

RANGE: Uplands of Northeastern states and eastern Canada, also south in the Appalachians.

HABITAT: Open woods and hummocks in swamps, in soils which, while varying in acidity, are usually cool.

CULTURE: The paler forms are desirable for cultivation in wild gardens where the soil does not heat up much in summer.

NOTES: This and other TRILLIUMS are often called WAKE-ROBIN. In the Midland states this species is replaced by the MIDLAND TRILLIUM (*T. glèasoni*). Its flower stalk is horizontal, its petals white or pink, and its scent agreeable. It grows in woodlands where the soil is rich and neutral, and can be cultivated in a partly shaded wild garden.

Trillium Family, concluded

Snow Trillium (*Tríllium nivàlè*) Pl. 1

FEATURES: Flower borne on an ascending stalk; petals white, rounded at tip; filaments as long as anthers; styles slender. Leaves roundish, short-stalked. Early spring.

RANGE: Midland states and adjacent parts of Northeastern ones.

HABITAT: Wooded slopes and rock ledges, in neutral soil.

CULTURE: The low stature and early blooming of this species, along with its preference for dryish neutral soil, render it especially desirable for limestone rock gardens.

Painted Trillium (*T. undulàtum*) Pl. 2

FEATURES: Flower borne on a nearly erect stalk; petals white with pink patch toward base; filaments equaling anthers; styles slender. Leaves short-stalked, broadest below middle, tapering to a sharp tip, often bronzy. Late spring.

RANGE: Uplands of our area and adjacent Canada, also south along the Appalachians.

HABITAT: Woods and swamps, in cold, peaty, strongly acid soil.

CULTURE: The most difficult TRILLIUM to cultivate successfully, requiring permanently acid humus soil which does not heat up during the summer; also requires protection from rodents.

Dayflower Family (*Commelinàceae*)

FEATURES: Plants with leafy stems bearing clusters of showy flowers which open one or two at a time and soon wither. Sepals 3, green or bronzy; petals 3, all or 2 of them showy; stamens 6; carpels 3, well united. Fruit a capsule.

Virginia Spiderwort (*Tradescántia virginiàna*) Pl. 3

FEATURES: Plant 1 to 2 ft. high. Flowers radial; sepals green, hairy; petals violet, purple, pink, or white; filaments covered with fuzzy hairs, to which the common name refers. Leaves long-tapering, bright green. Spring.

RANGE: Southern states and adjacent parts of our area.

HABITAT: Wooded slopes and flats, in rich neutral soil.

CULTURE: Extensively cultivated, both here and abroad, and often escapes from gardens into woodlands far beyond its native range.

Dayflower Family, concluded

Blue-leaf Spiderwort (*Tradescántia ohiénsis*) Pl. 3

FEATURES: Plant 1 to 2 ft. high. Flowers radial; sepals green, sparsely hairy; petals violet, purple, or sometimes white; filaments fuzzy-hairy. Leaves long and narrow, of a lustrous bluish-green hue. Late spring and early summer.

RANGE: Midland, Southern, and adjacent Northeastern states.

HABITAT: Grasslands, thickets, and open woods, in rich neutral or moderately acid soil.

CULTURE: Easily grown in any garden, and highly desirable.

NOTES: While not so frequently cultivated as the VIRGINIA SPIDERWORT, this species also escapes into wild lands far from its native haunts. The dull purple flowered SPIDERWORTS of old-fashioned gardens represent hybrids between these and other species.

Tall Dayflower (*Commelìna virgínica*) Pl. 3

FEATURES: Plant coarse, 2 or 3 ft. high. Flowers bilateral; petals blue, 2 large and 1 smaller; only 3 stamens normal. Flower cluster arising from a pair of partly united bracts. Leaves lance-shaped. Summer.

RANGE: Southern states and adjacent parts of our area.

HABITAT: Moist open woods and stream banks, in neutral soil.

CULTURE: Readily cultivated, but not especially attractive.

Low Dayflower (*C. diffùsa*) Pl. 3

FEATURES: Plant delicate, with branching stems which root at nodes. Flowers strongly bilateral; sepals bronzy, unequal; petals 3, blue, 1 very small; only 3 stamens normal. Flower cluster arising from a pair of bracts united up one side. Summer.

RANGE: Tropical America, southern United States, and the more southern parts of our area.

HABITAT: Thickets and open woods, in damp, rich, neutral soil.

CULTURE: Sometimes grown, but tends to become weedy.

NOTES: Other species of DAYFLOWER, differing in details of flowers and foliage, occur in our area. The rankest-growing one, *C. commùnis,* which has the lower petal white instead of blue, is believed to have been introduced from Asia but has become thoroughly naturalized.

Yellow-eye Family (*Xyridàceae*)

FEATURES: Tufted plants of bogs and moist acid sands, with grass-like leaves and wiry stalks tipped with a knob of overlapping brownish bracts. Sepals unequal, brownish; petals 3, radial, yellow; stamens 6 but only 3 normal; carpels 3, united; fruit a capsule.

Slender Yellow-eye (*Xỳris tòrta*)   Pl. 6

FEATURES: Stalk up to 1 ft. high, the inflorescence knob nearly spherical. Larger sepals bearing a low hairy keel. Base of stem a bulb. Summer.

RANGE: Over most of our area, also the Southern states.

HABITAT: Bogs and sandy flats, in strongly acid peaty soil.

CULTURE: Can be grown in a bog garden if kept acid.

Upland Yellow-eye (*X. montàna*)   Pl. 6

FEATURES: Stalk a few inches high, the inflorescence knob egg-shaped. Larger sepals bearing a winged, hairless keel. Base of stem not bulbous. Summer.

RANGE: Uplands of Northeastern states and adjacent Canada.

HABITAT: Sandy bog margins, in cool-climate regions.

CULTURE: Requires moist acid soil, kept cool in summer.

NOTES: Other species of YELLOW-EYE occur southward.

Pipewort Family (*Eriocaulàceae*)

FEATURES: Tufted plants of wet habitats, with short grass-like leaves, often translucent and conspicuously cross-veined, and wiry stalks tipped with a knob of minute grayish-white unisexual flowers, with their parts in threes or twos.

Northern Pipewort (*Eriocaúlon septangulàrè*)   Pl. 4

FEATURES: Stalk about 7-angled, a few inches high; knob of flowers ¼ in. thick, nearly spherical. Summer.

RANGE: Eastern half of North America; also northern Europe.

HABITAT: Clear ponds, the leaves forming rosettes on the bottom and the stalks lengthening until they extend well above the water surface.

CULTURE: Will grow in a clean garden pool.

NOTES: A coarser species with 10-angled stalk, *E. decangulàrè,* occurs toward the southern side of our area.

Pickerelweed Family (*Pontederiàceae*)

FEATURES: Aquatic plants with thick stems creeping in mud, rather large solitary leaves, and bracted spikes of delicate bilateral flowers.

Pickerelweed (*Pontedèria cordàta*)   Pl. 6

FEATURES: Plant 1 to 3 ft. high. Sepals and petals 3 each, blue, much alike, grouped to form two lips with bilateral symmetry. Leaf blades mostly heart-shaped, blunt-tipped. Summer.

RANGE: Eastern half of the United States and adjacent Canada.

HABITAT: Shallow water, borders of streams and ponds.

CULTURE: Desirable for water gardens.

Bunchlily Family (*Melanthiàceae*)

FEATURES: Plants with grass- or lily-like foliage and numerous small flowers, white, greenish, yellow, pinkish, etc. Sepals and petals 3 each, much alike, becoming firm and persistent; stamens 6; carpels 3, their ovaries incompletely united. Fruit a triangular or 3-lobed capsule.

Viscid Tofieldia (*Tofièldia glutinòsa*)   Pl. 4

FEATURES: Flowers greenish white, grouped in threes in a short inflorescence. Stalk a few inches high, sprinkled with dark glands; leaves grass-like, set edge to edge. Summer.

RANGE: Uplands of the eastern half of North America.

HABITAT: Thickets and grasslands, in cool, moist, neutral soil.

CULTURE: Can be grown in spots resembling its native haunts.

Poison-lily (*Amiánthium muscaetóxicum*)   Pl. 4

FEATURES: Flowers in a cylindric group on a smooth stalk 1 to 2 ft. high, opening white, and later turning bronzy green. Leaves grass-like, blunt, in a rosette arising from a bulb. Late spring and summer.

RANGE: Southern states and adjacent parts of our area.

HABITAT: Open woods, in strongly acid peaty soil.

CULTURE: May grow in an acid woodland garden.

NOTES: The tissues of this plant contain a very poisonous alkaloid, and cattle are often killed by eating the leaves. A sugar solution in which one of its bulbs has been crushed can be used to kill flies, suggesting the name FLY-POISON.

Bunchlily Family, continued

White-hellebore (*Veràtrum vìridè*)   Pl. 6

FEATURES: Plant 3 to 5 ft. high. Inflorescence compound; flowers medium-sized, with yellowish-green sepals and petals. Leaves short, broad, and veiny, resembling those of SLIPPER ORCHIDS, alternate up the stalk in 3 rows, withering early. Late spring.

RANGE: Over much of our area and adjacent Canada.

HABITAT: Swamps and wooded stream banks.

CULTURE: Can be grown in a moist-soil garden.

NOTES: The thick underground stem has medicinal value and is also dug commercially for use as an insecticide. This plant is not related to the true HELLEBORE, a European member of the BUTTERCUP FAMILY.

Bunchlily (*Melánthium virgìnicum*)   Pl. 5

FEATURES: Plant 3 to 4 ft. high, rough-hairy. Inflorescence compound; flowers medium-sized; sepals and petals stalked, greenish white with a pair of green dots at each blade base, becoming bronzy. Leaves coarse, grass-like, from the thick underground stem, with smaller ones alternate up the stalk. Summer.

RANGE: Southern, Midland, and adjacent Northeastern states.

HABITAT: Thickets in moist, strongly acid, peaty soil.

CULTURE: Worthy of a place in a bog garden, although it does not bloom every year.

NOTES: The related WIDE-LEAF BUNCHLILY (*M. latifòlium*) differs in having broader leaves, sepals, and petals; it grows in dryer, less acid soils, in the Appalachians and foothills.

Northern Camas (*Zygádenus chlworánthus*)   Pl. 5

FEATURES: Stalk 1 to 2 ft. high; inflorescence slender, of few medium-sized flowers with broad sepals and petals, greenish white with a green disk at base. Leaves gray-green, grass-like, from a bulb, and a few small ones on stalk. Summer.

RANGE: Northern North America and upper parts of our area.

HABITAT: Among grasses and bushes in limy meadows and damp hollows between limestone rocks.

CULTURE: Requires not only limy soil but also a situation in which the roots do not become heated up in summer.

Bunchlily Family, continued

Feather-fleece (*Stenánthium gramíneum*)   Pl. 5

FEATURES: Plant several feet high. Inflorescence compound, of small nodding flowers with narrow sepals and petals, white becoming green, some bisexual and some unisexual. Leaves grass-like, from a bulb, and smaller ones alternate up the stalk. Summer.

RANGE: Southern states and lower parts of our area.

HABITAT: Open rocky woods and sandy bogs, in strongly acid, usually humus-rich soil.

CULTURE: Desirable for cultivation in an acid-soil or bog garden, blooming more freely than its relatives.

NOTES: Varies considerably in stature, the coarser forms of moister soils being sometimes termed variety *robústum,* or even classed as a distinct species.

Turkey-beard (*Xerophýllum asphodeloìdes*)   Pl. 4

FEATURES: Plant 2 to 3 ft. high. Inflorescence a dense cylinder of small white flowers. Leaves numerous, wiry, in a rosette from the thick stem base. Late spring.

RANGE: Appalachian Mountains to the lowlands of New Jersey.

HABITAT: Open pine or oak woods, in strongly acid, sandy or gravelly soil, dry at the surface but moist in depth.

CULTURE: Difficult to cultivate unless its native conditions are closely matched; rarely blooms in the garden.

Swamp-hyacinth (*Helònias bullàta*)   Pl. 7

FEATURES: Stalk hollow, a few inches high when the flowers start to open; inflorescence dense; sepals and petals dull pink, and stamens lavender-blue; stalk elongating markedly and flowers becoming green in the course of the season. Leaves lily-like, in a rosette from a bulb. Early to late spring.

RANGE: Southern Appalachians, extending northeast in foothills and lowlands to southeastern New York.

HABITAT: Swamps and bog margins, in usually strongly acid, humus-rich soil.

CULTURE: Fairly easy to cultivate in a bog garden if the soil can be maintained in a moist though well-aerated and definitely acid condition.

Bunchlily Family, concluded

Fairy-wand (*Chamaelírium lùteum*) Pl. 5

FEATURES: Stalk wand-like, 2 to 3 ft. high. Inflorescence slender, of small white unisexual flowers, staminate on some plants and carpellate on others. Leaves lily-like, in a rosette on the thick underground stem. Early summer.

RANGE: Southern states, and over our area except far north.

HABITAT: Damp open woods in moderately acid, rather rich soil.

CULTURE: Desirable for cultivation in a woodland garden.

NOTES: Also inaptly termed BLAZING-STAR and DEVILS-BIT.

Bog-asphodel (*Narthècium americànum*) Pl. 7

FEATURES: Stalk up to 1 ft. high; inflorescence dense, of medium-sized flowers, with narrow yellow sepals and petals and hairy stamens; styles obsolete. Leaves small, grass-like, set edge to edge, mostly at stalk base. Early summer.

RANGE: Lowlands from South Carolina up to New Jersey.

HABITAT: Grassy thickets in moist, strongly acid, peaty soil.

CULTURE: Delicate and difficult to cultivate, but may grow in a well-maintained bog garden.

Arum Family (*Aràceae*)

FEATURES: Chiefly succulent plants of moist or occasionally dry soils, with the flowers fused together in a fleshy spike, which may be conspicuously bracted. Sepals and petals 3 or 2 each, often obsolete; stamens 6 or 4; carpels 3 or 2, united, maturing to a berry or sometimes a dry inflated fruit.

Goldenclub (*Oróntium aquáticum*) Pl. 7

FEATURES: Stalk white above, tipped by a club-like spike of yellow flowers, with very small sepals and petals; bract inconspicuous. Leaves floating or partly emersed, arising from a deep-seated creeping stem, veiny, covered with a grayish film which repels water. Early spring.

RANGE: Southern, and adjacent parts of Northeastern states.

HABITAT: Shallow water, margins of streams and ponds.

CULTURE: Spreads too rapidly to trust in a small garden pool.

NOTES: Sometimes known as FIRE-LEAF or NEVER-WET in reference to the ability of its leaves to shed water.

Arum Family, continued

Skunkcabbage (*Symplocárpus foétidus*)   Pl. 7

FEATURES: Flowers in a knob-shaped spike surrounded by a short-stalked, shell-like bract, mottled bronze and green. Sepals and petals 2 each, bronzy yellow. Leaves large, in a group from a thick stem base, developing as the flowers mature. Sap strong-scented, though more onion- than skunk-like. Late winter and early spring.

RANGE: Throughout our area and adjacent territory; also native in eastern Asia.

HABITAT: Swamps and bog margins, in wet, mucky soil.

CULTURE: Readily grown in a moist, shady garden, but requires considerable space.

Wild Calla (*Cálla palústris*)   Pl. 8

FEATURES: Flowers greenish, in a knob-shaped spike on a short stalk, backed by a shell-like white bract; sepals and petals obsolete; stamens about 6; carpel solitary, maturing to a red berry. Leaves heart-shaped, borne on a creeping stem. Early summer.

RANGE: Subarctic regions, extending south in North America into the northern parts of our area.

HABITAT: Swamps and bogs, in cold, wet, acid soil.

CULTURE: Can be grown in a bog garden if the soil is kept acid and the temperature does not rise much in summer.

Green-dragon (*Arisaèma dracóntium*)   Pl. 8

FEATURES: Stalk 2 to 3 ft. high, bearing a large leaf divided in somewhat spiral fashion into a number of leaflets. Flowers green, in a cylindric cluster at the base of a long axis, which extends as a sort of tail from the upper end of the tubular rolled green bract. Summer.

RANGE: Eastern half of the United States and adjacent Canada.

HABITAT: Open woods on flats along streams and on slopes underlain by limestone, in usually neutral soil.

CULTURE: Worth cultivating in a woodland garden, thriving best in a rather rich loamy soil.

NOTES: This and the species of *Arisaèma* on the following page have a tuberous root which, if tasted, burns the mouth severely.

Arum Family, concluded

Woodland Jack-in-the-pulpit (*Arisaèma triphýllum*) Pl. 10

FEATURES: Stalk 1 to 2 ft. high, bearing 1 or 2 leaves, their blade divided into 3 leaflets. Flowers green, in a cylindric group at the base of a long axis which extends up into a blunt, club-shaped "jack"; bract brown-striped, or in albino forms green-striped, arching over the flower cluster, and constituting the "pulpit." Sepals and petals obsolete; stamens about 4; carpel solitary, maturing to a red berry, the clusters of these forming conspicuous objects in the autumn woods. Leaflets gray-green beneath. Spring.

RANGE: Eastern half of the United States and adjacent Canada.

HABITAT: Woods and swamps, in various types of soil, though usually neutral or only moderately acid and rather rich.

CULTURE: One of the easiest of native plants to cultivate.

Swamp Jack-in-the-pulpit (*A. pusíllum*)   Pl. 10

FEATURES: Stalk around 1 ft. high, bearing a solitary leaf, or a large and a small one together, resembling a stunted form of the above species. Bract nearly black, or in albinos green, inside, bent abruptly and extending horizontally over the "jack." Leaflets bright green beneath. Early summer, often several weeks after the preceding species.

RANGE: Northeastern states, except far north.

HABITAT: Swamps and moist woods, in wet, mucky soil.

CULTURE: Suitable for a swampy wild garden.

Northern Jack-in-the-pulpit (*A..stewardsònii*)   Pl. 10

FEATURES: Similar to the next preceding, although the bract differs in bearing conspicuous white ridges outside and light brown stripes inside. Early summer.

RANGE: Eastern Canada and south through the uplands of the Northeastern states into the higher Appalachians.

HABITAT: Swamps and bog margins in cool acid soil.

CULTURE: Can be cultivated in moist, acid woodland gardens where the soil does not heat up much in summer.

NOTES: These plants are sometimes called INDIAN-TURNIP, in that the Indians are supposed to have used the tuberous roots for food, after thorough cooking to remove the extremely acrid principle they contain.

Rush Family (*Juncàceae*)

FEATURES: Plants more or less grass-like, but the stalks round and the leaves not set edge to edge. Flowers clustered, unlike grasses and sedges in having definite, though minute and brownish, sepals and petals, 3 of each. Stamens 6 or 3; carpels 3, well united, maturing to a capsule.

Wood-rush (*Lùzula campéstris*)   **Pl. 8**

FEATURES: Stalks a few inches high, bearing a compound group of flower clusters; stamens rather conspicuous. Leaves grass-like, loosely hairy, mostly in a rosette. Early spring.
RANGE: Northern Hemisphere; in our area represented by varieties which can be distinguished only by the specialist.
HABITAT: Wooded slopes, often in rather sterile soil.
CULTURE: May be cultivated in a wild garden.

Sedge Family (*Cyperàceae*)

FEATURES: Plants grass-like, but the stalks often triangular and the leaves in 3 rows. Flowers minute, clustered; sepals and petals obsolete; stamens 3; carpels 3 or 2, one maturing to a 1-seeded dry fruit.

Tawny Cotton-sedge (*Erióphorum virgínicum*)   **Pl. 8**

FEATURES: Flowers crowded in a tuft surrounded by copious buff, silky bristles on a wiry stalk 2 to 3 ft. high. Leaves grass-like, firm. Summer.
RANGE: Eastern half of North America.
HABITAT: Bogs and wet meadows in strongly acid, peaty soil.
CULTURE: Desirable for cultivation in an acid bog garden.
NOTES: Other species of COTTON-SEDGE have white bristles.

Grass Family (*Gramíneae*)

FEATURES: Plants with mostly narrow leaves set edge to edge and minute flowers. Sepals and petals obsolete; stamens 3; carpels 2, one maturing to a grain. Four of the more striking native species are figured here:

Bottle-brush Grass (*Hýstrix pátula*)   **Pl. 9**
Indian Grass (*Sorghástrum nùtans*)   **Pl. 9**
Spangle Grass (*Unìola latifòlia*)   **Pl. 9**
Wild-rice (*Zizània aquática*)   **Pl. 9**

Lily Family (*Liliàceae*)

FEATURES: Stem base bulbous. Leaves narrow or moderately broad. Flowers showy; sepals and petals 3 each; stamens 6; carpels 3, well united, maturing to a capsule.

Wood Lily (*Lílium philadélphicum*)   Pl. 10

FEATURES: Stalk 2 to 3 ft. high, bearing 1 or several upright orange-red flowers; sepal and petal blades stalked. Leaves in several whorls, and a few scattered. Summer.

RANGE: Eastern Canada, Northeastern states, and Appalachians.

HABITAT: Among grasses or bushes in strongly acid, humus-rich, gravelly or sandy soil.

CULTURE: Difficult to cultivate, unless the garden can be kept decidedly acid and rodents can be controlled.

NOTES: In the Midland states there grows a relative of the above LILY, differing in having the leaves mostly scattered. It is classed as variety or subspecies *andìnum*.

Yellow Canada Lily (*L. canadénsè*)   Pl. 11

FEATURES: Stalk several feet high, bearing a group of nodding yellow or reddish bell-shaped flowers; sepal and petal blades sessile; anthers about ⅓ in. long. Leaves in several whorls, their veins and margins bearing spicules. Early summer.

RANGE: Southeastern Canada and Northeastern states.

HABITAT: Meadows and thickets in neutral or somewhat acid soil.

CULTURE: Easy to grow if protected from rodents and blights.

NOTES: In uplands of the Northeastern and adjacent Midland states, and Appalachians, there grows a LILY, differing in its lower stature, redder flowers, and preference for thinly wooded slopes in rather acid soils. This is here figured as:

Upland Canada Lily (*L. canadénsè editòrum*)   Pl. 11

Midland Lily (*L. michiganénsè*)   Pl. 11

FEATURES: Like the preceding, except that the sepals and petals curve back until their tips touch. Early summer.

RANGE: Midland states and adjacent Canada.

HABITAT: Moist thickets and meadows, in neutral to moderately acid, humus-rich soils.

CULTURE: Can be grown in the pest-free wild garden.

Lily Family, concluded

Turks-cap Lily (*Lílium supérbum*)   Pl. 11

FEATURES: Stalk several feet high, bearing whorls of large nodding flowers. Sepals and petals orange-red, curved back so that their tips touch, displaying a central green star; anthers over ½ in. long. Leaves in several whorls, their margins and veins smooth. Late summer.

RANGE: Northeastern and Southern states.

HABITAT: Meadows and bog margins, in moist, acid, peaty soil.

CULTURE: Can be grown in acid-soil gardens, but needs protection against rodents and fungus diseases.

Eastern Troutlily (*Erythrònium americànum*)   Pl. 14

FEATURES: Flower a solitary nodding bell borne on a stalk a few inches high between 2 brown-mottled leaves arising from a deep-seated bulb. Sepals and petals yellow inside, bronzy outside; anthers red or yellow. Early spring.

RANGE: Eastern half of the United States and adjacent Canada.

HABITAT: Thinly wooded flats and slopes, in neutral or moderately acid soil.

CULTURE: In wild gardens offsets from the bulbs produce an abundance of small leaves but very few flowers.

NOTES: The related WHITE TROUTLILY (*E. álbidum*), has the bell white inside; it is more frequent in the Midland states, prefers rich neutral soil, and may bloom somewhat more freely. Toward the west side of the Midland states there grows the NARROW-LEAF TROUTLILY (*E. mesachòreum*); its flowers are also white, but its leaves are narrow and not mottled; it is the best bloomer of the three. In many books these little LILIES are known by the curiously inapt name of DOG-TOOTH-VIOLET.

Midland Camas-lily (*Camássia esculénta*)   Pl. 14

FEATURES: Flowers medium-sized, in a cylindric inflorescence on a stalk 1 to 2 ft. high; sepals and petals alike, lavender-blue, somewhat bilateral. Leaves grass-like. Spring.

RANGE: Midland, and adjacent Southern and Northeastern states.

HABITAT: Open woods on slopes and flats, often in neutral soil.

CULTURE: Desirable for cultivation in the woodland garden, but like the true LILIES needs protection from rodents.

Onion Family (*Alliàceae*)

FEATURES: Stem base bulbous; leaves basal, grass- or lily-like. Flowers small, in a cluster adjoining a papery bract. Sepals and petals 3 each, similar, radial; stamens 6; carpels 3, united, maturing to a few-seeded capsule.

Scentless-garlic (*Nothoscórdum biválvè*)   Pl. 12

FEATURES: Stalk 6 to 12 in. high. Flowers starry, white with yellow eye. Leaves grass-like. Sap odorless. Spring.

RANGE: Southern, and adjacent parts of Midland and North-eastern states.

HABITAT: Open woods, thickets, and grasslands, in loamy soil.

CULTURE: Suitable for cultivation in the rock garden; winter-hardy well north of its native range.

Wood-leek (*Allium tricóccum*)   Pl. 12

FEATURES: Bulb sending up in spring a solitary LILY-OF-THE-VALLEY-like leaf, which withers by summer, when the foot-tall stalk bearing a cluster of small white flowers appears. Sap intensely onion-flavored.

RANGE: Over our area, adjacent Canada, and Appalachians.

HABITAT: Wooded flats, slopes, and swamp margins, in usually neutral and rather rich soils.

CULTURE: Can be grown in a woodland garden; the leaves exceed the flowers in ornamental value.

NOTES: The bulbs are sometimes used as food, being collected, under the names of RAMSONS or RAMPS by the residents of the Appalachian region.

Spring Wild Onion (*A. canadénsè*)   Pl. 12

FEATURES: Stalk about 1 ft. high, bearing a group of mixed pale lavender flowers and bulblets. Leaves grass-like, few. Late spring.

RANGE: Eastern half of United States and adjacent Canada.

HABITAT: Open woods on flats and slopes, in neutral soil.

CULTURE: Can be cultivated, though scarcely attractive enough to deserve garden space.

NOTES: The somewhat similar GARLIC (*A. vineàlè*), a native of southern Europe, has become a serious weed in this country. It differs in having tubular leaves, some up the stalk.

Onion Family, concluded

Summer Wild Onion (*Állium cérnuúm*)   **Pl. 14**

FEATURES: Stalk about 1 ft. high, 2-ridged, curved at tip, the lilac flowers nodding. Summer.

RANGE: Uplands over the greater part of the United States.

HABITAT: Sunny or partly shaded rock ledges and gravelly slopes, in neutral or moderately acid soils.

CULTURE: Readily cultivated in the rock garden, spreading rapidly by both bulb offsets and seeds.

Autumn Wild Onion (*A. stellàtum*)   **Pl. 14**

FEATURES: Stalk 1 ft. or more high, round, holding the cluster of lilac flowers upright. Early autumn.

RANGE: Midland states, chiefly toward the western side.

HABITAT: Among grasses or bushes on slopes, in neutral to slightly acid gravelly soils.

CULTURE: Desirable as a rock-garden subject, especially in view of its late blooming season.

Lily-of-the-valley Family (*Convallariàceae*)

FEATURES: Main stem underground, ranging from long and slender to short and thick, sending up leafy stalks or leaf rosettes. Flowers small or medium-sized; sepals and petals 3 each, similar; stamens 6; carpels 3, the ovaries and often styles united, maturing to a berry or a capsule.

Sessile Merrybells (*Uvulària sessilifòlia*)   **Pl. 12**

FEATURES: Flowers solitary or paired, pale yellow, nodding near the tip of an angled 1-ft. stalk bearing small, thickish, sessile leaves which are grayish beneath and rough on the margins. Fruit a 3-angled capsule which remains closed through most of the season. Spring.

RANGE: Southern, Midland, and Northeastern states and adjacent Canada.

HABITAT: Open woods, in moderately acid, humus-rich soil.

CULTURE: Will spread into patches in a woodland garden.

NOTES: Placed by some taxonomists in the genus *Oakèsia,* and often assigned to the LILY FAMILY. This and related species are variously known as BELLWORT or STRAWBELL.

Lily-of-the-valley Family, continued

Great Merrybells (*Uvulària grandiflòra*).   Pl. 15

FEATURES: Flowers bright yellow, nodding, one at the tip of each fork of the round 1- to 2-ft. stalk. Leaves finely hairy beneath, their base ringing the stem. Fruit a 3-lobed capsule. Spring.

RANGE: Midland, and adjacent Southern and Northeastern states.

HABITAT: Wooded slopes, in usually neutral soil.

CULTURE: Desirable for cultivation in the wild garden; may even be grown in the border.

NOTES: SMOOTH MERRYBELLS (*U. perfoliàta*) differs in having the flowers paler yellow and the leaves gray-green and smooth beneath; it is found chiefly in the Northeastern and Southern states, growing in moderately acid woodlands.

Cucumber-root (*Medèola virginiàna*)   Pl. 15

FEATURES: Plant 1 to 2 ft. high, the loosely hairy stalk bearing a whorl of 6 or 7 leaves halfway up, and another of bracts at the tip. Flowers adjoining the bracts, greenish yellow, the sepals and petals alike, curved outward; styles free, curved. Fruit a purple berry. Late spring.

RANGE: Over our area, the Southern states, and southern Canada.

HABITAT: Moist woods, in moderately acid soil.

CULTURE: Can be grown in a swampy woodland garden, though does not bloom very freely.

NOTES: This plant is often placed in the TRILLIUM FAMILY, but differs from the TRILLIUMS in having the sepals and petals alike. In underground stem, leaves, and fruit, however, it is more like the members of the LILY-OF-THE-VALLEY FAMILY.

White Beadlily (*Clintònia umbellulàta*)   Pl. 13

FEATURES: Flowers numerous in a cluster on a 6- to 8-in. stalk; sepals and petals white with bronzy dots. Leaves 3 or 4 in a rosette from the thick underground stem, LILY-OF-THE-VAL-LEY-like, but hairy-margined. Fruit a blackish bead-like berry. Spring.

RANGE: Appalachians and western part of Northeastern states.

HABITAT: Wooded slopes, in moderately acid, rather rich soil.

CULTURE: Readily cultivated on a shaded slope.

Lily-of-the-valley Family, continued

Yellow Beadlily (*Clintònia boreàlis*)　　　　　**Pl. 15**
FEATURES: Flowers ¾ in. long, bell-shaped, pale yellow, in a
lax group on a 6- to 8-in. stalk. Leaves 2 or 3 in a rosette
from the thick underground stem, resembling those of LILIES
or ORCHIDS, but hairy-margined. Fruit a striking dark blue
bead-like berry, rather poisonous. Early spring.
RANGE: Eastern half of Canada, south into the upper part of
our area, also down the higher Appalachians.
HABITAT: Deep woods and hummocks in swamps, in cool,
strongly acid, peaty soil.
CULTURE: Difficult to cultivate far beyond its native haunts
because of its requirement for especially cool acid soils.
NOTES: The unusual color of the berries leads this plant to be
also called BLUEBEAD.

Fairybells (*Dísporum lanuginòsum*)　　　　　**Pl. 13**
FEATURES: Flowers solitary or paired, nodding at the tips of
branches of a leafy stalk 1 to 2 ft. high, bell-shaped, ¾ in.
long, greenish white speckled with bronzy dots. Leaves sessile, fine-hairy. Fruit a red berry. Late spring.
RANGE: Appalachians and north across the western parts of
the Northeastern states to southernmost Canada.
HABITAT: Wooded slopes, in neutral or moderately acid, usually
rich soil.
CULTURE: Desirable for cultivation in a woodland garden.

Solomon-plume (*Smilacìna racemòsa*)　　　　　**Pl. 13**
FEATURES: Flowers white, small, in a compound inflorescence
on an arching stalk 2 to 3 ft. high; stamens longer than the
petals. Leaves numerous, veiny, hairy-edged. Fruit a whitish
speckled berry, turning dull red. Late spring.
RANGE: Eastern half of the United States and adjacent Canada.
HABITAT: Wooded slopes, often in moderately acid soil.
CULTURE: Desirable in the wild garden or shady border.
NOTES: The members of this genus are sometimes called FALSE
SOLOMON-SEAL, since while the foliage resembles that of the
true SOLOMON-SEALS, the underground stems lack seal-like
scars. Another name in the books is FALSE SPIKENARD.

Lily-of-the-valley Family, continued

Starry Solomon-plume (*Smilacìna stellàta*) Pl. 13

FEATURES: Flowers white, fewer but larger than in the next preceding species, in a cylindric group on a stalk about 1 ft. high; stamens shorter than the petals. Leaves several, finely downy beneath. Fruit black-striped green berries, at maturity turning bronzy. Late spring.

RANGE: Northern Europe and North America, extending well down into our area.

HABITAT: Varied—moist meadows, swamp margins, wooded rocky slopes, sand dunes, etc., in often neutral soil.

CULTURE: Readily grown in the wild garden, spreading by its underground stems into large patches.

Bog Solomon-plume (*S. trifòlia*) Pl. 16

FEATURES: Flowers white, few, in a short group on a stalk 4 to 12 in. high. Leaves few, rather narrow, smooth. Fruit speckled berries which turn dull red. Late spring.

RANGE: Arctic regions of all continents, extending south into the cooler parts of our area.

HABITAT: Cold wet bogs, in strongly acid, peaty soil.

CULTURE: Difficult to cultivate, because of its requirement for strongly acid soils which do not heat up much in summer.

Heartleaf-lily (*Maiánthemum canadénsè*) Pl. 16

FEATURES: Flowers white, tiny, in a cylindric group on a stalk 4 to 6 in. high; unique in the family in having only 2 each sepals and petals, and 4 stamens. Leaves few, heart-shaped, 1 or 2 on the flowering stalk, and solitary ones arising from the underground stems. Fruit small whitish berries with bronzy spots, ultimately turning dull red. Spring.

RANGE: Northern North America, over our area, and a little farther south.

HABITAT: Woods and bog margins, in moderately acid humus-rich soil.

CULTURE: Suitable for a ground cover in an acid woodland.

NOTES: Called in the books FALSE LILY-OF-THE-VALLEY, although it does not resemble the true plant of that name. The latter is native in the southern Appalachians and enters our area in Virginia and West Virginia.

Lily-of-the-valley Family, continued

Great Solomon-seal (*Polygonàtum commutàtum*) Pl. 16

FEATURES: Flowers nodding, several in a group; sepals and petals greenish white, united to a tube about ¾ in. long, their tips flaring. Stalk 3 to 5 ft. high, inclined, bearing several alternate smooth leaves from the axils of which the flower groups arise. Fruit bluish berries. Late spring.

RANGE: Eastern half of the United States and adjacent Canada.

HABITAT: Wooded flats along streams and limestone slopes, in usually rich, neutral soil.

CULTURE: Readily grown in the woodland garden and even in the partly shaded perennial border.

NOTES: The common name of this and related species refers to the seal-like scars on the underground stem.

Hairy Solomon-seal (*P. pubéscens*) Pl. 16

FEATURES: Flowers nodding, solitary or paired; sepals and petals greenish white, united to a tube about ½ in. long. Stalk 1 to 2 ft. high, inclined, bearing several alternate leaves which are pale and downy beneath, with the flowers in their axils. Fruit bluish berries. Late spring.

RANGE: Eastern and adjacent parts of Midland states and Canada.

HABITAT: Wooded slopes, in moderately acid soil.

CULTURE: May be grown in an acid wild garden.

NOTES: SMOOTH SOLOMON-SEAL (*P. biflòrum*) is intermediate between the above two; it is common over our area.

Rosybells (*Stréptopus ròseus*) Pl. 15

FEATURES: Flowers open bell-shaped, nodding, on stalks which are kinked near the middle, bright rose-purple. Stalk 1 to 2 ft. high, branched, bearing several alternate hairy-margined leaves, from the axils of which the flowers arise. Fruit red berries. Late spring.

RANGE: Northeastern half of North America, extending in lowlands a short distance into our area and south in the mountains.

HABITAT: Cool woods and swamp margins, in moderately acid but usually rather rich soil.

CULTURE: Will thrive in woodland gardens beyond its native region only if the soil can be kept cool in summer.

Lily-of-the-valley Family, concluded

Twisted-stalk (*Stréptopus amplexifòlius*)   **Pl. 17**

FEATURES: Flowers open bell-shaped, greenish white, nodding on stalks which are conspicuously twisted near the middle, from the axils of smooth clasping leaves on a branched stalk 2 to 3 ft. high. Fruit red berries. Spring.

RANGE: Arctic North America, extending a short distance into our area in lowlands, and down the higher Appalachians.

HABITAT: Cold moist woods, in rather acid soil.

CULTURE: Can be grown in a swamp garden where the evaporating moisture keeps the surface cool.

Colic-root (*Áletris farinòsa*)   **Pl. 17**

FEATURES: Flowers small, tubular, white, granular-surfaced, in a cylindric group on a 1- to 2-ft. stalk. Leaves basal, in a rosette on a thick stem base. Fruit capsular. Summer.

RANGE: Over our area and more southern states.

HABITAT: Damp grassland, bog margins, and open woods, in strongly acid and often rather sterile soil.

CULTURE: Desirable for a moist, grassy, wild garden where the soil can be kept in strongly acid condition.

NOTES: Some authorities place this plant in the LILY, and others in the AMARYLLIS FAMILY. Its root masses have medicinal value and are gathered commercially.

Greenbrier Family (*Smìlacàceae*)

FEATURES: Plants more or less vine-like, often climbing by tendrils, sometimes thorny. Leaves short and broad, netted-veined. Flowers small, greenish, the male and female on separate individuals. Fruit blue-black berries.

Catbrier (*Smìlax rotundifòlia*)   **Pl. 17**

FEATURES: Flowers few, in clusters on short stalks in the axils of thickish subevergreen leaves. Stems woody and thorny, high-climbing. Summer.

RANGE: Eastern half of the United States and adjacent Canada.

HABITAT: Thickets in sterile, often acid soil.

CULTURE: Spreads rapidly by underground stems, and suitable only for garden barriers, remote from delicate plants.

Greenbrier Family, concluded

Carrion-flower (*Smìlax herbàcea*)   Pl. 17

FEATURES: Flowers putrid-scented, in rounded clusters on long
   stalks in the axils of heart-shaped leaves. Stems delicate, not
   thorny, climbing over bushes to 5 or 6 ft. Early summer.
RANGE: Eastern half of the United States and adjacent Canada.
HABITAT: Woods and thickets, in moderately acid soil.
CULTURE: Easily grown in a wild garden.
NOTES: The foul odor of the flowers attracts small flies, which
   carry pollen from the male to the female ones.

Amaryllis Family (*Amaryllidàceae*)

FEATURES: Plants small, arising from a bulb, with grass-like
   leaves and flat-topped groups of a few flowers. Sepals and
   petals 3 each; stamens 6; bases of all floral organs united.

Goldstar-grass (*Hypóxis hirsùta*)   Pl. 18

FEATURES: Flowers golden stars about ¾ in. across; leaves and
   outside of flowers loosely hairy. Fruit a capsule with a few
   round black seeds. Late spring and summer.
RANGE: Eastern half of United States and adjacent Canada.
HABITAT: Open woods and grassland, in acid soil.
CULTURE: Desirable in the acid rock or wild garden.

Iris Family (*Iridàceae*)

FEATURES: Plants with creeping stems shallowly buried in soil
   bearing grass-like leaves set edge to edge, and few short-lived
   showy flowers in bracted clusters. Sepals, petals, and stamens
   3 each, their bases united into a long tube coherent with the
   ovary, which has 3 cavities and supports 3 styles.

Copper Iris (*Ìris fúlva*)   Pl. 18

FEATURES: Flowers bright bronzy red, about 3 in. across, on
   stalks 2 ft. or so high; ovary 6-angled. Late spring.
RANGE: Midland and Southern states, close to the Mississippi.
HABITAT: Moist grassland and swamp margins, in neutral or
   moderately acid soil.
CULTURE: An attractive subject for the moist wild garden; can
   also be grown in the border.

Iris Family, continued

Blueflag Iris (*Íris versícolor*)   Pl. 18

FEATURES: Flowers lavender-blue, the sepal bases yellow with bronze veining, 3 to 4 in. across, on stalks 2 to 3 ft. high. Ovary bluntly angled. Late spring and early summer.

RANGE: Eastern half of North America, except far north.

HABITAT: Pond margins, marshes, and meadows, in neutral or moderately acid soil.

CULTURE: Readily grown in moist-soil gardens.

NOTES: The related GREAT BLUEFLAG IRIS (*I. virgínica*), differs in having downy sepal bases and broader leaves; it is chiefly found in the Midland states, but extends eastward in Virginia. Another relative, LONG-LEAF IRIS (*I. hexágona*), has long leaves on a low zigzag stem, large violet-blue flowers, and a 6-angled ovary; it occurs in the south Midland region. Both of these grow in moist neutral or slightly acid soil and are desirable for cultivation.

Narrow-leaf Iris (*I. prismática*)   Pl. 18

FEATURES: Flowers lavender-blue with yellow sepal bases, about 3 in. across, on slender stalks 1 to 2 ft. high. Leaves narrow. Capsule 3-angled. Early summer.

RANGE: Coastal lowlands from Georgia to Nova Scotia, extending a hundred miles inland in the Northeastern states.

HABITAT: Grassland and bog margins, in moist, acid, sandy, or peaty soil.

CULTURE: Can be grown in rock and wild gardens, being more particular that the soil be kept acid than moist.

Vernal Iris (*I. vérna*)   Pl. 19

FEATURES: Flowers lavender-blue varying to white, the sepal base bearing a smooth golden spot, about 2 in. across, rising only a few inches from the ground, violet-scented. Leaves narrow, rather straight-sided. Early spring.

RANGE: Southeastern and lower parts of Northeastern states.

HABITAT: Wooded slopes and grassy sand hills, in strongly acid and sterile sandy or gravelly soil.

CULTURE: The most difficult of the species here listed to keep growing in the garden, because of its acid soil requirements. In rich soil it soon succumbs to fungus attack.

Iris Family, concluded

Crested Iris (*Ìris cristàta*) Pl. 19

FEATURES: Flowers lavender-blue, varying to white, the sepal base bearing a yellow fringy crest, about 2½ in. across, rising to 4 or 6 in. in height. Leaves ½ to ¾ in. wide, the margins curved. Spring.

RANGE: Southern uplands, and adjacent parts of Midland and Northeastern states.

HABITAT: Sparsely wooded rocky or sandy slopes, in neutral or moderately acid soil.

CULTURE: Readily cultivated in rock and wild gardens, requiring only that its wiry running stems be shallowly covered, and spreading into large patches.

NOTES: A closely related though more compact species, the LAKES IRIS (*I. lacústris*), grows around the upper Great Lakes; it requires a garden which does not heat up much in summer.

Slender Blue-eyed-grass (*Sisyrínchium mucronàtum*) Pl. 19

FEATURES: Flowers violet-blue, about ½ in. across, the 3 sepals and 3 petals alike, borne on a wiry stalk about 8 in. high, well above the tuft of slender grass-like leaves. Late spring and early summer.

RANGE: Northeastern and adjacent Midland states.

HABITAT: Grasslands and open woods, in damp neutral to moderately acid soil.

CULTURE: Easily grown, spreading into patches by seeds.

Winged Blue-eyed-grass (*S. graminoìdes*) Pl. 19

FEATURES: Flowers violet-blue, about ¾ in. across, the sepals and petals alike, borne on a broadly winged stalk about 1 ft. high, moderately exceeding the tufted ¼-in.-wide grass-like leaves. Spring and early summer.

RANGE: Eastern half of the United States and adjacent Canada.

HABITAT: Woods margins and grasslands, in soil varying widely in acidity and moisture.

CULTURE: Will thrive in a partly shaded wild or rock garden, producing abundant seedlings.

NOTES: Several other species of BLUE-EYED-GRASS grow in our area, but study by a specialist is necessary to distinguish them.

Orchis Family (*Orchidàceae*)

FEATURES: Delicate plants with bilaterally symmetrical flowers, with 3 (rarely 2) green or colored sepals, a pair of lateral petals, and a markedly different medial petal, termed the lip. Stamens 2 or often only 1, united with the style. Bases of all floral organs fused with the ovary, which matures to a capsule containing numerous minute seeds. Most native orchids are difficult to cultivate, being highly susceptible to attack by pests such as parasitic fungi, slugs, and mice.

Moccasin Orchid (*Cypripèdium acaúlè*) **Pl. 22**

FEATURES: Flower solitary, 2 in. long; lip moccasin-shaped, pink with red veins or rarely white; petals and 2 sepals bronzy. Leaves 2, basal, hairy, 6 to 9 in. long. Late spring.

RANGE: Eastern half of Canada, Northeastern and east Midland states, and south in the Appalachians.

HABITAT: Woods and bogs, in soil which, whether wet or dry, is consistently rich in humus, well aerated, and strongly acid.

CULTURE: Difficult to cultivate, persisting in the garden only when high acidity can be maintained and pests controlled.

Queen Slipper Orchid (*C. regìnae*) **Pl. 22**

FEATURES: Flower solitary (or a pair), about 1½ in. long, borne on a leafy stalk 2 to 3 ft. high; lip inflated, white suffused with pink; petals and 2 sepals white. Leaves hairy, up to 7 in. long. Summer.

RANGE: Eastern half of North America, southward in uplands.

HABITAT: Swamps and grasslands in moist, humus-rich soil which, though acid at the surface, is neutral at root level.

CULTURE: Can be grown in cool, moist, pest-free wild gardens.

Yellow Slipper Orchid (*C. pubéscens*) **Pl. 22**

FEATURES: Flower solitary (or a pair), 1 to 3 in. long, borne on a leafy stalk 1 to 2 ft. high; lip inflated, yellow; 2 sepals and spiraled petals bronzy. Leaves hairy, up to 6 in. long. Spring.

RANGE: Widespread over North America.

HABITAT: Wooded slopes and hummocks in swamps.

CULTURE: The easiest native ORCHID to grow in the garden, often persisting for many years.

Orchis Family, continued

Golden Slipper Orchid (*Cypripèdium parviflòrum*) Pl. 22

FEATURES: Flowers 1 to 3 in a row, less than 1 in. long, fragrant, on a leafy stalk 1 to 1½ ft. high; lip inflated, deep yellow with purple spots; 2 sepals and spiraled petals bronzy. Leaves few, hairy, up to 4 in. long. Late spring.

RANGE: Eastern Canada, extending a short distance down into our area. (Reports from farther south represent stunted forms of the next-preceding species.)

HABITAT: Cold swamps and grasslands, in moist, humus-rich, neutral to moderately acid soil.

CULTURE: Difficult to cultivate much south of its native range, being sensitive to warm summer conditions and to pests.

NOTES: Some authorities group this and the next preceding one together, and some class them as American varieties of the LADY SLIPPER ORCHID of Europe, *C. calceòlus*.

Silver Slipper Orchid (*C. cándidum*) Pl. 20

FEATURES: Flower solitary (or a pair), about 1 in. long, on a leafy stalk up to 1 ft. high; lip inflated, white; 2 sepals and petals bronzy. Leaves few, rather crowded, up to 5 in. long. Late spring.

RANGE: Midland and locally in central Northeastern states.

HABITAT: Cool swamps and grasslands, in moist neutral soil.

CULTURE: Can be grown in a cool, limy, pest-free swamp garden.

NOTES: Another species, the RAMS-HEAD ORCHID (*C. arietìnum*), occurs in Canada and the northernmost parts of our area.

Showy Orchis (*Órchis spectábilis*) Pl. 23

FEATURES: Plant 5 to 9 in. high. Flowers several, about 1 in. long, leafy-bracted, fragrant; lip flat, white or purplish, bearing a pendent spur at base; sepals and petals mauve-purple, grouped into a hood. Leaves 2, basal, smooth and shining, 4 to 8 in. long. Spring.

RANGE: Over most of our area, adjacent Canada, and Appalachians.

HABITAT: Damp woods and swamp margins, in neutral or moderately acid, usually rather rich soil.

CULTURE: May grow in a woodland garden, but usually falls prey to pests before long.

Orchis Family, continued

One-leaf Orchis (*Órchis rotundifòlia*) Pl. 20

FEATURES: Plant 6 to 10 in. high. Flowers few, about ½ in. long; lip flat, lobed, bearing a short pendent spur at base, white with purple spots; sepals lilac and petals pink, spreading. Leaf solitary, basal, round, smooth, 1½ to 3 in. long. Early summer.

RANGE: Northern North America, extending into the northernmost parts of our area.

HABITAT: Cold swamps and moist open woods, in usually neutral or slightly acid, humus-rich soil.

CULTURE: Practically impossible to cultivate south of its native range, being sensitive to summer heat and to pests.

Tubercled Rein-orchid (*Habenària flàva*) Pl. 20

FEATURES: Stalk leafy, 1 to 2 ft. high. Flowers greenish yellow, ⅓ in. long, narrow-bracted, in a long slender inflorescence; lip oblong, bearing a medial tubercle to which the common name refers, and pendent at base a slender ¼-in. spur. Leaves narrow. Early summer.

RANGE: Eastern half of United States and adjacent Canada.

HABITAT: Moist grassland and swamps, in neutral or moderately acid, humus-rich soil.

CULTURE: Can be grown in a pest-free swamp garden.

Shy-flower Rein-orchid (*H. bracteàta*) Pl. 20

FEATURES: Stalk leafy, 1 to 2 ft. high. Flowers greenish, ⅓ in. long, conspicuously bracted, in a short inflorescence; lip oblong with notched tip and a short thick spur pendent at base. Leaves several, the lower 5 in. long. Summer.

RANGE: Northern North America and south across our area into the Appalachians. A close relative grows in Eurasia.

HABITAT: Cold damp woods and swamp margins, in acid soil.

CULTURE: May grow for a time in a pest-free wild garden which can be kept cool in summer and strongly acid.

NOTES: Some authors consider this not specifically distinct from the Eurasian FROG ORCHID, its technical name then becoming *H. víridis bracteàta;* it has also been assigned to a distinct genus, *Coeloglóssum*. The common name chosen here refers to the way the flowers hide under the bracts.

Orchis Family, continued

Club-spur Rein-orchid (*Habenària clavellàta*) Pl. 21

FEATURES: Stalk few-leaved, 8 to 16 in. high. Flowers greenish white, ⅓ in. long, few in a short broad group, often standing in an oblique position; lip wedge-shaped, toothed at tip, with a slender curved club-like ½-in. spur at base. Principal leaf near base, several inches long, the upper ones much smaller. Summer.

RANGE: Eastern half of North America.

HABITAT: Swamps and bogs, in moist, strongly acid soil.

CULTURE: Fairly easy to grow in a well-maintained bog garden.

NOTES: Two related southern species extend up to New Jersey.

One-leaf Rein-orchid (*H. obtusàta*) Pl. 21

FEATURES: Plant 6 to 9 in. high. Flowers greenish white, about ⅓ in. long, in a short inflorescence; lip tapering to a down-bent tip, bearing a short pendent spur at base. Leaf solitary, narrow, blunt, 3 to 4 in. long. Summer.

RANGE: Northern North America, extending down a short distance into our area; also in northwestern Europe.

HABITAT: Cold woods and swamps in moist, moderately acid soil.

CULTURE: Can scarcely be grown below its native range, being unable to withstand much summer heat or pests.

Pad-leaf Orchid (*H. orbiculàta*) Pl. 21

FEATURES: Stalk stout, bearing a few scale leaves, 1 to 2 ft. high. Flowers greenish white, about 1 in. long, in a short, broad inflorescence; lip oblong, blunt, with 1-in.-long spur pendent at base. Leaves 2, large, round, shiny, flat on the ground. Summer.

RANGE: Northern North America, across our area chiefly in uplands, and down the Appalachians.

HABITAT: Deep cool woods, in acid, humus-rich soil.

CULTURE: Difficult to cultivate, requiring cool acid conditions and being highly susceptible to pests.

NOTES: In the northern part of our area occurs the closely related LONGSPUR PAD-LEAF ORCHID, which has been named *H. macrophýlla,* although this epithet is inapt since the leaves are not notably large; its spur is 2 to 3 in. long.

Plate 1

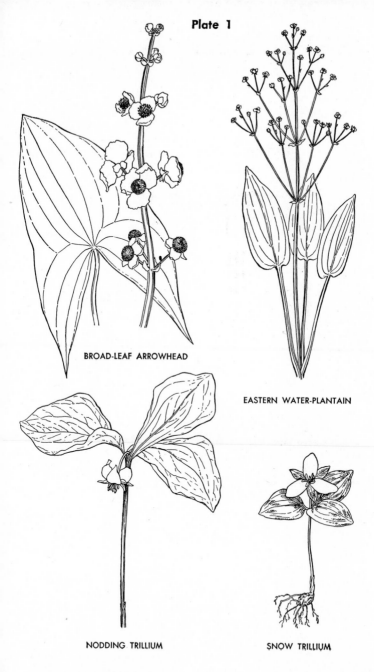

BROAD-LEAF ARROWHEAD

EASTERN WATER-PLANTAIN

NODDING TRILLIUM

SNOW TRILLIUM

Plate 2

TOAD TRILLIUM

GREAT TRILLIUM

WET-DOG TRILLIUM

PAINTED TRILLIUM

Plate 3

VIRGINIA
SPIDERWORT

BLUE-LEAF
SPIDERWORT

TALL DAYFLOWER

LOW DAYFLOWER

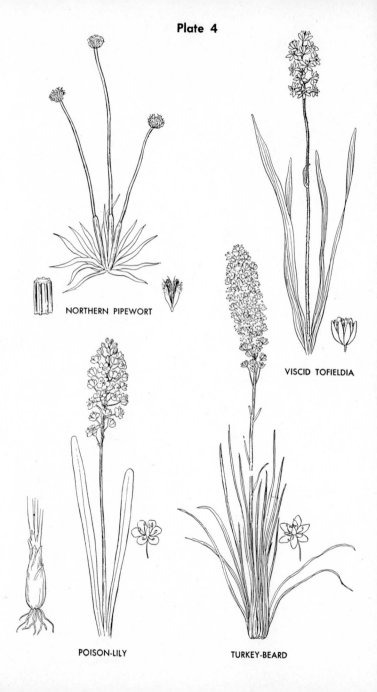

Plate 4

NORTHERN PIPEWORT

VISCID TOFIELDIA

POISON-LILY

TURKEY-BEARD

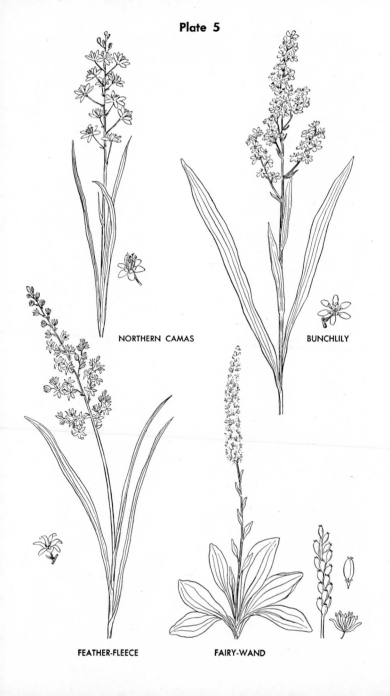

Plate 5

NORTHERN CAMAS

BUNCHLILY

FEATHER-FLEECE

FAIRY-WAND

Plate 6

SLENDER YELLOW-EYE

UPLAND YELLOW-EYE

PICKERELWEED

WHITE-HELLEBORE

Plate 7

SWAMP-HYACINTH

BOG-ASPHODEL

GOLDENCLUB

SKUNKCABBAGE

Plate 8

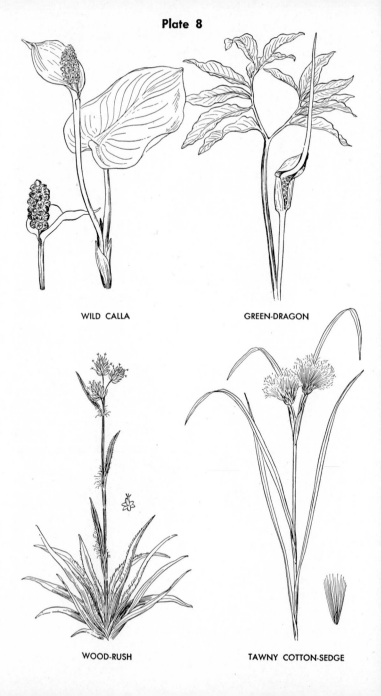

WILD CALLA

GREEN-DRAGON

WOOD-RUSH

TAWNY COTTON-SEDGE

Plate 9

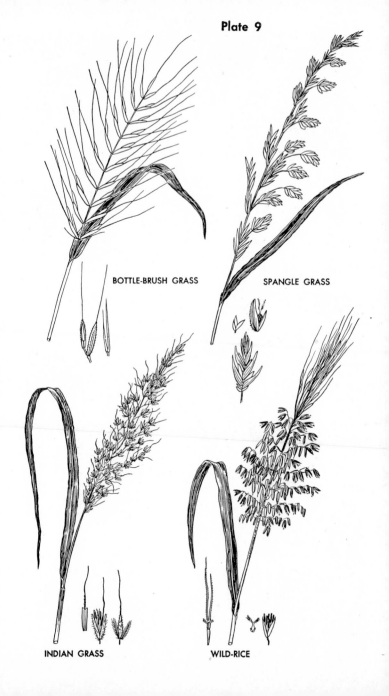

BOTTLE-BRUSH GRASS

SPANGLE GRASS

INDIAN GRASS

WILD-RICE

Plate 10

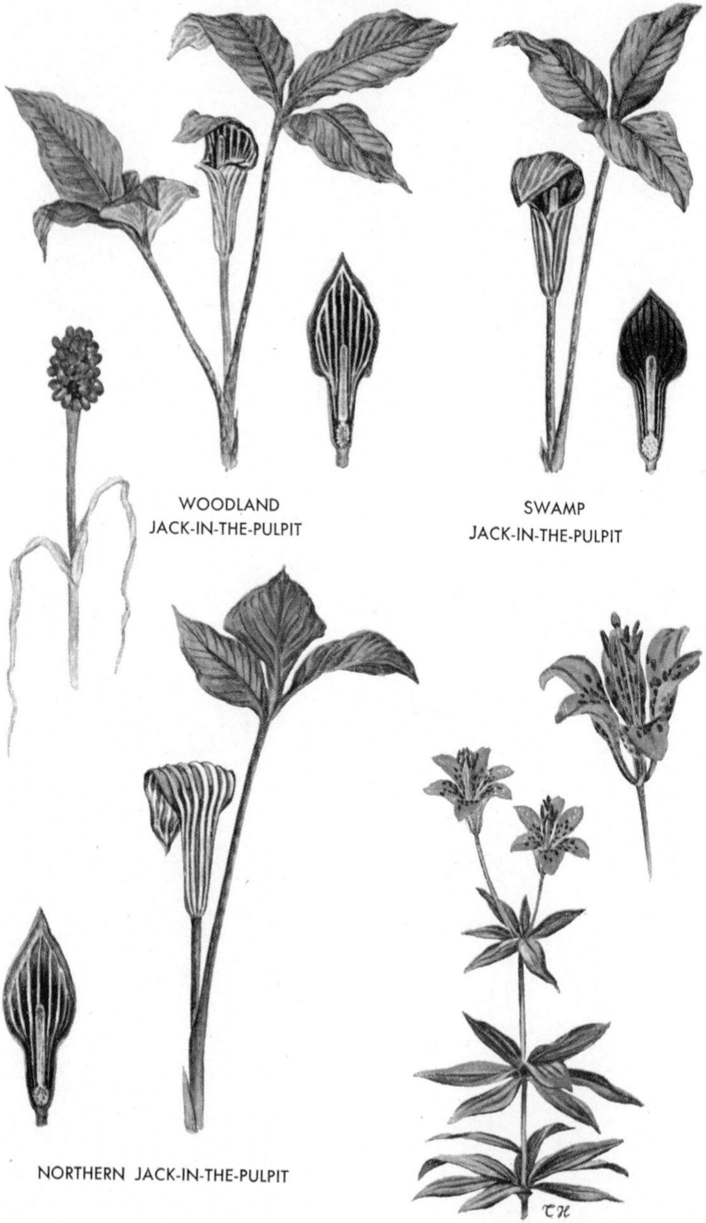

WOODLAND
JACK-IN-THE-PULPIT

SWAMP
JACK-IN-THE-PULPIT

NORTHERN JACK-IN-THE-PULPIT

WOOD LILY

Plate 11

YELLOW CANADA LILY

UPLAND CANADA LILY

MIDLAND LILY

TURKS-CAP LILY

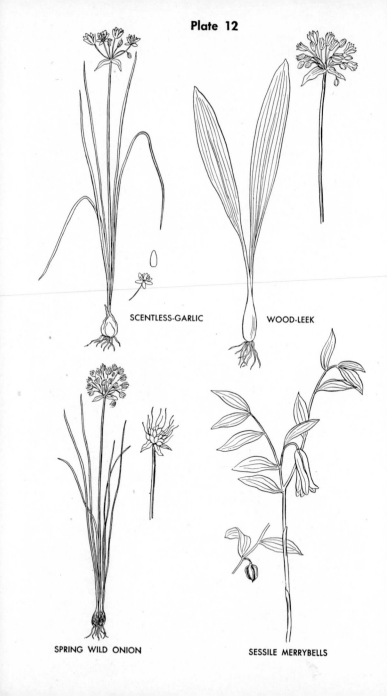

Plate 12

SCENTLESS-GARLIC

WOOD-LEEK

SPRING WILD ONION

SESSILE MERRYBELLS

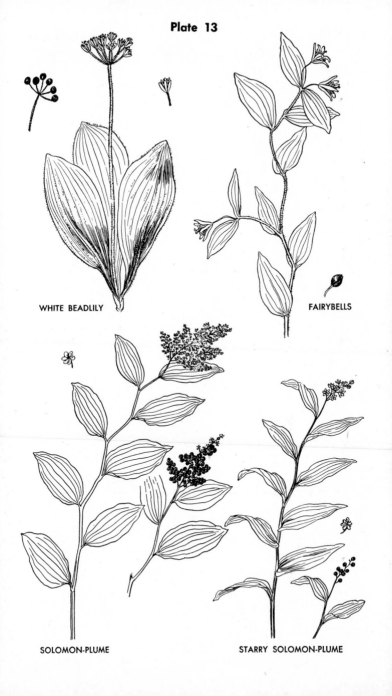

Plate 13

WHITE BEADLILY

FAIRYBELLS

SOLOMON-PLUME

STARRY SOLOMON-PLUME

Plate 14

EASTERN TROUTLILY

MIDLAND CAMAS-LILY

SUMMER WILD ONION

AUTUMN WILD ONION

Plate 15

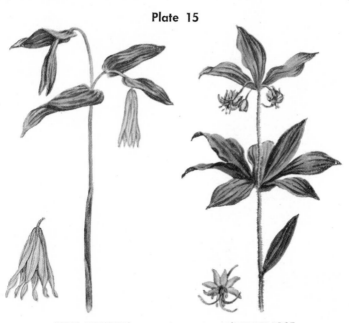

GREAT MERRYBELLS

CUCUMBER-ROOT

YELLOW BEADLILY

ROSYBELLS

Plate 16

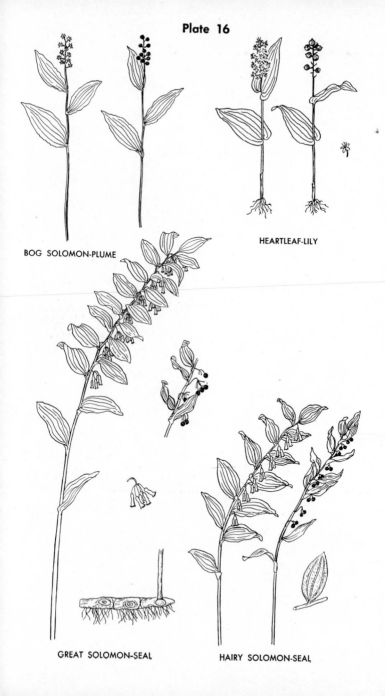

BOG SOLOMON-PLUME

HEARTLEAF-LILY

GREAT SOLOMON-SEAL

HAIRY SOLOMON-SEAL

Plate 17

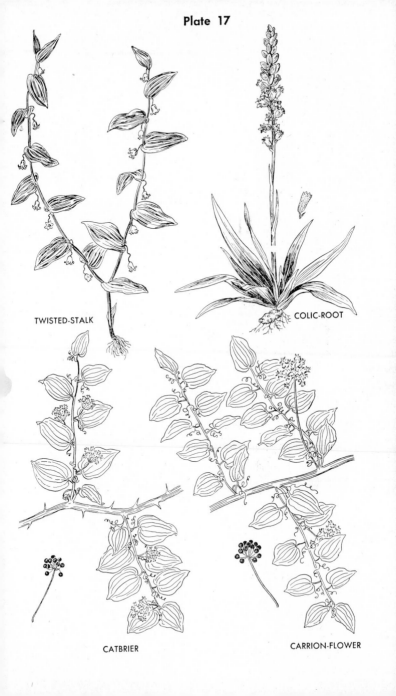

TWISTED-STALK

COLIC-ROOT

CATBRIER

CARRION-FLOWER

Plate 18

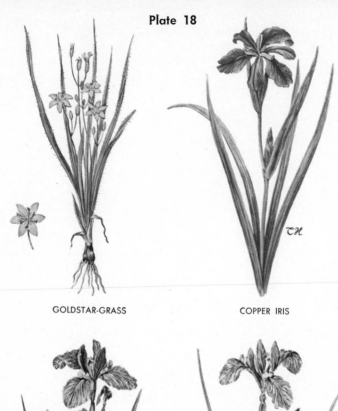

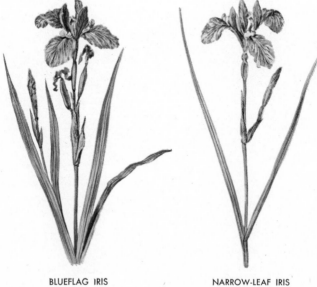

GOLDSTAR-GRASS

COPPER IRIS

BLUEFLAG IRIS

NARROW-LEAF IRIS

Plate 19

VERNAL IRIS

CRESTED IRIS

SLENDER BLUE-EYED-GRASS

WINGED BLUE-EYED-GRASS

Plate 20

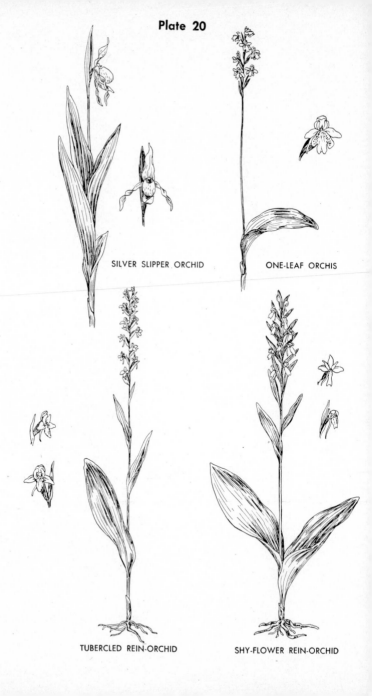

SILVER SLIPPER ORCHID

ONE-LEAF ORCHIS

TUBERCLED REIN-ORCHID

SHY-FLOWER REIN-ORCHID

Plate 21

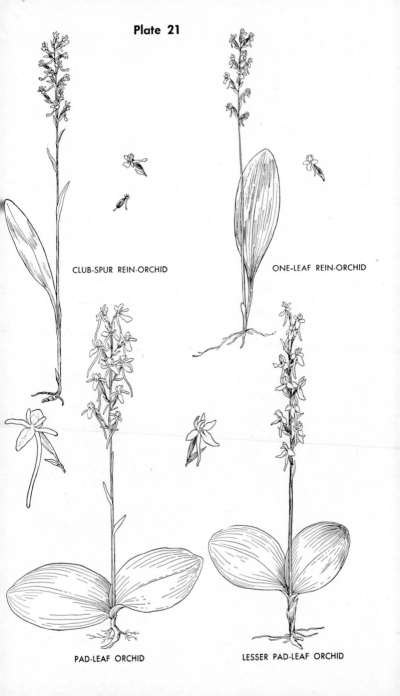

CLUB-SPUR REIN-ORCHID

ONE-LEAF REIN-ORCHID

PAD-LEAF ORCHID

LESSER PAD-LEAF ORCHID

Plate 22

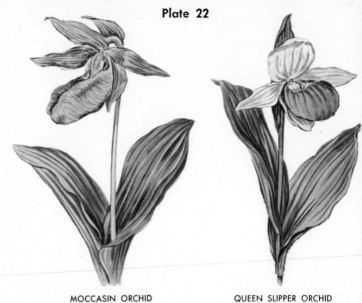

MOCCASIN ORCHID

QUEEN SLIPPER ORCHID

YELLOW SLIPPER ORCHID

GOLDEN SLIPPER ORCHID

Plate 23

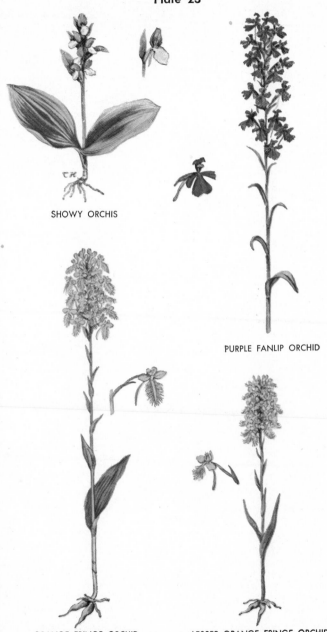

SHOWY ORCHIS

PURPLE FANLIP ORCHID

ORANGE FRINGE ORCHID

LESSER ORANGE FRINGE ORCHID

Plate 24

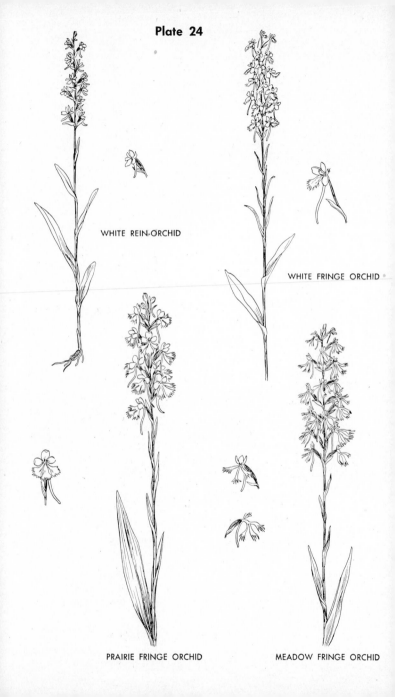

WHITE REIN-ORCHID

WHITE FRINGE ORCHID

PRAIRIE FRINGE ORCHID

MEADOW FRINGE ORCHID

Plate 25

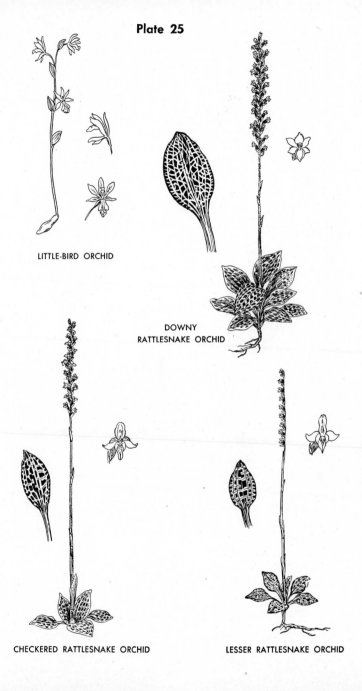

LITTLE-BIRD ORCHID

DOWNY
RATTLESNAKE ORCHID

CHECKERED RATTLESNAKE ORCHID

LESSER RATTLESNAKE ORCHID

Plate 26

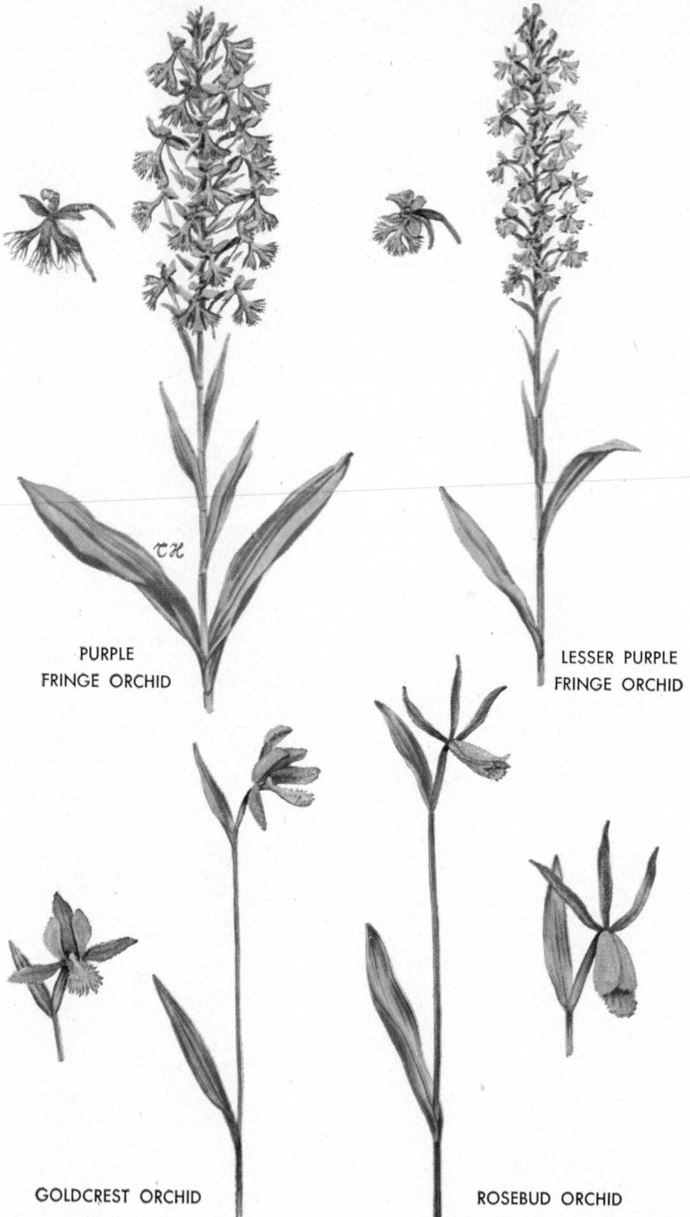

PURPLE
FRINGE ORCHID

LESSER PURPLE
FRINGE ORCHID

GOLDCREST ORCHID

ROSEBUD ORCHID

Plate 27

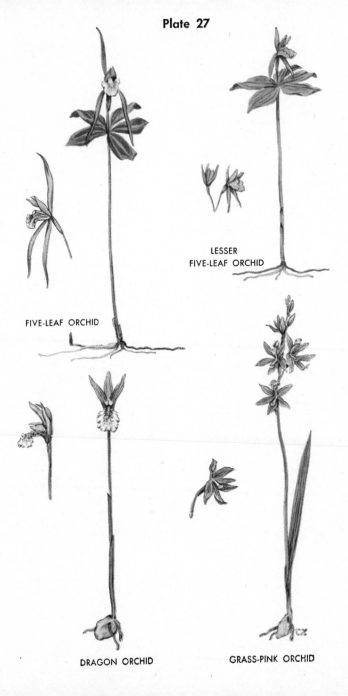

FIVE-LEAF ORCHID

LESSER
FIVE-LEAF ORCHID

DRAGON ORCHID

GRASS-PINK ORCHID

Plate 28

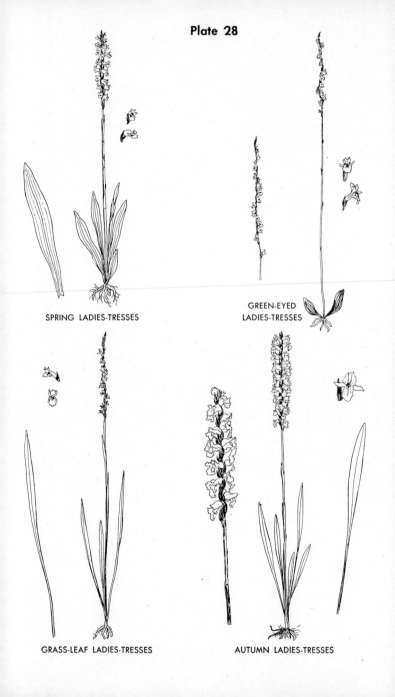

SPRING LADIES-TRESSES

GREEN-EYED
LADIES-TRESSES

GRASS-LEAF LADIES-TRESSES

AUTUMN LADIES-TRESSES

Plate 29

BROAD-LIP TWAYBLADE

NOTCH-LIP TWAYBLADE

LONG-LIP TWAYBLADE

AUTUMN CORALROOT

Plate 30

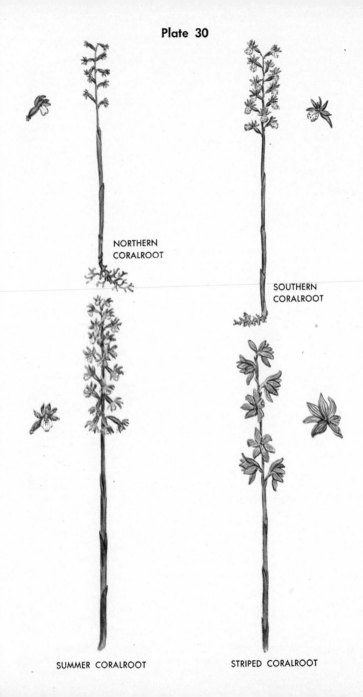

NORTHERN
CORALROOT

SOUTHERN
CORALROOT

SUMMER CORALROOT

STRIPED CORALROOT

Plate 31

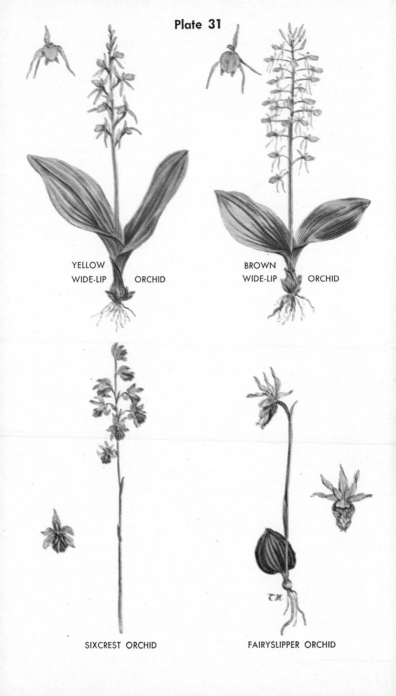

YELLOW
WIDE-LIP ORCHID

BROWN
WIDE-LIP ORCHID

SIXCREST ORCHID

FAIRYSLIPPER ORCHID

Plate 32

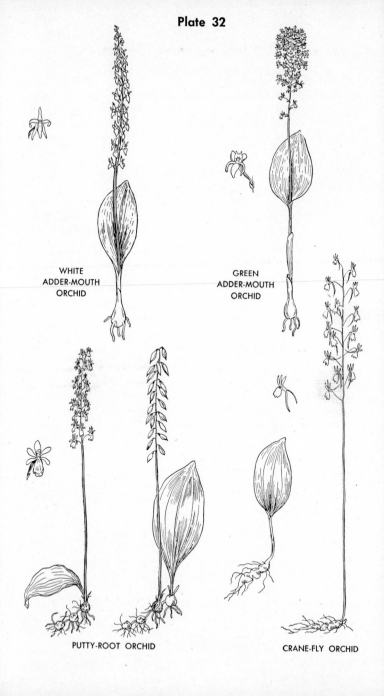

WHITE
ADDER-MOUTH
ORCHID

GREEN
ADDER-MOUTH
ORCHID

PUTTY-ROOT ORCHID

CRANE-FLY ORCHID

Orchis Family, continued

Lesser Pad-leaf Orchid (*Habenària hoókerì*)   Pl. 21

FEATURES: Stalk about 1 ft. high, leafless. Flowers several in a slender inflorescence, greenish yellow, about ¾ in. long; lip tapering to an upcurved point, bearing a slender ¾-in. spur pendent at base. Leaves 2, large and round, on the ground or ascending. Early summer.

RANGE: Northern part of our area and adjacent Canada.

HABITAT: Cool woods, in acid, humus-rich soil.

CULTURE: Rarely successfully cultivated, requiring especially cool acid soil and protection from pests.

White Rein-orchid (*H. dilatàta*)   Pl. 24

FEATURES: Stalk leafy, 1½ to 2½ ft. high. Flowers in a long slender inflorescence, white, about ½ in. long, fragrant; lip broad at base and tapering to a blunt point, bearing a slender ⅓-in. spur pendent at base. Leaves to 10 in. long. Late spring and summer.

RANGE: Northern North America, down a short distance into our area; also in the west American mountains and in northern Europe.

HABITAT: Cool swamps, bogs, and moist grasslands, in soil of widely varying texture and acidity.

CULTURE: Desirable for cultivation in a bog garden if this can be kept cool in summer and pests are controlled.

NOTES: This species grades into the GREEN REIN-ORCHID (*H. hyperbòrea*), which has greenish flowers with a narrower lip upcurved at tip. The two occupy about the same range and similar habitats.

White Fringe Orchid (*H. blephariglóttis*)   Pl. 24

FEATURES: Stalk leafy, 1 to 2 ft. high. Flowers numerous in a broad inflorescence, white, about ¾ in. long; lip oblong, fringed around the margin, with a slender 1-in. spur pendent at base. Leaves up to 8 in. long. Early summer.

RANGE: Eastern half of North America.

HABITAT: Sphagnum bogs and wet grasslands in strongly acid, peaty soil.

CULTURE: Can be cultivated only in bog gardens which are kept moist but well aerated and intensely acid.

Orchis Family, continued

Orange Fringe Orchid (*Habenària ciliàris*)   Pl. 23

FEATURES: Stalk leafy, 1½ to 2½ ft. high. Flowers numerous in a broad inflorescence, orange-yellow, about ¾ in. long; lip oblong, conspicuously fringed, bearing a slender 1-in. spur pendent at base. Leaves several, up to 8 in. long. Summer.

RANGE: Southern, Northeastern, and adjacent portions of the Midland states.

HABITAT: Moist thickets, bog margins, and grasslands, in sandy or clayey soil varying widely in acidity.

CULTURE: A fairly vigorous plant, this is one of the easier of the FRINGE ORCHIDS to cultivate, sometimes persisting in the wild garden if pests are not too active.

Lesser Orange Fringe Orchid (*H. cristàta*)   Pl. 23

FEATURES: Stalk leafy, 1 to 2 ft. high. Flowers numerous in a cylindric inflorescence, orange-yellow, about ½ in. long; lip narrow, upturned at tip, long-fringed, with a ¼-in. spur pendent at base. Leaves few, to 5 in. long. Summer.

RANGE: Southern states, north in coastal lowlands to lower New England.

HABITAT: Sphagnum bogs, thickets, and moist grasslands, in strongly acid, peaty soil.

CULTURE: Difficult to cultivate, requiring especially high soil acidity and freedom from parasites.

NOTES: The members of this group of FRINGE ORCHIDS tend to hybridize, so that intermediates between species are occasionally found.

Purple Fanlip Orchid (*H. peramoèna*)   Pl. 23

FEATURES: Stalk stout, leafy, 2 to 4 ft. high. Flowers numerous in a long thick inflorescence, bright purple, about 1 in. long; lip fan-shaped, split into 3 triangular divisions which are shallowly toothed at tip, bearing a 1-in. spur pendent at base. Leaves several, up to 8 in. long. Summer.

RANGE: Southern uplands and adjacent parts of our area.

HABITAT: Moist thickets and grasslands, rather deep-rooted in moderately acid, loamy soil.

CULTURE: Seems vigorous, but will not grow unless its soil conditions are closely matched and pests are controlled.

Orchis Family, continued

Purple Fringe Orchid (*Habenària fimbriàta*)   Pl. 26

FEATURES: Stalk leafy, 2 to 4 ft. high. Flowers in a broad cylindric inflorescence, mauve-purple, about 1 in. long; lip fanshaped, split into 3 triangular lobes deeply fringed at tip, bearing a slender 1½-in. spur pendent at base. Leaves several, up to 9 in. long. Early summer.

RANGE: Northeastern North America.

HABITAT: Cool moist woods and swamp margins, in moderately acid, humus-rich soil.

CULTURE: Rather difficult to grow in the wild garden, unless this is consistently cool, moist, and pest-free.

Lesser Purple Fringe Orchid (*H. psycòdes*)   Pl. 26

FEATURES: Stalk leafy, 1½ to 3 ft. high. Flowers in a narrow cylindric inflorescence, mauve-purple, about ¾ in. long; lip narrowly fan-shaped, split into 3 triangular fringed lobes, bearing a slender ¾-in. spur pendent at base. Leaves few, up to 8 in. long. Summer.

RANGE: Eastern half of North America, though in the south only in uplands.

HABITAT: Wet thickets and grasslands, in neutral or moderately acid soil.

CULTURE: Can be grown fairly well in a swamp garden if pests can be controlled.

NOTES: This and the next preceding species intergrade, so that it is often difficult to identify an isolated specimen.

Prairie Fringe Orchid (*H. leucophaèa*)   Pl. 24

FEATURES: Stalk stout, leafy, 3 to 4 ft. high. Flowers in a loose thick inflorescence, creamy white, fragrant, about 1 in. long; lip fan-shaped, cut into 3 wedge-shaped divisions with long fringes at tip, bearing a 1½-in. spur pendent at base. Leaves several, to 8 in. long. Early summer.

RANGE: Midland, rarely adjacent Northeastern states, and southern Canada.

HABITAT: Moist thickets and grasslands, in neutral to moderately acid, humus-rich soil.

CULTURE: Can scarcely be expected to grow in other than its native moist prairie habitat.

Orchis Family, continued

Meadow Fringe Orchid (*Habenària lácera*)   Pl. 24

FEATURES: Stalk leafy, 1 to 2 ft. high. Flowers numerous, greenish white, about ¾ in. long; lip fan-shaped, cut into 3 narrow wedge-shaped lobes with long fringe at tip, bearing a pendent ¾-in. spur at base. Leaves to 8 in. long. Summer.

RANGE: Eastern half of North America, except far south.

HABITAT: Moist grasslands and thickets around bog margins, in moderately to strongly acid soil.

CULTURE: Can be grown in a pest-free bog garden.

NOTES: Also known as the RAGGED ORCHID in reference to the strikingly fringed lip divisions.

Goldcrest Orchid (*Pogònia ophioglossoìdes*)   Pl. 26

FEATURES: Flower solitary (or paired) against a leafy bract on 1-ft.-high stalk bearing a solitary leaf about the middle, bright pink, fragrant; lip spoon-shaped, toothed at tip, bearing a yellow fringy crest. Late spring.

RANGE: Eastern half of North America; also northeastern Asia.

HABITAT: Sphagnum bogs, wet thickets, and grasslands, in strongly acid, humus-rich soil.

CULTURE: Difficult to transplant, since cutting the long, slender, humus-penetrating stems usually kills the plant; requires, too, a permanently moist, well-aerated, strongly acid soil.

NOTES: Known in various books by the peculiarly inapt name of SNAKE-MOUTH ORCHID.

Rosebud Orchid (*Cleìstes divaricàta*)   Pl. 26

FEATURES: Flower solitary, 1 to 2 in. long, above a leafy bract on a 1½- to 2-ft. stalk bearing a gray-green leaf above the middle; lip pink with bronze veins, trough-shaped, lobed at tip and bearing a granulate medial ridge; petals pink, short; sepals brown, long, narrow, spreading. Early summer.

RANGE: Southern states and adjacent parts of our area.

HABITAT: Dry or transiently wet grasslands and thickets, in strongly acid, humus-rich soil.

CULTURE: Extremely sensitive to pest attack.

NOTES: Also known as SPREADING CREST ORCHID, in reference to the conspicuous sepals. Some authorities assign it to the genus *Pogònia*.

Orchis Family, continued

Little-bird Orchid (*Triphòra trianthóphora*)   Pl. 25

FEATURES: Plant 4 to 8 in. high. Flowers few, suggesting, as the common name implies, tiny birds on the wing, lilac to whitish; lip roundish, ½ in. long, lobed at tip and bearing a granulate purple-and-green crest. Leaves few, small, roundish, pale or bronzy. Early autumn.

RANGE: Eastern half of United States.

HABITAT: Woods, in mostly neutral, rich loamy soil.

CULTURE: Plants die after blooming, but may produce tubers which remain dormant in the soil for some years, and then, if not meanwhile eaten by mice, send up blooming stalks.

NOTES: Also known as THREE BIRD ORCHID.

Five-leaf Orchid (*Isòtria verticillàta*)   Pl. 27

FEATURES: Stalk 8 to 10 in. high, smooth, purplish, tipped with a whorl of 5 leaves and the solitary or rarely paired 2-in.-long flowers; lip yellowish, lobed at tip, bearing a medial crest; short lateral petals and long forward-pointing sepals bronzy-green. Early spring.

RANGE: Eastern half of United States and adjacent Ontario.

HABITAT: Woods, usually of pine or oak, and bog margins, in strongly acid, humus-rich soil.

CULTURE: Difficult to transplant, since injury to the long, slender, running underground stems often kills the plant; also requires strongly acid, pest-free soil.

NOTES: A book name for this orchid is WHORLED POGONIA.

Lesser Five-leaf Orchid (*I. affìnis*)   Pl. 27

FEATURES: Stalk 6 to 8 in. high, gray-green, smooth except for bronzy scales near the base, tipped with a whorl of 5 lax leaves and paired or solitary 1-in. flowers; lip yellow, lobed at tip, bearing a broad crest; petals and sepals short, greenish yellow with bronze shading. Late spring.

RANGE: Northeastern states, apparently very rare.

HABITAT: Woods, in moderately acid, humus-rich soil.

CULTURE: Although the underground stem system of this orchid does not spread widely, and can be lifted intact, the plant is too delicate for successful cultivation; indeed it is very erratic in its reappearance even in its native haunts.

Orchis Family, continued

Dragon Orchid (*Arethùsa bulbòsa*)   Pl. 27

FEATURES: Flower solitary above small bracts on a smooth stalk 5 to 10 in. high, about 1½ in. long, suggesting the open mouth of some beast; lip whitish with conspicuous purple spots and yellowish crests; petals and sepals bright purple-pink. Leaf solitary, basal, grass-like, arising from the small white bulb as the flower matures. Spring.

RANGE: Eastern half of North America, except far southward.

HABITAT: Wet sphagnum bogs and hummocks of litter in swamps, in strongly acid, peaty soil.

CULTURE: Difficult to cultivate, for even if the soil acidity can be maintained, rodents soon eat the bulbs. It has, however, been grown by planting in a clump of sphagnum on a plank floating well out in a garden pool.

Grass-pink Orchid (*Calopògon pulchéllus*)   Pl. 27

FEATURES: Flowers several, magenta-pink or rarely white, about 1 in. long, on an 8- to 15-in. stalk; lip spoon-shaped, bearing a golden fringed crest, standing up at the back of the flower. Leaf solitary, like a broad veiny grass blade, from a white bulb. Summer.

RANGE: Eastern half of North America.

HABITAT: Bog margins and moist, thinly wooded slopes, in strongly acid sandy or gravelly soil.

CULTURE: Can be grown in a pest-free bog garden.

Downy Rattlesnake Orchid (*Goodyèra pubéscens*)   Pl. 25

FEATURES: Flowers small, white, numerous in a cylindric group on a downy stalk 8 to 15 in. high; lip cupped. Leaves several, basal, gray-green with conspicuous white netted veins to which the common name refers. Summer.

RANGE: Eastern half of United States and adjacent Ontario.

HABITAT: Wooded slopes, mostly under pine or oak trees, in acid, humus-rich soil.

CULTURE: May grow for a time in a shady acid-soil garden.

NOTES: This is called in books RATTLESNAKE PLANTAIN, but there seems nothing to be gained by naming a delicate orchid for a coarse weed. Alternative genus epithets are also in use as *Epipáctis* and *Peràmium*.

Orchis Family, continued

Checkered Rattlesnake Orchid (*Goodyèra tesselàta*) Pl. 25

FEATURES: Flowers small, white, several in a loosely spiraled inflorescence on a stalk 5 to 10 in. high; lip cupped, with flaring margin. Leaves several, basal, about 2 in. long, dull green with gray, irregularly netted veins. Summer.

RANGE: Eastern Canada, Northeastern, and north Midland states.

HABITAT: Cool wooded slopes, in acid, humus-rich soil.

CULTURE: More difficult to grow than the next preceding species, requiring soil which does not heat up much in summer.

Lesser Rattlesnake Orchid (*G. ophioìdes*) Pl. 25

FEATURES: Flowers small, white, in a straight or somewhat twisted row on a 6- to 8-in. scaly stalk; lip sac-like, with a down-bent tip. Leaves several, basal or 1 on stalk, ½ to 1 in. long, green with a few broadly white-bordered veins. Summer.

RANGE: Northern North America, extending in uplands across our area into the Appalachians.

HABITAT: Cold bog margins and deep moist woods, in strongly acid, humus-rich soil.

CULTURE: Capable of cultivation only in an especially cool, acid, and pest-free garden.

NOTES: Some authorities class this orchid as a variety of the European *G. rèpens,* but they differ markedly in inflorescence plan and leaf marking. Hybrids between the three American species are occasionally found.

Spring Ladies-tresses (*Spiránthes lùcida*) Pl. 28

FEATURES: Flowers in an irregularly spiraled group on a leafy stalk 6 to 8 in. high, about ¼ in. long, white except for a yellow stripe down the lip. Leaves several, chiefly basal, up to 5 in. long. Spring.

RANGE: Over our area and adjacent Canada.

HABITAT: Moist grasslands, in neutral, rather rich soil.

CULTURE: May grow for a time in a wild garden, but likely to be soon destroyed by pests.

NOTES: The members of this genus are also known as PEARL-TWISTS. Alternative technical epithets are sometimes used.

Orchis Family, continued

Green-eyed Ladies-tresses (*Spiránthes grácilis*)　　Pl. 28

FEATURES: Flowers tiny, in a spiraled row on a leafless stalk 1 to 2 ft. high, white except for an intense green central spot on the lip. Leaves few, basal, roundish, developing as the flowers mature, evergreen. Roots fleshy, 2 or 3 in a radiating group. Summer.

RANGE: Eastern half of United States and adjacent Canada.

HABITAT: Grasslands, in dryish, moderately acid soil.

CULTURE: Can be grown in a grassy wild garden, but likely to succumb to pests or to more vigorous competing plants.

NOTES: Northern and southern phases of this have been classed as separate species, but seem only varietally distinct. The chief one in our region, which has been named *S. lácera,* has the flowers rather widely spaced and little spiraled, and the leaves thinnish and long-persistent. The related WHITE LA-DIES-TRESSES (*S. gràyi*) has pure white flowers and a soli-tary taproot. It grows in strongly acid soils in the southern part of our area.

Grass-leaf Ladies-tresses (*S. vernàlis*)　　Pl. 28

FEATURES: Flowers small, in a spiraled row on a leafy stalk 1 to 2 ft. high, creamy white with a yellowish stripe down the lip. Leaves several, grass-like. Summer.

RANGE: Southern states and lower parts of our area.

HABITAT: Damp grasslands, in neutral or moderately acid soil.

CULTURE: Will grow in some wild gardens.

NOTES: This grades into a supposedly distinct species, *S. prae-cox,* which differs, however, only in obscure details.

Autumn Ladies-tresses (*S. cérnua*)　　Pl. 28

FEATURES: Flowers in 3 or 4 somewhat spiraled rows on a leafy stalk 6 to 12 in. high, white, about ⅓ in. long, more or less fragrant. Leaves grass-like. Autumn.

RANGE: Eastern half of North America.

HABITAT: Marshes, moist grasslands, springy slopes, and sum-mer-dry open woods, in moderately or strongly acid soil.

CULTURE: Though perhaps the easiest of the LADIES-TRESSES to grow, this is not immune to destruction by pests.

NOTES: SWEET LADIES-TRESSES is a large, fragrant variety.

Orchis Family, continued

Broad-lip Twayblade (*Listèra convallarioìdes*)   Pl. 29

FEATURES: Plant 4 to 8 in. high. Flowers numerous, bronzy green, about ½ in. long; lip lobed near tip and base. Leaves 2, roundish, opposite or nearly so about the middle of stalk. Early summer.

RANGE: Northern North America, extending a short distance down into our area.

HABITAT: Cold moist woods and swamp margins, in neutral or moderately acid, humus-rich soil.

CULTURE: Unlikely to succeed far from its native haunts.

NOTES: The related APPALACHIAN TWAYBLADE (*L. smállii*) has broader, more pointed leaves and a deeply notched lip. It grows in bogs and RHODODENDRON thickets in the Appalachians and uplands of the Northeastern states. Its soil is strongly acid, and it may grow in a well-maintained bog garden.

Notch-lip Twayblade (*L. cordàta*)   Pl. 29

FEATURES: Plant 3 to 6 in. high. Flowers few, bronzy green, tiny, the lip deeply notched and V-shaped. Leaves 2, heart-shaped, subopposite near middle of stalk. Late spring.

RANGE: Around the world in all lands bordering the Arctic, and down in the uplands of our area.

HABITAT: Cold bogs and moist woods, in strongly or sometimes only slightly acid soil.

CULTURE: Too susceptible to pests for cultivation.

Long-lip Twayblade (*L. austràlis*)   Pl. 29

FEATURES: Plant 4 to 8 in. high. Flowers few, bronzy green, up to ½ in. long; lip deeply cleft into two narrow parallel divisions. Leaves 2, roundish, subopposite halfway up stalk. Late spring.

RANGE: Southern and Northeastern states and adjacent Ontario.

HABITAT: Moist woods and bog margins, in moderately to strongly acid soil.

CULTURE: Somewhat more amenable to cultivation than the other species listed, though only in pest-free bog gardens.

NOTES: The common name of the genus *Listèra,* Scotch for "two-blade," refers to the paired leaves on the stalk.

Orchis Family, continued

Northern Coralroot (*Corallorhìza trìfida*)   Pl. 30

FEATURES: Plant leafless, though bearing a few scales on the greenish 4- to 12-in. stalk. Flowers few, small, greenish yellow with more or less purple-spotted white lip, lobed toward tip and base. Underground system a cluster of fleshy-branched coral-like stems, to which the common name of this and related species refers. Spring.

RANGE: Northern Europe and North America, south in the uplands of the Northeastern states into the Appalachians.

HABITAT: Deep cool woods and swamps in humus of varying reaction.

CULTURE: The CORALROOT ORCHIDS lack chlorophyl in their tissues, and obtain all their nourishment from the humus into which their underground stems extend. Like saprophytes in general, they cannot be transplanted, although they sometimes appear where seeds have been sown in humus years previously.

Southern Coralroot (*C. wisteriàna*)   Pl. 30

FEATURES: Plant leafless, bearing a few scales on the bronzy 8- to 15-in. stalk. Flowers several, about ⅓ in. long, bronzy or rarely yellowish; lip white, usually purple-spotted, wavy-margined, not lobed. Underground stems coral-like. Spring.

RANGE: Southern states and adjacent parts of our area, also extending into the Rocky Mountain region.

HABITAT: Wooded slopes and flats in mostly neutral humus.

Summer Coralroot (*C. maculàta*)   Pl. 30

FEATURES: Plant leafless, bearing scales on the bronzy 8- to 15-in. stalk. Flowers numerous, up to ¾ in. long, bronzy; lip white with purple spots, large and squarish, with a lobe on either side toward the base. Underground stems coral-like. Summer.

RANGE: Over most of the United States and southern Canada.

HABITAT: Woods, in humus of usually moderate acidity.

NOTES: This is commonest of the CORALROOTS. These ORCHIDS live in an especially critical state of equilibrium with root-investing fungi, and so are very erratic in their reappearance from year to year.

Orchis Family, continued

Autumn Coralroot (*Corallorhìza odontorhìza*)   **Pl. 29**

FEATURES: Plant leafless, bearing a few scales on the bronzy 4- to 6-in. stalk. Flowers few, tiny, their parts scarcely spreading, bronzy or rarely yellow; lip white with purple spots, roundish. Stalk enlarged at base to a globular tuber from which slender coral-like underground stems extend. Autumn.

RANGE: Eastern half of the United States and adjacent Ontario, becoming rare northward.

HABITAT: Woods, in moderately to strongly acid humus.

CULTURE: As with other saprophytes, cannot be transplanted.

NOTES: This diminutive plant is probably commoner than is usually supposed, the inconspicuous flowers rendering it easily overlooked.

Striped Coralroot (*C. striàta*)   **Pl. 30**

FEATURES: Plant leafless, but bearing scales on the bronzy 9- to 18-in. stalk. Flowers numerous, about ½ in. long, bronzy with bright purple stripes on lip, petals, and sepals. Underground system a large group of coral-like stems. Spring.

RANGE: Northern North America, barely entering the northernmost parts of our area.

HABITAT: Cool woods and swamp margins, in neutral or somewhat acid humus.

NOTES: The largest and showiest CORALROOT.

Sixcrest Orchid (*Hexaléctris spicàta*)   **Pl. 31**

FEATURES: Plant leafless, but bearing scales on the bronzy 1- to 2-ft. stalk. Flowers few, nearly 1 in. long, bronzy with conspicuous purple stripes; lip roundish, lobed at tip, bearing about 6 purple-tipped ridges, to which both common and technical genus names refer. Underground system a radiating group of fleshy, somewhat coral-like stems. Summer.

RANGE: Southern states and adjacent parts of our area.

HABITAT: Wooded slopes and rock ledges, in usually neutral soil, which may be gravelly, sandy, or clayey, with a humus content seeming rather low for a saprophyte.

CULTURE: Not transplantable.

NOTES: While this and the next preceding are placed in separate genera, their coloring is strikingly similar.

Orchis Family, continued

Yellow Wide-lip Orchid (*Líparis loesélii*)   **Pl. 31**

FEATURES: Flowers few, ¼ in. long, greenish yellow, on an angled stalk 2 to 8 in. high; lip oblong, thinnish, grooved. Leaves 2, basal, 3 to 5 in. long, smooth and shining, arising from a shallowly set bulb. Early summer.

RANGE: Northern North America and Europe, down into the uplands of our area.

HABITAT: Damp woods, swamp margins, and moist grasslands, in moderately acid, humus-rich soil.

CULTURE: Difficult to cultivate, the bulbs being a favorite food of burrowing rodents.

NOTES: In some books members of the genus *Líparis* are termed TWAYBLADES, but this belongs to *Listèra*, discussed above. The name for the present species in Europe is FEN ORCHID.

Brown Wide-lip Orchid (*L. liliifòlia*)   **Pl. 31**

FEATURES: Flowers rather numerous, ½ in. long, greenish brown, on an angled stalk 4 to 8 in. high; lip relatively broad, roundish, translucent, brown with purple veins. Leaves 2, basal, 3 to 5 in. long, smooth and shining, arising from a nearly superficial greenish bulb. Late spring.

RANGE: Over our area and uplands of the Southern states.

HABITAT: Open woods in moderately acid, humus-rich soil.

CULTURE: Can be grown in a woodland garden and may survive for a time, but rodents will ultimately find it.

White Adder-mouth Orchid (*Maláxis brachýpoda*)   **Pl. 32**

FEATURES: Plant 3 to 6 in. high. Flowers greenish white, short-stalked, about ¼ in. long, in a slender inflorescence; lip gradually tapering to a point. Leaf solitary, borne near the stalk base, which is somewhat bulbous. Early summer.

RANGE: Northern and upland parts of our area and adjacent Canada.

HABITAT: Cool swamps and moist grassland, in usually neutral, humus-rich soil.

CULTURE: Delicate and susceptible to garden pests.

NOTES: This species is sometimes confused with the European *M. monophýllos*, which differs in having the lip standing erect at the back of the flower.

Orchis Family, continued

Green Adder-mouth Orchid (*Maláxis unifòlia*)   Pl. 32

FEATURES: Plant 3 to 8 in. high. Flowers green, minute, long-stalked in a blunt cylindric group, often twisted so as to lie sidewise. Leaf solitary, borne about the middle of the stalk. Underground system a small greenish bulb. Summer.

RANGE: Eastern half of the United States and adjacent Canada.

HABITAT: Open woods and bog margins, in strongly acid, humus-rich, often sandy soil.

CULTURE: Difficult to cultivate, because of its requirement for high acidity and also its attractiveness to rodents.

NOTES: A relative of this, differing in the longer and narrower inflorescence, has recently been named *M. bayárdi*, but seems only varietally distinct; it is rare, being known in north-eastern Pennsylvania, southeastern Virginia, and the Appalachians of North Carolina. Another relative, the SOUTHERN AD-DER-MOUTH ORCHID (*M. floridàna*), differs in having 2 leaves alternate on the stalk and larger flowers with a yellow center; it extends from Florida up to ravines of southeastern Virginia, where beds of fossil shells outcrop.

Fairyslipper Orchid (*Calýpso bulbòsa*)   Pl. 31

FEATURES: Flower solitary, showy, about 1 in. long, on a stalk 3 to 6 in. high; lip inflated, with a translucent cover, white blotched with purple, and bearing yellowish hairs in front; petals and sepals narrow, bronzy purple. Leaf solitary, basal, withering early. Underground system a small tuber. Late spring.

RANGE: In all northern lands, extending down a short distance into our area.

HABITAT: Cold damp woods, in neutral to moderately acid, humus-rich soil.

CULTURE: The northeastern form of this species seems never to have been successfully cultivated far from its native haunts, requiring exceptionally cool and pest-free conditions. The Rocky Mountain form (offered by dealers in wild flowers) is somewhat easier to grow, yet it too disappears without warning.

NOTES: One of our loveliest native orchids, fast vanishing with the cutting of northern forests.

Orchis Family, concluded

Putty-root Orchid (*Apléctrum hyemàlè*) **Pl. 32**

FEATURES: Flowers several, ½ in. long, bronzy, borne on a leafless stalk 10 to 20 in. high; lip oblong, lobed toward tip, white with purple blotches. Leaf solitary, basal, 4 to 6 in. long, dark green with prominent pale veins, appearing in autumn, remaining green through winter, and withering as the flowers develop. Underground system a group of round tubers connected by slender stems; contents of tubers putty-like, suggesting the common name. Late spring.

RANGE: Over our area, adjacent Canada, and southern uplands.

HABITAT: Damp woods, in humus-rich soil, usually neutral or slightly acid.

CULTURE: In the wild garden may produce leaves each autumn for a few years, until rodents discover the tubers, but rarely blooms unless the soil is closely similar to that of its native haunts.

NOTES: Another common name, ADAM-AND-EVE ORCHID, refers to the way the tubers grow side by side.

Crane-fly Orchid (*Tipulària discolor*) **Pl. 32**

FEATURES: Flowers bronzy, numerous, all opening about the same time, turned obliquely sideways on individual stalks, in a long inflorescence on a leafless main stalk 1 to 2 ft. high; lip consisting of a long narrow strip with a short basal lobe on either side, bearing at base a long slender spur. Leaf solitary, basal, 3 to 4 in. long, dark green above and purple beneath, somewhat plaited along a few veins, appearing in autumn and remaining normal during winter, but withering well before the flowers appear. Underground system a chain of pillow-shaped tubers. Late summer.

RANGE: Southern states and adjacent parts of our area.

HABITAT: Pine or oak woods, in humus-rich soil of rather strongly acid reaction.

CULTURE: May grow in an acid wild garden, but the tubers are often likely to be located and destroyed by rodents before a flowering stalk can develop.

NOTES: The flowers resemble long-legged insects, suggesting both the common name and genus epithet.

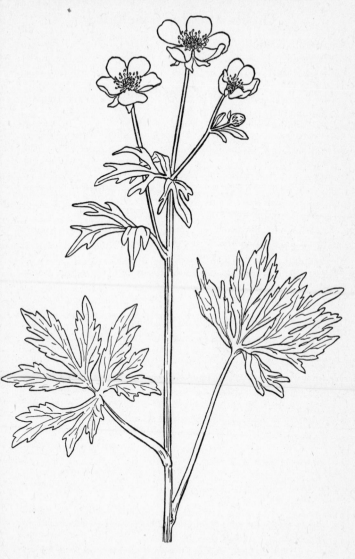

Dicots: Classification

As noted in the general discussion of classification on page xv, the second main group of flowering plants, known as the Dicots, is characterized by having the floral symmetry most frequently based on the number 5, and the chief veins of the leaves divergent, with heavy cross connections. The Dicots in turn are separable into two subdivisions, on the basis of corolla characters. In the first of these the petals are free from one another, or else have in the course of evolution become obsolete. In the second, the petals are more or less united into a disk, a cup, or a tubular corolla.

If preliminary inspection indicates an unknown plant to be a Dicot, the next step is, then, to examine the corolla, and to allocate the specimen to one or the other of these subdivisions. When the petals are conspicuous, it is an easy matter to establish whether they are free or not: pull one of them and see if it comes off without disturbing the adjoining ones or if it tends to bring others with it.

To tell whether the petals are obsolete will require close examination, for in such cases the sepals often become petaloid, their normal green color changing to white, yellow, pink, etc. When there is but a solitary whorl of organs attached to the receptacle below the stamens, that whorl represents the calyx, and its organs are sepals, no matter what their coloration.

In the 45 pages and 32 plates which follow, the members of the Free-petal Subdivision are treated. A key to families is given first, although it is to be noted that the relations of the groups of Dicots are rather complex, so that many exceptions to the descriptions given in key lines are likely to be encountered.

Since the sequence in which the families in this subdivision are taken up is different from that used in most current reference works, a discussion of the evolutionary ideas on which arrangement is based is in order.

CARPELS few, yielding a capsule.
    LEAVES opposite; flowers
        large . . **Four-o'clock** F.
    LEAVES alternate; flowers
        small . . . **Buckwheat** F.
    SEPALS obsolete also . . **Lizard-tail** F.
FLORAL SYMMETRY bilateral.
    FRUIT a legume; stamens 10.
    STAMENS separate, some imperfect;
        petals nearly alike . . . **Senna** F.
    STAMENS more or less united, all per-
        fect; petals of 3 sorts . . . **Pea** F.
    FRUIT a capsule.
    SEPALS all green; petals 5, showy **Violet** F.
    SEPALS in part colored like petals.
    COLORED SEPALS 2, lateral **Candyroot** F.
    COLORED SEPAL 1, basal **Snapweed** F.
    FLOWERS lacking sepals and petals, the stamens and
    carpels in a cup-shaped receptacle **Spurge** F.
FLOWER PARTS more or less united at base.
UNION involving calyx, corolla, and stamens **Loosestrife** F.
UNION involving carpels also.
  UNITED PARTS forming a mere disk.
    CARPELS numerous . . . . **Rose** F.
    CARPELS few.
    CARPEL NUMBER 4; carpels well united **Parnassia** F.
    CARPEL NUMBER 2; carpels little united **Saxifrage** F.
  UNITED PARTS forming a cup or cylinder.
    SEEDS small, numerous in each cavity; carpels 4.
    STIGMAS 4 . . . . . . **Evening-primrose** F.
    STIGMA 1 . . . . . . **Meadow-beauty** F.
    SEEDS large, few or solitary in each cavity.
    PETALS present.
    PLANTS consisting of huge fleshy stems **Cactus** F.
    PLANTS otherwise.
    FRUIT dry . . . . . . **Carrot** F.
    FRUIT fleshy.
    STAMEN NUMBER 5 . . **Ginseng** F.
    STAMEN NUMBER 4 . . **Dogwood** F.
    PETALS obsolete.
    SEPALS 5; plant parasitic . . **Sandalwood** F.
    SEPALS 3; plant not parasitic . **Wild-ginger** F.

Waterlily Family (*Nymphaeàceae*)

FEATURES: Aquatic plants with coarse stems creeping in mud, and large flowers and leaves. Sepals few; petals numerous, grading into stamens; carpels numerous, bulky.

American Lotus (*Nelúmbo lùtea*)   Pl. 33

FEATURES: Flowers borne high above water, pale yellow, 4 to 8 in. across; sepals 4 or 5; carpels in pits in a hemispheric receptacle. Leaves 1 to 2 ft. across, their stalk attached centrally. Summer.

RANGE: Southern states, extending north locally in our area, in widely separated places.

HABITAT: Lakes and slow-moving streams.

CULTURE: Readily cultivated in water gardens.

NOTES: Both the fleshy stems and the seeds of this plant were used as food by the Indians. It is not to be confused with the ASIATIC LOTUS, which has larger, pink flowers, and is not winter-hardy in much of our area.

White Waterlily (*Nymphaèa odoràta*)   Pl. 33

FEATURES: Flowers floating, white or pinkish, about 4 in. across, fragrant; sepals 4; carpels united into a globular ovary tipped by a whorl of stigmas. Leaves round, 5 to 10 in. across, floating. Summer.

RANGE: Eastern half of North America.

HABITAT: Lakes, ponds, and stream margins.

CULTURE: Waterlilies are extensively cultivated.

NOTES: While primitive in some respects, this is specialized in having the bases of petals and stamens united to the ovary.

Spatterdock (*Nùphar ádvena*)   Pl. 34

FEATURES: Flowers floating or emersed, 2 to 3 in. across, yellow; sepals 5 or 6; petals small; carpels united into a flask-shaped ovary tipped by a disk bearing radiating stigmas. Leaves 6 to 12 in. long, floating or emersed. Summer.

RANGE: Eastern half of North America.

HABITAT: Muddy shores and shallow waters generally.

CULTURE: Spreads rather rapidly for a small garden pool.

NOTES: One or more related species, differing in minor details, grow in our area also.

Buttercup Family (*Ranunculàceaè*)

FEATURES: Flower parts separate; petals few or obsolete, the sepals then bright-colored and petal-like; stamens numerous; carpels varying from numerous and spirally arranged to few and whorled or to solitary.

Swamp Buttercup (*Ranúnculus septentrionàlis*)   Pl. 34

FEATURES: Flowers an inch across, borne on long arching stems; petals 5, longer than sepals, broadened upward, bright yellow; carpels numerous. Leaves long-stalked, divided into 3 lobed and toothed leaflets. Stem hairy, rooting at nodes. Late spring and summer.

RANGE: Over our area and adjacent regions.

HABITAT: Swamps and wet thickets, in humus-rich soil.

CULTURE: Will spread into a large patch in a moist woodland.

NOTES: About 20 other species of this genus occur in our area; the most conspicuous are weeds introduced from Europe.

Hepatica (*Hepática americàna*)   Pl. 34

FEATURES: Flowers ½ in. across, on slender hairy 4 to 6 in. stalks; sepals 5 to 9, white, pink, lilac, or lavender-blue; petals obsolete; bracts 3, sepal-like, borne on stalk just behind flower; carpels several. Leaves basal, with 3 or 5 rounded lobes. Early spring.

RANGE: Eastern half of the United States and adjacent Canada.

HABITAT: Wooded slopes in mostly moderately acid soil.

CULTURE: Should be in every shady wild garden.

NOTES: The related SHARP-LOBE HEPATICA (*H. acutilòba*), with somewhat showier flowers, occurs in the Appalachians and adjacent parts of our area, in often neutral soil.

Pasque-flower (*Anémone pàtens*)   Pl. 34

FEATURES: Flower 2 in. across, on a 4- to 8-in. hairy stalk bearing lacy-cut bracts; sepals 5 to 7, lavender-blue; petals obsolete; carpels numerous, maturing to feathery tailed fruits. Leaves basal, hairy, with many slender divisions. Early spring.

RANGE: High plains and adjacent Midland states.

HABITAT: Grasslands and open woods on plains and hillsides.

CULTURE: Can be grown in rock gardens beyond its native range.

NOTES: Sometimes known as WILD-CROCUS.

Buttercup Family, continued

Many-ray Anemone (*Anémone caroliniàna*)   **Pl. 36**

FEATURES: Flower 1¼ in. across, on a stalk 4 to 8 in. high, bearing 3 sessile, deeply cut bracts below the middle; sepals 10 to 15, lilac to lavender or whitish; petals obsolete; carpels numerous, woolly. Leaves basal, with 3 much-cut divisions, arising from a small tuber. Spring.

RANGE: Midland and Southern states.

HABITAT: Open woods and grasslands, in varied soils.

CULTURE: Readily grown in the rock garden, and the most desirable of the species here treated.

Broad-leaf Anemone (*A. canadénsis*)   **Pl. 36**

FEATURES: Flowers 1¼ in. across, on branches of a stout 1- to 2-ft. stalk bearing sessile, broad, cut-toothed bracts; sepals 5, white; petals obsolete; carpels several, hairy. Leaves basal, broad, cut-toothed. Late spring to summer.

RANGE: Over our area and northward.

HABITAT: Damp open woods and thickets, in varied soils.

CULTURE: Spreads rapidly by underground stems into colonies. Preferably kept out of the rock garden.

Thimble Anemone (*A. virginiàna*)   **Pl. 37**

FEATURES: Flowers ¾ to 1½ in. across, on branches of a stout 2- to 3-ft. stalk, bearing whorls of stalked, cut-lobed and toothed bracts; sepals 5, somewhat greenish white; petals obsolete; carpels numerous, woolly, in a thimble-shaped group. Summer.

RANGE: Over our area and adjoining regions.

HABITAT: Dry open woods and gravelly slopes, in neutral or moderately acid, rather sterile soil.

CULTURE: Readily grown in the rock garden.

NOTES: The related LONG-FRUITED ANEMONE (*A. cylíndrica*) has its fruits in a cylindric group and narrower leaf divisions; it is commoner in the Midland states. Several other species enter the margins of our area. Notable is the BRONZE ANEMONE (*A. hudsoniàna*), with flowers 1 in. across, of 5 to 9 bronzy-green sepals, and bracts and leaves cut into narrow divisions; it occurs along our northern borders and adjacent Canada.

Buttercup Family, continued

Wood Anemone (*Anémone quinquefòlia*)   Pl. 36

FEATURES: Flower 1 in. across, on a stalk 4 to 8 in. high, bearing about the middle a whorl of 3 stalked, 3- to 5-parted sharp-toothed bracts; sepals 5 to 7, white or lavender-tinged; petals obsolete; carpels few. Leaves basal, similar to the bracts though larger. Early spring.

RANGE: Over our area, also Appalachians and eastern Canada.

HABITAT: Open woods in often moderately acid soil.

CULTURE: Can be grown in a wild garden but blooms sparsely.

NOTES: The related APPALACHIAN ANEMONE (*A. lancifòlia*) is a stouter plant about twice as high, with the 3 bract and leaf divisions only shallowly toothed; it ranges through the Appalachians as far north as southern Pennsylvania. In Virginia there is another relative, the LEAST ANEMONE (*A. mínima*), differing in its smaller stature and hairy foliage.

Rue-anemone (*Anemonélla thalictroìdes*)   Pl. 36

FEATURES: Flowers about ¾ in. across, several in a group arising from a whorl of bracts with 3 stalked, rounded, blunt-toothed divisions on a 6- to 8-in. stalk; sepals 5 to 10, white or pink-tinged; petals obsolete; carpels several, grooved. Leaves basal, compound, the roundish leaflets with a few blunt teeth. Roots tuberous, clustered. Early spring.

RANGE: Eastern half of the United States.

HABITAT: Open woods in moderately acid soil.

CULTURE: Readily cultivated in a woodland garden.

Midland Isopyrum (*Isopỳrum biternàtum*)   Pl. 33

FEATURES: Plant similar in aspect to the next preceding, but the flowers borne in axils of small bracts alternate on a sparingly leafy stalk; sepals 5, white, delicate and soon falling; petals obsolete; carpels few, maturing to small divergent, pointed, pear-shaped fruits, containing several seeds. Leaves compound, the leaflets shallowly blunt-lobed. Roots slender, swollen at intervals to tiny tubers. Spring.

RANGE: Midland and Southern states.

HABITAT: Open woods, in rich, often neutral soils.

CULTURE: Desirable for the wild garden.

NOTES: Sometimes known as FALSE MEADOW-RUE.

Buttercup Family, continued

Tall Meadow-rue (*Thalictrum polýgamum*)   Pl. 33

FEATURES: Flowers numerous in a large compound inflorescence, whitish, in part unisexual, on a leafy stalk 4 to 8 ft.
high; sepals few, greenish, falling early; petals obsolete; filaments club-shaped; carpels several, maturing to spindle-
shaped 1-seeded fruits. Leaves compound, repeatedly divided
in threes, the leaflets rounded, blunt-lobed. Summer.

RANGE: Northeastern and Southeastern states, adjacent Midlands and southern Canada.

HABITAT: Moist meadows and thickets, in various soils.

CULTURE: Desirable for cultivation in a swamp garden.

NOTES: Several other species of MEADOW-RUE, differing in details of leaves and flowers, occur in our area; most widespread
is the EARLY MEADOW-RUE (*T. diòicum*) of wooded slopes.

Virgins-bower (*Clématis virginiàna*)   Pl. 37

FEATURES: Flowers numerous in a compound inflorescence on a
high climbing stem; sepals 4 or 5, white; petals obsolete;
carpels numerous, maturing to plumy-tailed 1-seeded fruits.
Leaves opposite, compound, with 3 sharp-lobed leaflets; stalks
twining around other plants for support. Late summer.

RANGE: Over our area and adjoining regions.

HABITAT: Damp thickets, in moderately acid soils.

CULTURE: Often grown in gardens.

Rock Clematis (*C. verticillàris*)   Pl. 35

FEATURES: Flowers few, about 3 in. across, on a climbing stem;
sepals 4, large, veiny, lavender-blue; petals present but inconspicuous; carpels numerous, maturing to plumy-tailed 1-
seeded fruits. Leaves opposite, compound, with 3 few-lobed
leaflets; stalks twining. Spring.

RANGE: Northeastern North America, down into the cooler
parts of our area and the Appalachians.

HABITAT: Woods and thickets, in our area often on shaded rock
slides with cold air pockets, in humus-rich soil.

CULTURE: Can be grown in a rock garden kept cool in summer.

NOTES: Other species of CLEMATIS in our area include the
LEATHER-FLOWER (*C. viórna*), in which the bronzy sepals are
markedly thickened; its range is southerly.

Buttercup Family, continued

Marsh-marigold (*Cáltha palústris*)   Pl. 35

FEATURES: Flowers few, 1 to 1½ in. across, on a thick, hollow, 1- to 2-ft. stalk; sepals 5, bright yellow; petals obsolete; carpels several in a whorl, maturing to many-seeded fruits ¼ in. long. Leaves broadly heart-shaped. Early spring.

RANGE: Northeastern North America and Appalachians.

HABITAT: Wet meadows, swamps, and stream banks, in humus-rich soil varying widely in acidity.

CULTURE: Readily cultivated in a wet-soil garden.

NOTES: Also known as AMERICAN COWSLIP, and by various other local names. Sometimes cooked and eaten as "greens."

Eastern Globe-flower (*Tróllius láxus*)   Pl. 37

FEATURES: Flowers few, 1 to 1½ in. across, on a slender stalk 1 to 2 ft. high; sepals 5 to 7, greenish yellow; petals present but minute and inconspicuous; carpels several, whorled, maturing to tubular, many-seeded fruits ⅓ in. long. Leaves rather large, palmately divided into cut-toothed lobes. Spring to early summer.

RANGE: Rare in a few scattered localities, chiefly in the middle and western portions of the Northeastern states.

HABITAT: Swamps and wet thickets, in rather acid, peaty soil.

CULTURE: May grow in a bog garden, but short-lived.

Goldthread (*Cóptis trifòlia*)   Pl. 37

FEATURES: Flowers solitary, about ½ in. across, on slender leafless stalks a few inches high; sepals 5 or 6, white; petals tiny, trough-shaped; carpels few, whorled, maturing to stalked, spreading, spindle-shaped, several-seeded fruits. Leaves basal, divided into 3 rounded, sharp-toothed lobes, evergreen. Underground stem slender, golden yellow, referred to in the common name. Spring.

RANGE: Northern North America down into the cooler parts of our area and the Appalachians.

HABITAT: Cold damp woods and bog margins, in acid, peaty soil.

CULTURE: Can be grown in a wild garden which is kept acid and does not heat up much in summer.

NOTES: The underground stems contain astringent principles.

Buttercup Family, continued

Goldenseal (*Hydrástis canadénsis*)   Pl. 40

FEATURES: Flower solitary, above 2 large cut-lobed bracts on a 1-ft. stalk; sepals 3, greenish white, falling early; petals obsolete; stamens prominent; carpels several in a knob, maturing to red berry-like fruits. Leaf large, basal, palmately cut into broad sharp-toothed lobes. Underground stem short and thick, bright yellow. Early spring.

RANGE: Appalachians and over our area except far northeastward.

HABITAT: Wooded slopes, in rich, often neutral soil.

CULTURE: Readily cultivated in partial shade.

NOTES: The underground stem contains valuable medicinal principles, and the plant is grown commercially.

White Baneberry (*Actaèa álba*)   Pl. 40

FEATURES: Flowers small, whitish, in a short-cylindric group on a 1- to 2-ft. stalk; sepals few, falling early; petals minute; stamens conspicuous; carpel solitary, maturing to a white berry with purple spot at tip, on a thick red stalk. Leaves large, compound, with sharp-toothed leaflets. Spring.

RANGE: Over our area and adjacent regions.

HABITAT: Wooded slopes, in rich neutral or somewhat acid soil.

CULTURE: Can be grown in a woodland garden.

NOTES: The related RED BANEBERRY (*A. rùbra*) has red berries on slender stalks; there are also intermediates between the two. The berries of both are poisonous.

Fairy-candles (*Cimicífuga racemòsa*)   Pl. 40

FEATURES: Flowers small, white, in long slender groups in a compound inflorescence on a leafy 4- to 6-ft. stalk; sepals few, falling early; petals minute; stamens conspicuous; carpel solitary, maturing to a several-seeded ellipsoidal dry fruit. Leaves large, compound, sharp-toothed. Summer.

RANGE: Over our area, adjacent Ontario, and Appalachians.

HABITAT: Wooded slopes, in moderately acid soil.

CULTURE: Desirable for the large wild garden.

NOTES: The flowers are rank-scented. APPALACHIAN FAIRY-CANDLES (*C. americàna*) differs in having several carpels in a group; it blooms in late summer and its flowers are scentless.

Buttercup Family, continued

Eastern Columbine (*Aquilègia canadénsis*)   **Pl. 35**

FEATURES: Flowers 1½ in. long, nodding at tips of branches on a 1- to 2-ft. stalk, red with yellow face; sepals 5, small, petal-like; petals 5, extended backward into conspicuous spurs; stamens extending beyond flower face; carpels 5, maturing to tubular, many-seeded dry fruits. Leaves compound, the leaflets lobed and blunt-toothed. Spring.

RANGE: Eastern half of the United States and adjacent Canada.

HABITAT: Shaded rocks and banks, in various types of soil.

CULTURE: One of the easiest wild flowers to cultivate.

Spring Larkspur (*Delphínium tricòrnè*)   **Pl. 38**

FEATURES: Plant about 1 ft. high. Flowers 1 to 1½ in. long, in a cylindric inflorescence; sepals 5, violet-blue to whitish, the upper one bearing a hollow conical spur; petals inconspicuous; carpels few, maturing to divergent, tubular, many-seeded dry fruits. Leaves cut into 5 to 7 slender-lobed divisions. Roots tuberous. Spring.

RANGE: Midland and adjacent Northeastern states.

HABITAT: Prairies and rocky slopes, in rich neutral soil.

CULTURE: Easily cultivated in the rock garden.

Tall Larkspur (*D. exaltàtum*)   **Pl. 40**

FEATURES: Flowers ¾ in. long, downy, bilateral, numerous in a long slender inflorescence on a leafy stalk 2 to 4 ft. high; sepals 5, lavender-blue, the upper one spurred; petals inconspicuous; carpels 3, maturing to subparallel, tubular dry fruits. Leaves cut into 5 narrow, few-toothed divisions. Roots thickish. Summer.

RANGE: Midland states and adjacent regions.

HABITAT: Wooded slopes, in neutral or somewhat acid soil.

CULTURE: Will grow in a partly shaded garden.

NOTES: Several other species, differing in details of flowers and leaves, occur in our area. Notable is the PRAIRIE LARKSPUR (*D. viréscens*), which is intermediate between the two here described, having whitish flowers and narrow leaf segments; it grows in the western part of the Midland states, also farther west. European species sometimes escape, notably the FIELD LARKSPUR (*D. ajàcis*), an annual with deep blue flowers.

Buttercup Family, concluded

Summer Aconite (*Aconītum uncinàtum*)   **Pl. 35**

FEATURES: Flowers 1 in. across, bilateral, grouped at branch tips of a weak 2- to 4-ft. leafy stalk; sepals 5, violet-blue, the upper one enlarged into a "helmet"; petals inconspicuous; carpels few, maturing to tubular, many-seeded dry fruits. Leaves divided into 3 or 5 cut-toothed lobes. Summer.

RANGE: Midland and adjacent Northeastern and Southern states.

HABITAT: Damp thickets, in moderately acid soil.

CULTURE: Desirable for growing in a thickety wild garden.

Barberry Family (*Berberidàceae*)

FEATURES: Leaves few, large. Sepals and petals few; stamens as many or twice as many as the petals. Carpel solitary.

May-apple (*Podophýllum peltàtum*)   **Pl. 41**

FEATURES: Flower large, solitary, nodding in the fork of a pair of leaves on a stalk a foot or so high; sepals 6, falling early; petals 6 to 9, white or pinkish; stamens twice as many; carpel maturing to a large yellow berry, the "apple" to which the common name refers. Leaves deeply divided into coarse, cut-toothed lobes. Underground stem long and thick. Late spring.

RANGE: Eastern half of the United States and adjacent Canada.

HABITAT: Damp open woods in neutral or somewhat acid soil.

CULTURE: Spreads too rapidly for any but the largest gardens.

NOTES: While the roots and herbage contain highly poisonous principles, the fruit, when fully ripe in summer, is edible.

Twin-leaf (*Jeffersònia diphýlla*)   **Pl. 41**

FEATURES: Flowers solitary on 5- to 10-in. leafless stalks; sepals about 4, falling early; petals about 8, white; stamens 8, one above each petal; carpel maturing to a pear-shaped dry fruit. Leaves basal, about 1 ft. high, the blade deeply divided into 2 wings, to which the common name refers. Early spring; flowers lasting but a day.

RANGE: Midland and adjacent Northeastern states.

HABITAT: Damp open woods, in rich, often neutral soil.

CULTURE: Desirable for the wild garden.

Barberry Family, concluded

Blue Cohosh (*Caulophýllum thalictroìdes*)   **Pl. 41**

FEATURES: Flowers small, in a compound inflorescence on a 1- to 2-ft. stalk bearing a bract and a larger leaf; sepals 6, bronzy green; petals inconspicuous, 1 above each sepal; carpel soon bursting and displaying a pair of large stalked blue seeds. Leaves compound; leaflets few-lobed. Underground system a thick running stem. Spring.

RANGE: Over our area and adjacent regions.

HABITAT: Moist woods, in rich, often neutral soils.

CULTURE: Can be grown in the cool woodland garden.

Poppy Family (*Papaveràceae*)

FEATURES: Delicate plants with cloudy juice. Flowers large; sepals 2; petals 4 or multiples of 4; stamens numerous; carpel solitary, maturing to a many-seeded dry fruit.

Bloodroot (*Sanguinària canadénsis*)   **Pl. 41**

FEATURES: Flower solitary on a leafless stalk a few inches high; sepals falling early; petals numerous, white or pinkish. Leaf basal, broad, round-lobed, gray-green. Underground system a thick horizontal stem containing bright red juice, to which the common name refers. Earliest spring.

RANGE: Eastern half of the United States and adjacent Canada.

HABITAT: Wooded slopes, in rich neutral or moderately acid soil.

CULTURE: Widely grown in wild gardens.

Gold-poppy (*Stylóphorum diphýllum*)   **Pl. 38**

FEATURES: Flowers few, on a leafy stalk a foot or so high; sepals falling early; petals 4, bright yellow; carpel maturing to a rough-hairy, spindle-shaped dry fruit. Leaves whitish beneath, divided into several toothed lobes. Underground stem thick, its juice yellow. Spring.

RANGE: Midland and adjacent Northeastern states.

HABITAT: Open woods, in rich, often neutral soil.

CULTURE: Desirable for the wild garden or shady border.

NOTES: This native is more attractive than the similar European CELANDINE (*Chelidònium màjus*), which is a weed on wooded slopes in our area; its flowers are smaller and fruit smooth.

Fume-root Family (*Fumariàceae*)

FEATURES: Delicate herbs with small bilateral or oblique flowers; sepals 2, minute; petals 2 large and 2 small; stamens 6, in two groups of 3 each; carpels 2, well united.

Dutchmans-breeches (*Dicéntra cucullària*)   Pl. 44

FEATURES: Flowers nodding in a row on a leafless arching stalk a few inches high; larger petals expanded into spurs resembling a pair of breeches, white or pinkish with yellow tip. Leaves basal, repeatedly divided in a lacy pattern. Underground system a knobby bulb. Early spring.

RANGE: Over our area and adjacent regions.

HABITAT: Wooded rocky slopes and stream banks or terraces, in rich neutral or slightly acid soil.

CULTURE: Will grow in a wild garden, but bloom only sparsely.

Squirrel-corn (*D. canadénsis*)   Pl. 44

FEATURES: Flowers nodding on a leafless stalk 6 to 8 in. high, fragrant; larger petals expanded into rounded spurs, white with pink tinge; smaller petals bearing yellowish crests. Leaves basal, lacy like those of the preceding, but grayer on the back. Underground system a group of small yellow tubers, to which the common name refers. Early spring.

RANGE: Over our area and adjacent regions, except in lowlands.

HABITAT: Shaded rocky slopes, in cool, rich, neutral soil.

CULTURE: Can be grown for a time in a woodland garden, but rodents usually soon consume the tubers.

Mountain-fringe (*Adlùmia fungòsa*)   Pl. 44

FEATURES: Flowers clustered on branches of a climbing leafy stem several feet long; petals pink, coherent in a nodding tubular corolla. Leaves repeatedly compound, the small leaflets few-lobed, the stalks twining around twigs or rocks for support. Duration biennial, the seedlings forming striking rosettes the first season, elongating the second season, and dying after maturing seeds. Summer.

RANGE: Over our area and adjacent uplands.

HABITAT: Cool rocky woods and thickets in somewhat acid soils.

CULTURE: Often cultivated in shady wild gardens.

NOTES: The coherent petals are anomalous in this Dicot group.

Fume-root Family, concluded

Pink Fume-root (*Corýdalis sempérvirens*)   **Pl. 38**

FEATURES: Flowers pink with yellow tip, about ½ in. long, numerous in a compound inflorescence on a smooth branching stalk 6 to 12 in. high; symmetry bilateral, the upper petal short-spurred. Leaves gray-green, much divided, the ultimate lobes blunt. Duration biennial; first-year rosettes conspicuous; roots when crushed exhaling a nitrous odor, to which the family name refers. Spring and summer.

RANGE: Northern North America, and down the Appalachians.

HABITAT: Open rocky or gravelly slopes in moderately acid soil.

CULTURE: Readily grown from seed in a cool rock garden.

Golden Fume-root (*C. aúrea*)   **Pl. 38**

FEATURES: Flowers bright yellow, ½ in. long, in cylindric groups at branch tips of a leafy stalk 6 to 12 in. high; symmetry bilateral, the upper petal long-spurred. Leaves much divided, the ultimate lobes wedge-shaped, acute. Duration biennial; roots pungent-scented. Spring.

RANGE: Northern North America and down across the Midlands.

HABITAT: Sparse woodland, in often rich neutral soil.

CULTURE: Desirable for cultivation in a woodland garden.

NOTES: Several related species, differing in details of foliage, flowers, and seeds, occur in our area.

Cress Family (*Crucíferae*)

FEATURES: Sepals 4; petals 4, their blades spreading in a symmetrical cross, to which the family epithet refers; stamens 6, with 4 longer than the other 2; carpels 2, well united.

Wild Rocket (*Iodánthus pinnatífidus*)   **Pl. 39**

FEATURES: Flowers light violet, about ⅓ in. across, numerous in a branched inflorescence on a leafy stalk 1 or 2 ft. high; seed pod long, slender, and roundish. Leaves large and broad, coarsely toothed and basally lobed. Late spring.

RANGE: Midland and adjacent Northeastern and Southern states.

HABITAT: Wooded slopes and flats along streams, in rich, often neutral soil.

CULTURE: Can be grown in a shady wild garden.

Cress Family, continued

Low Rock-cress (*Árabis lyràta*)　　　　　　Pl. 45

FEATURES: Flowers white, about ⅓ in. across, in groups at
tip of 4- to 8-in. stalks bearing sparse narrow leaves, arising
from a rosette of blunt-lobed basal leaves; seed pods about
1 in. long, slender, flattened. Spring and early summer.

RANGE: Over our area except far northeast; also in northwestern North America and northeastern Asia.

HABITAT: Rock ledges, gravelly slopes, and sandy banks, in well-
drained, often sterile, acid or neutral soil.

CULTURE: Suitable for the rock garden.

NOTES: Several other members of this genus occur in our area;
they mostly have rather small flowers, although the seed pods
are often long and conspicuous.

Marsh Bittercress (*Cardámine bulbòsa*)　　　　Pl. 45

FEATURES: Flowers white, about ½ in. across, in a slender inflorescence on a smooth leafy stalk 9 to 18 in. high; seed pod
1 in. long, erect, flattened, tapering toward both ends. Stem
leaves sessile, toothed; basal leaves stalked, roundish. Underground system a knobby tuber. Spring.

RANGE: Eastern half of the United States, except far northeast.

HABITAT: Marshes, wet meadows, and open swamps, in often
muddy, moderately acid soil.

CULTURE: Readily grown in a swamp garden, spreading by seed
into large patches.

Lavender Bittercress (*C. douglássii*)　　　　　Pl. 39

FEATURES: Flowers lavender, about ½ in. across, in a slender
inflorescence on a hairy 6- to 12-in. stalk; seed pod 1 in. long,
ascending, flattened, tapering. Stem leaves coarsely few-
toothed, rather crowded; basal leaves stalked, their blades
round-heart-shaped. Underground system a group of slender
tubers. Early spring.

RANGE: Northern North America and down over our area,
though rare eastward.

HABITAT: Moist open woods and rocky slopes, in neutral soil.

CULTURE: Can be grown in a moist, shady, wild garden, and
desirable for its early blooming and the attractiveness of the
flowers.

Cress Family, concluded

Two-leaf Crinkle-root (*Dentària diphýlla*) **Pl. 45**

FEATURES: Flowers white, about ½ in. across, few on a 6- to 12-in. stalk bearing about the middle a pair of leaves divided into 3 broad, blunt-toothed leaflets; seed pods flattened, short-tapering. Underground system a fleshy horizontal stem, crinkled but scarcely jointed. Spring.

RANGE: Over our area and adjacent Canada, also down the Appalachians; rare eastward.

HABITAT: Open rocky woods and thickets, in moderately acid soil.

CULTURE: Can be grown in a cool woodland garden.

Three-leaf Crinkle-root (*D. laciniàta*) **Pl. 45**

FEATURES: Flowers pinkish, about ½ in. across, few on an 8- to 15-in. hairy stalk bearing about the middle a whorl of 3 leaves, divided into 3 narrow sharp-toothed or lobed leaflets; seed pods flattened, long-tapering. Underground system a fleshy, jointed, horizontal stem. Early spring.

RANGE: Eastern half of the United States and adjacent Canada.

HABITAT: Wooded slopes, in neutral or slightly acid soil.

CULTURE: Readily grown in a wild garden.

Sundew Family (*Droseràceae*)

FEATURES: Small plants with bronzy foliage bearing tentacles tipped with viscid globules which entrap insects, gradually digested by the plant. Flower parts mostly in fives.

Round-leaf Sundew (*Drósera rotundifòlia*) **Pl. 44**

FEATURES: Plant a rosette of leaves consisting of a small disk-shaped blade on a 1- to 2-in. stalk, from which unrolls a stalk a few inches high bearing small white flowers. Summer.

RANGE: Over much of North America except the hottest and driest regions; also northern Europe and Asia.

HABITAT: Wet, acid, sterile, sandy or peaty soil in bogs, swamps, and along streams.

CULTURE: May grow in a well-maintained acid bog garden.

NOTES: SPOON-LEAF SUNDEW (*D. intermèdia*) grows in similar but even wetter places. There is also a THREAD-LEAF SUNDEW (*D. filifórmis*), with lavender flowers, in southern New Jersey.

Pitcherplant Family (*Sarraceniàceae*)

FEATURES: Plant a rosette of bronzy tubular leaves, containing water in which insects drown and are digested. Flowers solitary, nodding, their parts mostly in fives.

Northern Pitcherplant (*Sarracènia purpùrea*) **Pl. 39**
FEATURES: Leaves several inches long, upcurved. Petals bronzy, delicate, soon falling. Early summer.
RANGE: Northeastern half of North America and down across our area, though becoming rare southward.
HABITAT: Bogs and swamps, in peaty soil, either strongly acid or neutral, but in either case highly sterile.
CULTURE: Worth growing in the acid bog garden.

Mallow Family (*Malvàceae*)

FEATURES: Sepals 5, basally united; petals 5, showy; stamens numerous, united to a cylindric group; carpels united, the separate stigmas projecting beyond the stamen cylinder.

Rose-mallow (*Hibíscus palústris*) **Pl. 39**
FEATURES: Plant several feet high. Flowers 4 or 5 in. across, pink; carpels 5, maturing to a 1-in. capsule. Leaves large, 3-lobed. Summer.
RANGE: Great Lake and Atlantic lowland parts of our area.
HABITAT: Thickets along streams, in often neutral mud.
CULTURE: Readily grown in a water garden.
NOTES: Other species, and hybrids, are extensively cultivated.

Flax Family (*Linàceae*)

FEATURES: Sepals, petals, and stamens 5 each; carpels 5, their ovaries united, maturing to a large-seeded capsule.

Woodland Flax (*Lìnum virginiànum*) **Pl. 43**
FEATURES: Plant 1 to 2 ft. high, the slender stalks branched. Flowers yellow, delicate, in axils of tiny bracts. Leaves small, oblong, sessile, entire. Summer.
RANGE: Northeastern and adjacent Midland and Southern states.
HABITAT: Open woods in moderately acid soil.
CULTURE: Suitable for the shady wild garden.
NOTES: Several other species occur in our area also.

Oxalis Family (*Oxalidàceae*)

FEATURES: Flowers solitary or few in a cluster; sepals and petals 5 each; stamens 10; carpels 5, united, maturing to a cylindric or prismatic capsule. Leaves long-stalked, the blades divided into 3 inversely heart-shaped leaflets.

Wood-sorrel (*Óxalis montàna*)   Pl. 42

FEATURES: Flowers about ¾ in. across, white with pink veins, solitary on 3- or 4-in. stalks. Underground system a scaly, fleshy horizontal stem. Spring and early summer.

RANGE: Northeastern North America down into the northern parts of our area, and the higher Appalachians.

HABITAT: Deep woods in cold, acid, humus-rich soil.

CULTURE: Difficult to grow in low-level gardens unless the soil can be kept acid and cool in summer.

NOTES: A related species, the original WOOD-SORREL (*O. acetosélla*), grows in Europe and Asia; it is one of the plants to which the name SHAMROCK is applied.

Violet Oxalis (*O. violàcea*)   Pl. 42

FEATURES: Flowers few, on leafless stalks 4 to 6 in. high, ½ in. across, lavender-purple. Underground system a brown scaly bulb. Spring and early summer.

RANGE: Eastern half of the United States, except far north.

HABITAT: Open woods and grasslands, in slightly acid soil.

CULTURE: Spreads rapidly by runners from the bulbs, so undesirable in a small garden.

Great Oxalis (*O. grándis*)   Pl. 43

FEATURES: Flowers 1 in. across, bright yellow, several in a group on a leafy stalk 1 to 2 ft. high. Leaflets 1 in. across, bronzy-margined. Underground system a slender horizontal stem. Spring and early summer.

RANGE: Southern parts of our area and adjacent Southern states.

HABITAT: Open or thinly wooded gravelly or sandy slopes, in neutral or moderately acid soil.

CULTURE: Spreads into large patches by underground stems.

NOTES: Several related species of lower stature and smaller flowers occur in our area; two of these, natives of Europe, may become troublesome weeds.

Geranium Family (*Geraniàceae*)

FEATURES: Sepals and petals 5; stamens 10; carpels 5, united, maturing to a cylindric capsule which splits at base into divergent strips at maturity.

Wood Geranium (*Geràniuum maculàtum*)   Pl. 42

FEATURES: Flowers 1¼ in. across, lavender-purple, at branch tips of a 1- to 2-ft. leafy stalk. Leaves broad, deeply cut into sharp-toothed divisions. Late spring to summer.
RANGE: Over our area, adjacent Canada, and Southern states.
HABITAT: Open woods in neutral or moderately acid soil.
CULTURE: Readily grown in the wild garden or border.

Musk Geranium (*G. robertiànum*)   Pl. 42

FEATURES: Flowers ½ in. across, lilac-purple, at branch tips of a weak 1-ft. leafy stalk. Leaves compound, the 3 leaflets deeply cut and toothed, musk-scented. Summer.
RANGE: Northern parts of our area and adjacent Canada; also in Europe and Asia.
HABITAT: Woods and thickets on cool rocky or sandy slopes, in neutral or somewhat acid soil.
CULTURE: Can be grown in a cool shady rock garden.
NOTES: Several weedy GERANIUMS also occur in our area.

Snapweed Family (*Balsaminàceae*)

FEATURES: Flowers bilateral, 2-lipped; sepals 3, the lower one a petal-colored spur; petals 5; fruit a capsule which when mature splits violently into 5 spiraled valves. Leaves alternate, toothed. Stem hollow, weak, 2 or 3 ft. high.

Touch-me-not (*Impàtiens biflòra*)   Pl. 43

FEATURES: Flowers orange with purple spots; spur sepal conical, longer than wide. Summer.
RANGE: Eastern half of North America.
HABITAT: Marshes, swamps, and damp woods, in various soils.
CULTURE: Spreads rather rapidly for garden use.
NOTES: PALE TOUCH-ME-NOT (*I. pállida*) has yellow flowers with wider spur sepal; it prefers cooler and richer soils. These plants are also known as JEWELWEED and SNAPWEED. Their juice is an excellent remedy for ivy poisoning.

St. Johnswort Family (*Hypericàceae*)

FEATURES: Sepals and yellow or bronzy petals 4 or 5, often somewhat oblique; stamens numerous; carpels few, united. Leaves small, entire, opposite, black-dotted. Stems often angled.

Great St. Johnswort (*Hypéricum áscyron*)   Pl. 43

FEATURES: Flowers bright yellow, 1½ in. across, borne at branchlet tips of a 3- or 4-ft. stalk; carpels 5, united below, yielding a pear-shaped capsule with 5 cavities. Summer.

RANGE: Northern parts of our area and adjacent Canada; also in Europe.

HABITAT: Wooded rocky slopes, usually along streams, in neutral or moderately acid soil.

CULTURE: Desirable for a cool wild garden.

NOTES: There are also a number of smaller species here.

St. Andrews-cross (*Ascy̆rum hypericoìdes*)   Pl. 46

FEATURES: Flowers in upper leaf axils of sprawling woody-based stems; sepals 4, one pair enlarged; petals 4, pale yellow, forming an oblique cross to which the name refers; carpels 2, united below. Summer.

RANGE: Southeastern United States and adjacent parts of our area; reported to grow also in the West Indies.

HABITAT: Open woods and thickets on dry sandy or rocky slopes in rather acid sterile soil.

CULTURE: Can be grown in an acid rock garden.

Rock-rose Family (*Cistàceae*)

FEATURES: Flowers radially symmetrical; sepals and delicate yellow petals usually 5; stamens numerous; carpels 3, united, yielding a partitionless capsule.

Woolly Gold-heather (*Hudsònia tomentòsa*)   Pl. 46

FEATURES: Flowers small but numerous. Plant densely tufted; leaves scale-like, crowded, woolly. Late spring and summer.

RANGE: Great Lake and Atlantic coast portions of our area.

HABITAT: Sandy slopes and dunes, in the open or under sparse shrubs; soil sterile and neutral or moderately acid.

CULTURE: Difficult to cultivate except in a sand barren.

NOTES: A less woolly species, *H. ericoìdes,* known as GOLD-HEATHER or CLOTH-OF-GOLD, grows in Atlantic pinelands.

Rock-rose Family, concluded

Frostwort (*Heliánthemum canadénsè*)   **Pl. 46**

FEATURES: Flowers of two kinds, a few 1 in. across and showy, and several lacking petals and inconspicuous, borne on slender stems a foot or so high. Leaves small, elliptic-oblong, well spaced. Late spring.

RANGE: Over our area, adjacent Canada, and Southern states.

HABITAT: Sandy or rocky slopes, in the open or under thin woods, in sterile acid soil.

CULTURE: In cultivation produces mostly inconspicuous flowers.

NOTES: The common name refers to the development, on frosty mornings, of striking ice ribbons around the shrubby stem bases.

Violet Family (*Violàceae*)

FEATURES: Small plants with strongly bilateral flowers, their lower petals extended backward into a hollow spur. Sepals, petals, and stamens 5; capsule 3-valved.

Birdfoot Violet (*Vìola pedàta*)   **Pl. 47**

FEATURES: Plant low, the leaves and flowers arising from a short, knobby, fleshy underground stem. Flowers 1 to 1½ in. across, the petals lilac, or sometimes the upper pair purple-black. Leaves fan-shaped, with multiple narrow divisions, to which the common name refers. Spring.

RANGE: Over our area and Southern states, except far northeast.

HABITAT: Open woods and grasslands, on rocky, sandy, or clayey slopes; soil sterile and acid.

CULTURE: Does not survive long in cultivation unless the soil can be maintained in a decidedly acid condition.

Larkspur Violet (*V. pedatífida*)   **Pl. 47**

FEATURES: Plant low, the leaves and flowers arising from a short, knobby, fleshy underground stem. Flowers 1 in. across, violet-purple. Leaves fan-shaped. Spring.

RANGE: Midland states and adjacent regions.

HABITAT: Open woods and grasslands, in neutral or somewhat acid, often humus-rich soil.

CULTURE: Can be grown in well-drained parts of the wild garden.

Violet Family, continued

Longspur Violet (*Vìola rostràta*) Pl. 47

FEATURES: Plant leafy-stemmed, about 6 in. high. Flowers borne in axils of leafy bracts, lavender, ¾ in. across, the spur ½ in. long. Leaves heart-shaped. Late spring.

RANGE: Southeastern Canada, northern parts of our area, and down the Appalachians to Georgia.

HABITAT: Cool rocky woods, in rather rich, often neutral soil.

CULTURE: May grow in a cool woodland garden.

Smooth Yellow Violet (*V. eriocárpa*) Pl. 46

FEATURES: Plant leafy-stemmed, a foot or so high. Flowers yellow, ¾ in. across, borne in axils of leafy bracts. Leaves heart-shaped. Spring.

RANGE: Eastern half of the United States and adjacent Canada.

HABITAT: Open woods, in rich neutral or slightly acid soil.

CULTURE: Desirable for culture in a woodland garden.

NOTES: This smooth, leafy species grades into the HAIRY YELLOW VIOLET (*V. pubéscens*), which has fewer leaves and is much more hairy. EARLY YELLOW VIOLET (*V. rotundifòlia*) has the flowers and leaves arising from a fleshy underground stem.

Canada Violet (*V. canadénsis*) Pl. 48

FEATURES: Plant leafy-stemmed, about 1 ft. high. Flowers white with yellow eye, lilac-shaded on back of petals, ¾ in. across, in axils of leafy bracts. Leaves heart-shaped. Late spring and summer.

RANGE: Southern Canada, down into the cooler parts of our area and the Appalachians.

HABITAT: Cool, moist, wooded slopes, in neutral or moderately acid, humus-rich soil.

CULTURE: Can be grown in a woodland garden if kept cool.

NOTES: There remain to be discussed several stemless VIOLETS. The white one treated on the following page grades on the one hand into the NARROW-LEAF VIOLET (*V. lanceolàta*) and on the other into the NORTHERN WHITE VIOLET (*V. pállens*), in which the leaves are heart-shaped. Commonest of the violet-hued species is the DOORYARD VIOLET (*V. papilionàcea*) which spreads by seed so rapidly as to become a weed.

Violet Family, concluded

Primrose Violet (*Vìola . primulifòlia*)   Pl. 48

FEATURES: Plant low, the flowers and leaves arising from a slender creeping stem. Flowers white with purple lines on the lower petals, ½ in. across, pungently fragrant. Leaves elliptic, tapering into their stalks. Spring.
RANGE: Eastern United States and adjacent Canada.
HABITAT: Bogs, meadows, and open woods in moist acid soil.
CULTURE: Readily grown in a bog garden.

Candyroot Family (*Polygalàceae*)

FEATURES: Small plants with bilateral flowers; sepals 5, the two lateral ones enlarged and petal-like; petals 3, coherent into a tube, the lower one crested at tip; stamens about 8; carpels 2, united, each producing 1 hairy seed.

Gay-wings (*Polýgala paucifòlia*)   Pl. 47

FEATURES: Flowers purple with pinkish tube and bronzy fringed crest, ¾ in. long, in axils of leafy bracts. Leaves elliptic, the largest toward stem tip. Underground system long slender branching stems. Late spring and early summer.
RANGE: Over our area, though rare southeastward, adjacent Canada, and down the Appalachians.
HABITAT: Wooded slopes in cool, moderately acid, humus-rich soil.
CULTURE: Difficult to cultivate, being susceptible to attack by slugs, fungi, and other garden pests.
NOTES: Sometimes known as FRINGED MILKWORT, but not milky; also as FLOWERING WINTERGREEN.

Purple Candyroot (*P. sanguínea*)   Pl. 50

FEATURES: Flowers bronzy purple to greenish, tiny, in dense short-cylindric groups on leafy stems 5 to 10 in. high. Leaves narrow, scattered. Duration annual. Underground system a tuft of small roots, exhaling when crushed a wintergreen odor, to which the common name refers. Summer.
RANGE: Over our area, adjacent Canada, and Southern states.
HABITAT: Damp grassland, in moderately acid soil.
CULTURE: Will sometimes grow from seed sown in a meadow.

Candyroot Family, concluded

Yellow Candyroot (*Polýgala lùtea*)   **Pl. 50**

FEATURES: Flowers orange-yellow, tiny, in dense rounded groups
on a leafy stem 5 to 10 in. high. Leaves narrow, scattered.
Duration biennial, the first year producing a rosette of
rounded leaves. Summer.

RANGE: Southern states, extending north along the Atlantic
slope to Long Island.

HABITAT: Bogs and wet sandy flats, in strongly acid soil.

CULTURE: First-year rosettes, transplanted to a bog garden, may
yield flowers the following season.

NOTES: Other CANDYROOTS, differing in details, occur here.
The members of this genus are often called by the translation
of its epithet, MILKWORT, but the name referring to the wintergreen flavor of the roots is preferred here.

Spurge Family (*Euphorbiàceae*)

FEATURES: Small plants with milky juice. Flowers consisting
of a cup with several petal-like marginal lobes, in which arise
stalked groups of several stamens or of 3 carpels.

Snow-on-the-mountain (*Euphòrbia marginàta*)   **Pl. 48**

FEATURES: Plant annual, 1 to 2 ft. high, with elliptic leaves.
Inflorescence a flat-topped group of greenish flowers accom-
panying conspicuous white-margined bracts, to which the
common name refers. Summer and fall.

RANGE: West part of Midland states to Rocky Mountain foothills and escaping from cultivation eastward.

HABITAT: Dry grassland in mostly neutral soil.

CULTURE: Widely grown in gardens.

White Spurge (*E. corollàta*)   **Pl. 48**

FEATURES: Plant perennial, 1 to 2 ft. high, with small oblong
leaves. Inflorescence branching; bracts small; flower lobes
conspicuous, white. Summer.

RANGE: Eastern half of the United States and adjacent Canada.

HABITAT: Dry grassy slopes and open thickets; soil various.

CULTURE: Desirable for the rock or wild garden.

NOTES: Other SPURGES occur in our area, most of them weedy.

Pink Family (*Caryophyllàceae*)

FEATURES: Sepals and petals 5; stamens 5 or 10; carpels 3 to 5, the ovaries united, yielding a capsule mostly lacking partitions, with numerous small seeds.

Starry Cerastium (*Ceràstium arvénsè*) Pl. 49

FEATURES: Plant a few inches high. Flowers several in a forked inflorescence, about ½ in. across; petals white, shallowly notched; capsule cylindric to horn-shaped, opening at tip, with several teeth. Leaves narrow. Spring and early summer.

RANGE: Over much of North America, though rare southward; also in Europe and Asia.

HABITAT: Open rocky or sandy slopes, in neutral or moderately acid soil.

CULTURE: Can be grown in a dry rock garden.

NOTES: Several other members of this genus are weeds.

Wood Starwort (*Stellària pùbera*) Pl. 49

FEATURES: Stems up to 1 ft. long, weak. Flowers in a few-forked bracted inflorescence; petals white, so deeply notched that there seem to be 10; styles 3; capsule egg-shaped, splitting into 6 valves. Leaves elliptic-oblong. Late spring.

RANGE: Southern part of our area and adjacent Southern states.

HABITAT: Wooded rocky slopes, in neutral or moderately acid, humus-rich soil.

CULTURE: Easily grown and spreading rapidly in a wild garden.

NOTES: There are several other members of this genus in our area, differing in details of flowers and leaves. The more weedy ones are commonly called CHICKWEEDS.

Blunt-leaf Sandwort (*Arenària lateriflòra*) Pl. 49

FEATURES: Stems about 8 in. high. Flowers few, ⅓ in. across; petals white, rounded at tip; styles 3; capsule splitting into 3 valves. Leaves small, elliptic-oblong. Late spring and early summer.

RANGE: Northern North America, down part way across our area; also in Europe and Asia.

HABITAT: Open woods and moist grassy thickets, in cool neutral or moderately acid soil.

CULTURE: Suitable for the cool woodland garden.

Pink Family, continued

Rock Sandwort (*Arenària strícta*)   Pl. 49

FEATURES: Stems tufted, 6 to 10 in. high. Inflorescence forked, the flowers long-stalked; flowers ⅓ in. across; petals white, rounded at tip; styles 3; capsule egg-shaped, splitting into 3 valves. Leaves needle-like, with rosettes of smaller ones in their axils. Summer.

RANGE: Over our area and adjacent regions, but rare southward.

HABITAT: Dry rocky slopes and cliffs, in often neutral soil.

CULTURE: Desirable for rock gardens.

NOTES: Other species of SANDWORT occur in our area also; all have small white flowers, but the plant habit and leaf characters are different.

Pink Catchfly (*Silènè pennsylvánica*)   Pl. 51

FEATURES: Plant low, tufted. Flowers about 1 in. across; sepals united into a long tube, covered with sticky hairs, to which the common name refers; petals pale to deep pink, consisting of an erect "claw" and a broader spreading blade shallowly toothed at tip; styles 3; capsule becoming bell-shaped, opening at tip with 3 rounded teeth. Basal leaves about 3 in. long, widest toward tip. Spring.

RANGE: Northeastern states and adjacent regions.

HABITAT: Dry rocky and sandy slopes, in moderately acid soil.

CULTURE: Can be grown in a well-drained wild garden.

Red Catchfly (*S. virgínica*)   Pl. 51

FEATURES: Stem a foot or more long, weak and reclining at base. Flowers about 1½ in. across; sepals united into a long sticky tube; petals bright red, consisting of an erect "claw" and a spreading blade toothed at tip; styles 3; capsule becoming bell-shaped, opening with 6 teeth. Lower leaves widest toward tip. Spring and summer.

RANGE: Midland and adjacent Northeastern states, also down the Appalachians.

HABITAT: Open woods and thickets on rocky and sandy slopes, the soil varying from neutral to decidedly acid.

CULTURE: May grow in a wild garden, though susceptible to attack by fungi and other pests, especially in damp areas.

Pink Family, concluded

Star Silene (*Silène stellàta*)   Pl. 52

FEATURES: Stems 2 to 3 ft. high. Flowers ⅔ in. across, numerous; sepals united into a bell-shaped minutely hairy tube; petals white, the blade fringed; styles 3; capsule globular, opening with 6 rounded teeth. Leaves whorled in fours. Summer.

RANGE: Over our area except far northeastward, and down the Appalachians.

HABITAT: Open woods, in moderately acid soil.

CULTURE: Desirable for the woodland garden.

NOTES: A few other members of this genus occur in our area.

Portulaca Family (*Portulacàceae*)

FEATURES: Plants fleshy. Sepals 2; petals 5, showy but short-lived; carpels 3, the ovaries united, yielding a partitionless capsule splitting into 3 valves.

Sunbright (*Talìnum teretifòlium*)   Pl. 51

FEATURES: Plant low, tufted. Inflorescence forked, on a slender stalk several inches high. Flowers ½ in. across, deep carmine-pink, opening for a few hours around midday; stamens numerous. Leaves rod-shaped, basal, in a rosette. Underground system a knobby tuber. Summer.

RANGE: Appalachians and adjacent parts of our area.

HABITAT: Dry rocky or gravelly slopes, in slightly acid soil.

CULTURE: Suitable for the rock garden.

NOTES: Other species, differing in flower details, occur in the Midland states.

Spring-beauty (*Claytònia virgínica*)   Pl. 52

FEATURES: Stem several inches high, bearing a pair of long narrow leaves. Inflorescence long and narrow; flowers ½ in. across, white to pink with deep pink veining; stamens 5. Underground system a deep-seated tuber. Spring.

RANGE: Eastern half of the United States and adjacent Canada.

HABITAT: Moist open woods and grassy thickets; soil various.

CULTURE: Should be grown in every woodland garden.

NOTES: The northern BROAD-LEAF SPRING-BEAUTY (*C. caroliniàna*) has fewer flowers, which appear even earlier.

Poke Family (*Phytolaccàceae*)

FEATURES: Coarse plants several feet high with branched groups of small flowers. Sepals 5, white, firm; petals obsolete; stamens 10; carpels 10, united, yielding a deep purple berry.

Pokeweed (*Phytolácca americàna*)   Pl. 52

FEATURES: As described under the family.
RANGE: Eastern half of the United States and adjacent Mexico.
HABITAT: Open woods and thickets, often in disturbed soil.
CULTURE: Weedy and worth growing only for bird food.
NOTES: The berries and underground parts are poisonous, although the young leafy shoots are edible when well cooked.

Four-o'clock Family (*Nyctaginàceae*)

FEATURES: Plants with opposite entire leaves and complex inflorescences of small flowers. Sepals 5, united below, the free part colored and petal-like; petals obsolete; stamens 3 to 5; carpel solitary, 1-seeded.

Wild Four-o'clock (*Oxýbaphus nyctagíneus*)   Pl. 50

FEATURES: Plant 2 to 3 ft. high. Flowers small, 2 or 3 together on a star of 5 pale bracts; sepals red. Summer.
RANGE: Midland states and adjacent regions; also spreading as a weed into the Northeastern states.
HABITAT: Grasslands and thickets on sandy or gravelly neutral to slightly acid soil.
CULTURE: Suitable for rather barren places.

Buckwheat Family (*Polygonàceae*)

FEATURES: Plants with alternate entire leaves, whose points of attachment are covered with a brown sheath. Flowers small; sepals 5 or 6, green or somewhat petal-like; petals obsolete; stamens 6; fruit 1-seeded.

Ladys-thumb (*Polýgonum amphíbium*)   Pl. 51

FEATURES: Plant aquatic. Flowers pink, numerous in a dense ellipsoidal group. Leaves oblong, 2 or 3 in. long. Summer.
RANGE: Over much of northern North America and Europe.
HABITAT: Pond and lake margins.
CULTURE: Spreads rather rapidly to be used in a small pool.

Buckwheat Family, concluded

Jumpseed (*Tovàra virginiàna*)   Pl. 52

FEATURES: Plant up to 3 ft. high. Flowers whitish, well spaced on a long slender stalk. Leaves elliptic, up to 4 or 5 in. long. Autumn.

RANGE: Eastern half of the United States and adjacent Canada.

HABITAT: Open woods in rich, moderately acid soil.

CULTURE: Readily cultivated in a woodland garden.

NOTES: The common name refers to the way the mature fruits spring from the stalk when touched.

Sand Jointweed (*Polygonélla articulàta*)   Pl. 53

FEATURES: Plant a slender annual with jointed stems 5 to 10 in. high. Flowers numerous, tiny, in a compound inflorescence; sepals 5, white, pink, or bronzy. Autumn.

RANGE: Atlantic and Great Lakes lowlands.

HABITAT: Sandy banks in the open or in sparse woodland; soil well drained, sterile, and acid.

CULTURE: Seed sown in an acid rock garden will sometimes grow.

NOTES: Many other members of this family occur in our area, some of them active weeds; those belonging to the genus *Polýgonum* are known as KNOTWEED or SMARTWEED, those to the genus *Rùmex* (not treated individually here) as DOCK or SORREL.

Lizard-tail Family (*Saururàceae*)

FEATURES: Coarse herbs with broad entire leaves. Flowers minute, fragrant, in long curvy spikes; sepals and petals obsolete; stamens 6 to 8, white; carpels 3 or 4, united at base.

Lizard-tail (*Saurùrus cérnuús*)   Pl. 53

FEATURES: As given for the family.

RANGE: Southern states and over our area except far northeast.

HABITAT: Shaded marshes and stream margins, in muddy soil.

CULTURE: Spreads too rapidly for use in a small garden.

NOTES: In some classifications this is regarded as the most primitive of the Dicots, but here interpreted as a derivative from some normal family through loss of sepals and petals.

Rose Family (*Rosàceae*)

FEATURES: A large and varied group, with mostly radially symmetric flowers. Sepals usually 5, united at base and borne on a disk; petals often 5; stamens numerous. Many important ornamental and food plants belong here.

Bowman-root (*Gillènia trifoliàta*)   Pl. 56

FEATURES: Plant about 3 ft. high. Flowers few, slender-stalked, about ¾ in. across; petals white or pinkish, narrow, somewhat oblique; carpels 5, maturing to divergent, tubular, few-seeded fruits. Leaves divided into 3 toothed lobes and a pair of stipules. Late spring and early summer.
RANGE: Central parts of our area and adjacent Southern states.
HABITAT: Open woods and thickets, in rather acid soil.
CULTURE: Can be grown in an acid wild garden.

Golden Avens (*Gèum strictum*)   Pl. 50

FEATURES: Plant about 3 ft. high. Flowers few, ¾ in. across; petals yellow; carpels numerous, separate, the styles hooked at tip, at maturity forming a globular bristly mass. Leaves pinnately divided into broad, toothed leaflets, the terminal one largest; larger leaflets of basal leaves interspersed with tiny ones. Summer.
RANGE: Northern North America and northeastern Asia.
HABITAT: Moist woods and thickets in moderately acid soil.
CULTURE: Readily grown in the wild garden.

White Avens (*G. canadénsè*)   Pl. 53

FEATURES: Plant about 2 ft. high. Flowers few, ½ in. across; petals white; carpels as in the next preceding species. Basal leaves with a large, lobed terminal leaflet and several much smaller lateral ones; stem leaves divided into 3 toothed lobes, sessile. Summer.
RANGE: Eastern half of the United States and adjacent Canada.
HABITAT: Open woods in neutral or somewhat acid soil.
CULTURE: Easy; desirable more for its foliage than its flowers.
NOTES: Several other species of *Gèum* occur in our area; they differ in details of foliage and flowers. A striking one in the Midland states and westward is PRAIRIE-SMOKE (*G. triflòrum*), named for its long, plumy, smoke-colored styles.

Rose Family, continued

Barren-strawberry (*Waldsteìnia fragarioìdes*)   **Pl. 54**

FEATURES: Plant a few inches high. Flowers ½ in. across; sepals
  united into a top-shaped cup; petals yellow; stamens about
  8; carpels few, separate, maturing to small, dry, 1-seeded
  fruits. Leaves basal, long-stalked, divided into 3 broad, toothed
  leaflets. Late spring.
RANGE: Cooler parts of our area and adjacent regions.
HABITAT: Wooded slopes and hummocks in swamps, in rather
  acid, humus-rich soil.
CULTURE: Can be grown in a cool, acid, woodland garden.
NOTES: The common name refers to the fact that, while the
  plant has the general aspect of a STRAWBERRY, neither receptacle nor fruits become fleshy at maturity.

Wine-leaf Cinquefoil (*Potentílla tridentàta*)   **Pl. 53**

FEATURES: Plant a few inches high, tufted on a woody crown.
  Flowers few in a flat-topped group, about ⅓ in. across; petals
  white, roundish; stamens about 20; carpels numerous, maturing to globular 1-seeded fruits. Leaves divided into 3 narrow,
  thick, shining leaflets, 3-toothed at tip, turning wine-red in
  late season (to which the common name refers). Summer.
RANGE: Northeastern North America, down across our area on
  mountain summits and bleak rocky outcrops.
HABITAT: Open rocky and gravelly situations, in acid soil.
CULTURE: Desirable for the cool acid rock garden.

Silver-and-gold (*P. anserìna*)   **Pl. 54**

FEATURES: Plant low, spreading into patches by slender arching stems. Flowers solitary, long-stalked in bract axils; petals
  5 to 7, golden yellow, blunt; stamens about 20; carpels
  numerous, separate, maturing to small 1-seeded fruits. Leaves
  pinnately divided into numerous oblong, toothed leaflets, dark
  green above and silvery-hairy beneath. Summer.
RANGE: In all lands bordering on the Arctic, and down into
  cool northern parts of our area.
HABITAT: Shores, salt marshes, and meadows, in neutral, more
  or less saline or limy soil.
CULTURE: Can be grown in a moist, limy situation.
NOTES: Also known as SILVER-WEED and GOOSE-WEED.

Plate 33

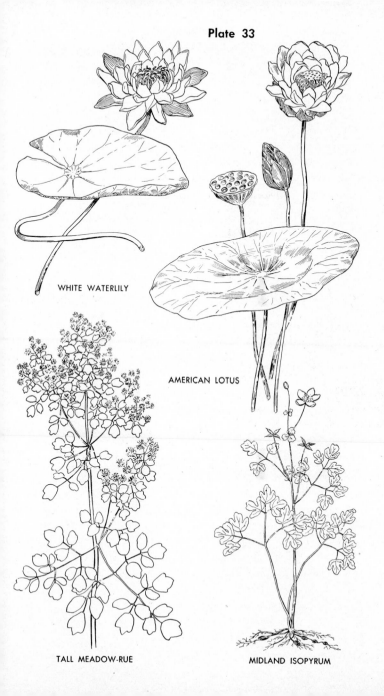

WHITE WATERLILY

AMERICAN LOTUS

TALL MEADOW-RUE

MIDLAND ISOPYRUM

Plate 34

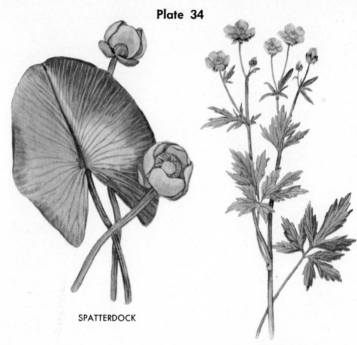

SPATTERDOCK

SWAMP BUTTERCUP

PASQUE-FLOWER

HEPATICA

Plate 35

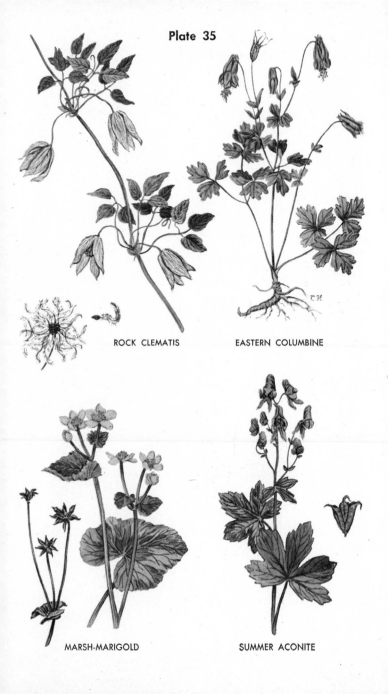

ROCK CLEMATIS

EASTERN COLUMBINE

MARSH-MARIGOLD

SUMMER ACONITE

Plate 36

MANY-RAY ANEMONE

BROAD-LEAF ANEMONE

WOOD ANEMONE

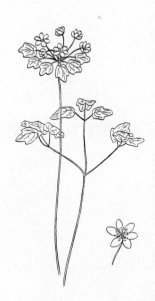

RUE-ANEMONE

Plate 39

WILD ROCKET

LAVENDER BITTERCRESS

NORTHERN PITCHERPLANT

ROSE-MALLOW

Plate 40

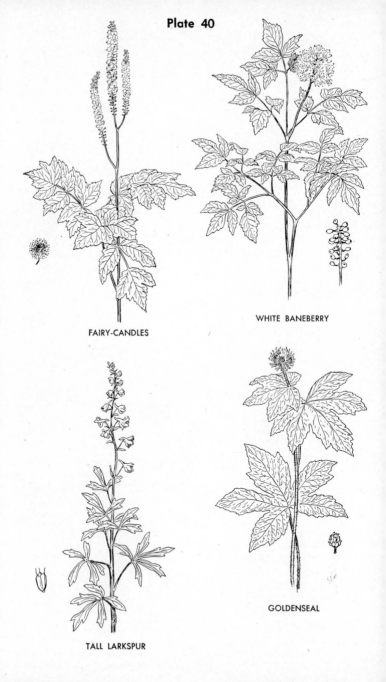

FAIRY-CANDLES

WHITE BANEBERRY

TALL LARKSPUR

GOLDENSEAL

Plate 45

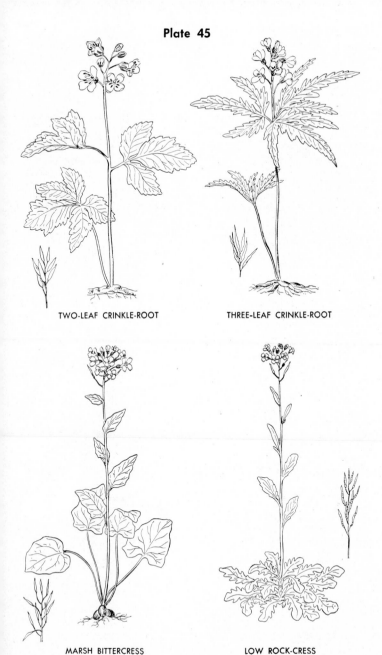

TWO-LEAF CRINKLE-ROOT

THREE-LEAF CRINKLE-ROOT

MARSH BITTERCRESS

LOW ROCK-CRESS

Plate 46

ST. ANDREWS-CROSS

WOOLLY GOLD-HEATHER

FROSTWORT

SMOOTH YELLOW VIOLET

Plate 49

BLUNT-LEAF SANDWORT

ROCK SANDWORT

WOOD STARWORT

STARRY CERASTIUM

Plate 50

PURPLE CANDYROOT

YELLOW CANDYROOT

WILD FOUR-O'CLOCK

GOLDEN AVENS

Plate 51

PINK CATCHFLY

RED CATCHFLY

LADYS-THUMB

SUNBRIGHT

Plate 52

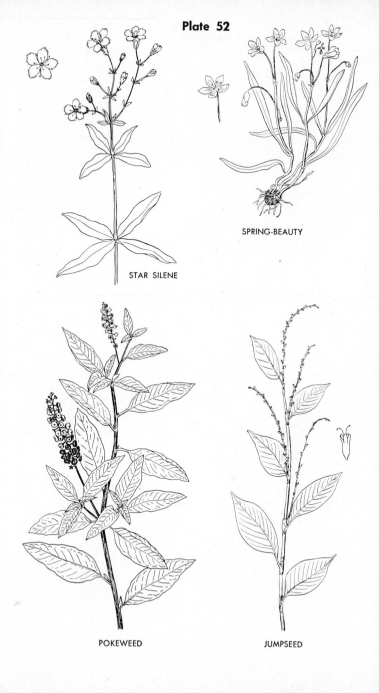

STAR SILENE

SPRING-BEAUTY

POKEWEED

JUMPSEED

Plate 53

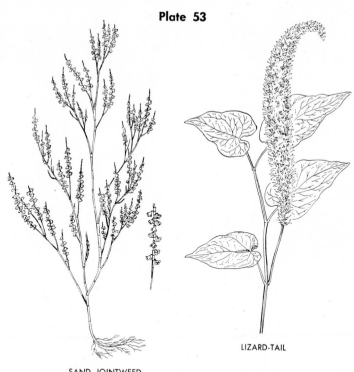

LIZARD-TAIL

SAND JOINTWEED

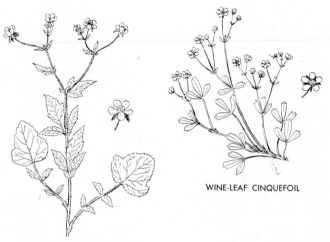

WINE-LEAF CINQUEFOIL

WHITE AVENS

Plate 54

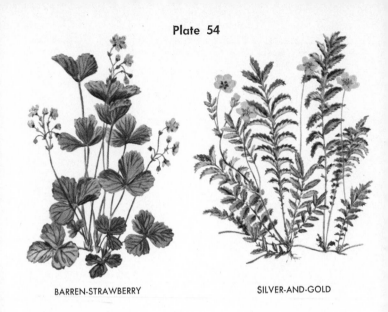

BARREN-STRAWBERRY

SILVER-AND-GOLD

FIELD CINQUEFOIL

YELLOW WILD-INDIGO

Plate 55

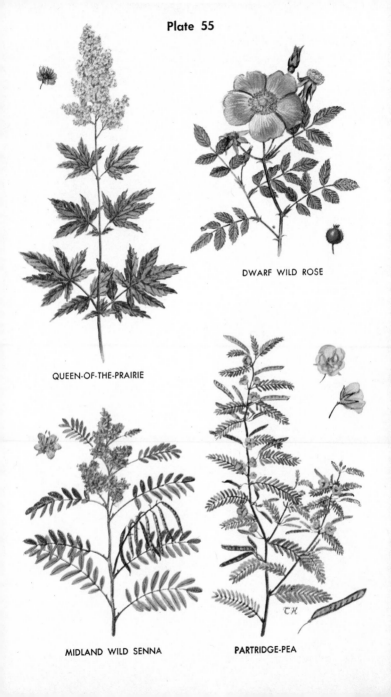

QUEEN-OF-THE-PRAIRIE

DWARF WILD ROSE

MIDLAND WILD SENNA

PARTRIDGE-PEA

Plate 56

WILD STRAWBERRY

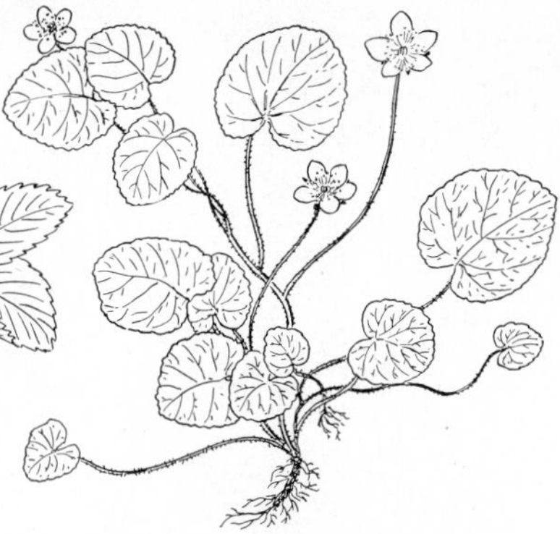

STAR-VIOLET

BOWMAN-ROOT

AMERICAN BURNET

Plate 57

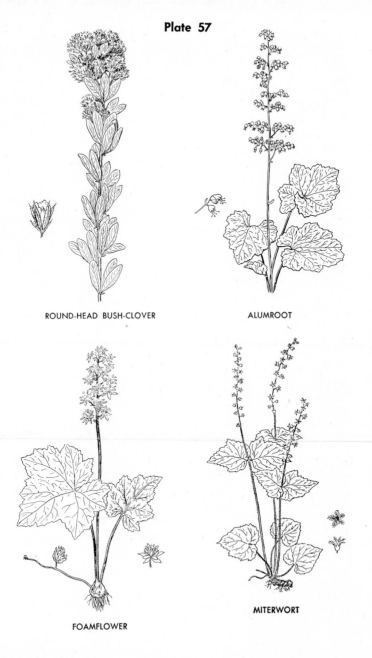

ROUND-HEAD BUSH-CLOVER

ALUMROOT

FOAMFLOWER

MITERWORT

Plate 58

BLUE WILD-INDIGO

EASTERN LUPINE

AMERICAN VETCH

BEACH-PEA

Plate 59

DEVILS-SHOESTRING

POTATO-BEAN

THICKET-BEAN

GROUND-BEAN

Plate 60

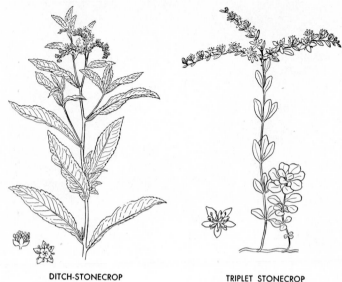

DITCH-STONECROP

TRIPLET STONECROP

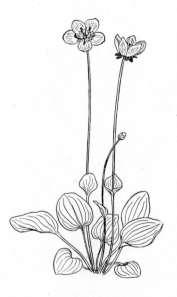

EARLY SAXIFRAGE

EASTERN PARNASSIA

Plate 61

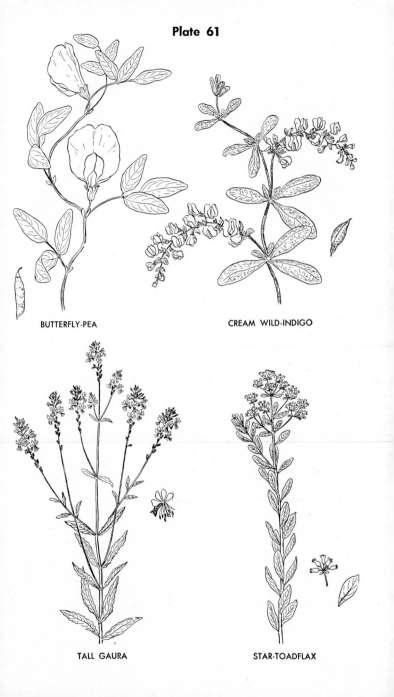

BUTTERFLY-PEA

CREAM WILD-INDIGO

TALL GAURA

STAR-TOADFLAX

Plate 62

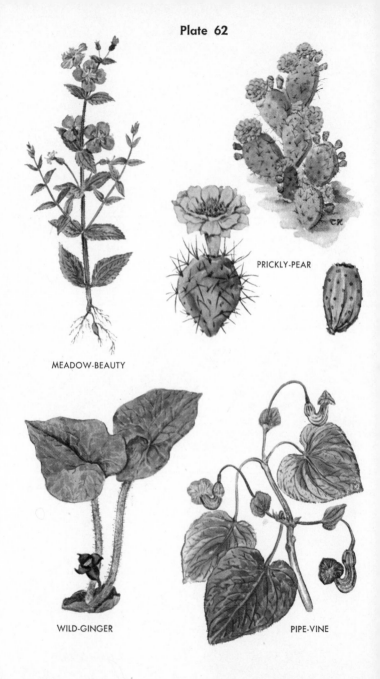

MEADOW-BEAUTY

PRICKLY-PEAR

WILD-GINGER

PIPE-VINE

Plate 63

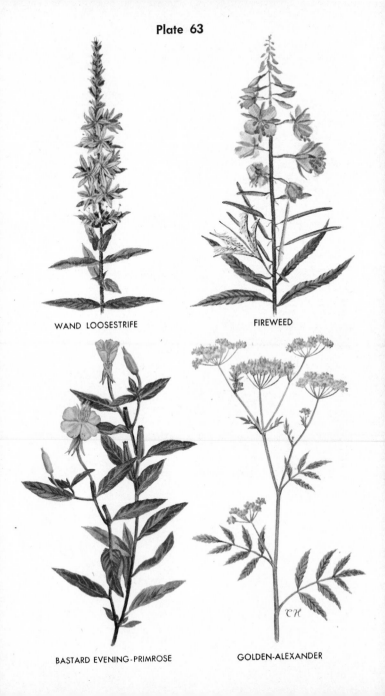

WAND LOOSESTRIFE

FIREWEED

BASTARD EVENING-PRIMROSE

GOLDEN-ALEXANDER

Plate 64

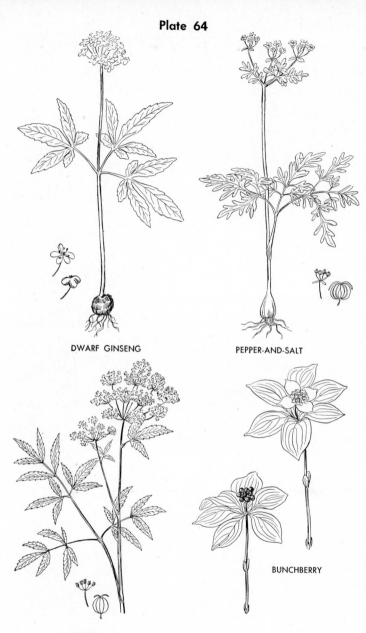

DWARF GINSENG

PEPPER-AND-SALT

AMERICAN POISON-HEMLOCK

BUNCHBERRY

Rose Family, continued

Field Cinquefoil (*Potentílla canadénsis*)   Pl. 54

FEATURES: Plant low, spreading into patches by long running leafy stems. Flowers solitary, long-stalked in bract axils, about ⅓ in. across; petals yellow, broad, blunt; stamens 20; carpels numerous, separate, maturing to tiny, dry, 1-seeded fruits. Leaves palmately divided into 5 toothed leaflets. Late spring and summer.

RANGE: Eastern half of the United States and adjacent Canada.

HABITAT: Grasslands and barrens, in dry, sterile, acid soil.

CULTURE: Spreads too rapidly for the small wild garden, but desirable for covering barren spots.

NOTES: Additional species, mostly weedy, occur in our area.

Queen-of-the-prairie (*Filipéndula rùbra*)   Pl. 55

FEATURES: Plant 3 to 5 ft. high. Flowers small, numerous; petals pink; stamens numerous; carpels several, maturing to dry, tubular, 1-seeded fruits. Leaves coarse, pinnately divided into lobed and toothed leaflets. Summer.

RANGE: Midland states and adjacent regions.

HABITAT: Damp grasslands and thickets, in neutral or slightly acid soil.

CULTURE: Often grown as a garden perennial.

Wild Strawberry (*Fragària virginiàna*)   Pl. 56

FEATURES: Plant low, spreading into patches by slender runners. Flowers few, clustered at the tip of a long stalk, about ¾ in. across; petals white; stamens numerous; carpels numerous, borne separately on a conical receptacle which at maturity becomes red, pulpy, and sweet, constituting the "berry." Leaves basal, long-stalked, divided into 3 elliptic, toothed leaflets. Late spring.

RANGE: Eastern half of North America.

HABITAT: Grassy slopes and open thickets in rather sterile, moderately acid soil.

CULTURE: Readily grown on a dry slope.

NOTES: There are really several species in our area, but they differ in minor details and are difficult to distinguish. The cultivated STRAWBERRIES are hybrids between these and foreign species.

Rose Family, concluded

American Burnet (*Sanguisórba canadénsis*) **Pl. 56**

FEATURES: Plant 3 to 5 ft. high. Flowers small, in dense spikes; sepals 4, whitish; petals obsolete; stamens 4, white, conspicuous; carpel solitary, maturing to a 1-seeded dry fruit. Leaves large, pinnately divided into toothed oblong leaflets. Summer and early autumn.

RANGE: Eastern Canada, uplands of our area, and down the higher Appalachians.

HABITAT: Marshes, meadows, and wet thickets, in acid soil.

CULTURE: Can be grown in a cool bog garden.

Dwarf Wild Rose (*Ròsa carolìna*) **Pl. 55**

FEATURES: Plant 1 to 2 ft. high. Flowers in axils of leafy bracts; sepals united to an urn-shaped structure which becomes red and fleshy; petals 5, pink, showy; stamens numerous; carpels numerous, separate, maturing to 1-seeded fruits inside the hollow calyx. Leaves pinnately divided into 5 or 7 toothed leaflets. Summer.

RANGE: Eastern half of the United States.

HABITAT: Gravelly or sandy slopes in moderately acid soil.

CULTURE: Readily grown in a sunny wild garden.

NOTES: Other species of ROSES occur in our area, some native and some escaped from gardens. They are distinguished by details of thorn position, sepal outline, etc.

Star-violet (*Dalibárda rèpens*) **Pl. 56**

FEATURES: Plant low, tufted. Flowers solitary on long stalks, about ⅓ in. across; sepals 5 or 6, unequal, united to a cup; petals small, white; stamens numerous; carpels few, separate, maturing to small, 1-seeded, fleshy fruits. Leaves roundish heart-shaped, blunt-toothed. Summer.

RANGE: Cooler parts of our area and adjacent regions.

HABITAT: Woods and bogs, in moist acid soil.

CULTURE: Suitable for the cool bog garden.

NOTES: The common name refers to the fact that, although the leaves look like those of a VIOLET, the flowers are starry. An alternative name, DEWDROP, refers to the pearly buds. Closely related are BLACKBERRIES and RASPBERRIES, but these, being shrubby, are not treated here.

Senna Family (*Caesalpiniàceae*)

FEATURES: Herbs with mostly pinnately compound leaves. Flowers slightly bilateral; sepals 5, united at base; petals 5; stamens 10; carpel solitary, maturing to a legume, a long, tubular, several-seeded pod splitting into 2 valves.

Midland Wild Senna (*Cássia marilándica*)   Pl. 55

FEATURES: Plant perennial, 4 or 5 ft. high. Flowers ¾ in. across; petals yellow; stamens in part imperfect. Fruit flat, segmented, 3 or 4 in. long. Summer.
RANGE: Midland states and adjacent regions.
HABITAT: Thickets on gravelly slopes, in moderately acid soil.
CULTURE: Desirable for the wild garden or border.

Partridge-pea (*C. chamaecrísta*)   Pl. 55

FEATURES: Plant annual, 1 to 2 ft. high. Flowers in sparse clusters in leaf axils, 1 in. across; petals yellow, some with purple spot near base; stamens part purple and part yellow; fruit 2 in. long. Summer.
RANGE: Eastern half of United States.
HABITAT: Open thickets in neutral to acid sandy soil.
CULTURE: Readily grown from seed.

Pea Family (*Leguminòsae*)

FEATURES: Plants with pinnately or palmately compound or, rarely, simple leaves. Flowers strongly bilateral: petals 5, one erect at back of flower, 2 forming lateral wings, and 2 more united to a boat-shaped keel around the reproductive organs; stamens 10; fruit a legume. A large and varied family, including many ornamental and food plants, notably peas and beans.

Yellow Wild-indigo (*Baptísia tinctòria*)   Pl. 54

FEATURES: Plant 2 to 3 ft. high. Flowers in sparse groups, about ½ in. long; sepals united to a bell-shaped tube; petals yellow; stamens 10, separate; fruit stalked, spindle-shaped. Leaves with 3 leaflets, about 1 in. long. Summer.
RANGE: Eastern half of the United States.
HABITAT: Open woods and barrens, in acid sandy soil.
CULTURE: Difficult to transplant, but may grow in acid gardens.

Pea Family, continued

Cream Wild-indigo (*Baptísia bracteàta*)   **Pl. 61**

FEATURES: Plant a foot or so high. Flowers in drooping inflorescences; petals cream color, 1 in. long; stamens 10, separate; fruit spindle-shaped. Leaves with 3 leaflets 2 in. long. Late spring.

RANGE: Midland and Southern states.

HABITAT: Grasslands and marginal thickets in often neutral soil.

CULTURE: Can be grown in a dry, open wild garden or rock garden, and very desirable.

NOTES: This species is unusual in the way its flower clusters point toward the ground.

Blue Wild-indigo (*B. austràlis*)   **Pl. 58**

FEATURES: Plant 3 to 4 ft. high. Flowers about ¾ in. long, in erect cylindrical groups; petals violet-blue; stamens 10, separate; fruit short-stalked, 1 in. long. Leaves with 3 leaflets 1 to 2 in. long. Summer.

RANGE: Southern states and adjacent parts of our area.

HABITAT: Rocky slopes and stream banks, in often neutral soil.

CULTURE: A desirable garden border subject.

NOTES: One or two other species occur in the Midland states. Especially striking is the WHITE WILD-INDIGO (*B. leucántha*), a tall, smooth plant with white flowers in erect groups.

Eastern Lupine (*Lupìnus perénnis*)   **Pl. 58**

FEATURES: Plant 1 to 2 ft. high. Flowers about ⅔ in. long, in a narrow cylindric group; petals lavender-blue; stamens 10, united to a cylinder; fruit hairy, about 1½ in. long. Leaves palmately divided into about 8 narrow leaflets. Spring.

RANGE: Eastern half of the United States.

HABITAT: Thickets and open woods in dry, sandy or gravelly, sterile and acid soil.

CULTURE: This LUPINE develops an extensive root system and is correspondingly very difficult to transplant from the wild to a garden. It can, however, be introduced into open, sterile, acid, sandy tracts by sowing seed. This must be collected when barely ripe, and kept from drying out, preferably by packing in damp soil from the base of the parent plant.

Pea Family, continued

Devils-shoestring (*Tephròsia virginiàna*)   Pl. 59

FEATURES: Plant 1 to 2 ft. high. Flowers ¾ in. long, in compact groups; petals showy, pink and buff; stamens 10, united at base, but one nearly distinct from the tube formed by the other 9; fruit narrow, hairy, 1½ in. long. Leaves pinnate with oblong leaflets. Summer.

RANGE: Eastern half of the United States.

HABITAT: Open woods on dry acid soil.

CULTURE: Can be grown in an acid wild garden.

NOTES: The common name refers to the long, tough, stringy roots; these contain rotenone, an insecticide. A number of genera of legumes occurring in grasslands of the Midland states are not discussed here. Their flower and fruit characters show that they belong to this family, but in general only a specialist can assign them to the correct genus and species.

Round-head Bush-clover (*Lespedèza capitàta*)   Pl. 57

FEATURES: Plant 3 or 4 ft. high. Flowers small, in dense globular heads; sepals long and narrow; petals cream color, the upper one with a lilac spot at base; fruit disk-shaped, with a solitary seed. Summer.

RANGE: Eastern half of the United States and adjacent Canada.

HABITAT: Grasslands and thickets in dry, rather sterile, moderately acid soil.

CULTURE: Suitable for barren areas.

NOTES: Other species of BUSH-CLOVER grow in our area, differing in stature and flower characters, but alike in fruit.

American Vetch (*Vìcia americàna*)   Pl. 58

FEATURES: Plant a vine climbing by tendrils at the tip of the pinnate leaves. Flowers ¾ in. long, in sparse groups; petals violet-purple; stamens 10, with one separate from the tube formed by the other 9; fruit flat, about 1 in. long, with a few round seeds. Late spring and summer.

RANGE: Widespread in central North America.

HABITAT: Moist thickets, in neutral or moderately acid soil.

CULTURE: Will grow in a moist woodland garden.

NOTES: Several other species of VETCH grow here also, but they differ in rather minor details.

Pea Family, continued

Beach-pea (*Láthyrus marítimus*)   Pl. 58

FEATURES: Plant a trailing vine, with tendrils at the tip of the pinnate leaves. Flowers ¾ in. long, in compact groups; petals violet and purple; stamens 10, with 1 separate from the tube of the other 9; fruit flat, about 2 in. long, veiny. Leaves rather thick and fleshy. Summer.

RANGE: In all lands bordering the Arctic, extending in our area around the Great Lakes and the Atlantic coast.

HABITAT: Beaches and gravelly slopes in neutral soil.

CULTURE: Can be grown under conditions resembling its native haunts.

NOTES: Several other species are known in our area. The RIVERBANK-PEA (*L. venòsus*), with less fleshy but more veiny leaves and somewhat smaller flowers, is desirable for a shady rock or wild garden.

Butterfly-pea (*Clitòria mariàna*)   Pl. 61

FEATURES: Plant trailing or twining over bushes. Flowers solitary, showy, about 2 in. long; sepals united below into a tube; petals lavender-blue; stamens 10, united; fruit about 1 in. long, few-seeded. Leaves divided into 3 leaflets 1 to 2 in. long. Summer.

RANGE: Southern United States and adjacent parts of our area.

HABITAT: Open woods and thickets in rather sterile and acid sandy or gravelly soil.

CULTURE: Difficult to grow except in a situation matching its native habitat closely.

Potato-bean (*Àpios americàna*)   Pl. 59

FEATURES: Plant twining over bushes to a height of several feet. Flowers fragrant, about ½ in. long, in compact groups; sepals united to a bell-shaped tube; petals brownish purple; stamens 10, one nearly separate from the other 9; fruit 2 or 3 in. long, many-seeded. Leaves pinnately divided into 5 or 7 pointed leaflets. Summer.

RANGE: Eastern half of the United States and adjacent Canada.

HABITAT: Moist thickets in neutral to moderately acid soil.

CULTURE: Spreads rapidly by underground runners, so undesirable for the small garden.

NOTES: The name refers to edible tubers produced.

Pea Family, concluded

Thicket-bean (*Phaséolus polystàchyus*)   Pl. 59

FEATURES: Plant twining over bushes. Flowers ⅓ in. long, in slender inflorescences; petals lilac; stamens 10, 1 separate from the other 9; keel strongly spiraled at tip; fruit about 2 in. long, containing 4 or 5 small brown beans. Leaves divided into 3 broad, pointed leaflets. Summer.
RANGE: Southern states and adjacent parts of our area.
HABITAT: Thickets on moderately acid soil.
CULTURE: Suitable for the brushy wild garden.
NOTES: This is the only close relative of the cultivated beans native to our area. The seeds are edible and were used for food by the Indians.

Ground-bean (*Strophostýles hélvola*)   Pl. 59

FEATURES: Plant trailing or ascending, several feet long. Flowers about ½ in. long, in compact clusters on long stalks from leaf axils; petals dull pink; stamens 10, 1 separate from the other 9; keel curved; fruit a slender cylindric pod 2 in. long. Leaves divided into 3 loby leaflets. Summer.
RANGE: Over our area except far northeastward.
HABITAT: Thickets and barrens in rather acid sandy soil.
CULTURE: Can be grown in a sandy wild garden.

Saxifrage Family (*Saxifragàceae*)

FEATURES: Low plants with groups of small flowers. Sepals 5, united below into a cup; petals 5; stamens 5 or 10; carpels 2, more or less united to one another and to a supporting disk.

Early Saxifrage (*Saxífraga virginiénsis*)   Pl. 60

FEATURES: Plant a rosette of broad, few-toothed, rather fleshy leaves, with a branched inflorescence a few inches high. Flowers small white fragrant stars with the golden anthers of the 10 stamens conspicuous; carpels divergent. Early spring.
RANGE: Over our area and adjacent regions.
HABITAT: Partly shaded rocky or loamy slopes; acidity varying.
CULTURE: Desirable for the shady rock garden.
NOTES: Several other SAXIFRAGES grow in our area, some on dry rocks and some in wet swamps.

Saxifrage Family, concluded

Alumroot (*Heuchèra americàna*)   Pl. 57

FEATURES: Plant with a thick underground stem bearing lobed, blunt-toothed leaves and a branched inflorescence 1 to 2 ft. high. Flowers tiny but numerous; sepals united into a conspicuous cup; petals minute, bronzy; stamens 5, elongate; carpels well united, forming a 2-valved capsule. Late spring.

RANGE: Appalachians and adjacent parts of our area.

HABITAT: Open woods on rocky or gravelly slopes, in moderately acid soil.

CULTURE: Readily grown on a well-drained slope.

NOTES: Additional species present here differ in cutting and pubescence of leaves, blooming period, and floral symmetry. Most frequent in the Midland states is MIDLAND ALUMROOT (*H. richardsónii*) with leaf stalks and undersurfaces of blades conspicuously pubescent, and distinctly bilateral flowers about ⅓ in. long.

Foamflower (*Tiarélla cordifòlia*)   Pl. 57

FEATURES: Plant low, spreading into patches by arching stems. Flowers small, in a cylindric group at tip of a 6- to 8-in. stalk; petals white; stamens 10, conspicuous; carpels maturing to a capsule with 2 unequal valves. Leaves heart-shaped, shallowly lobed and toothed. Spring.

RANGE: Northern parts of our area, and adjacent Canada and Appalachians.

HABITAT: Cool woods, in rich neutral or moderately acid soil.

CULTURE: Desirable as a ground cover in a woodland garden.

NOTES: The common name refers to the foamy stamens.

Miterwort (*Mitélla diphýlla*)   Pl. 57

FEATURES: Plant low, with basal heart-shaped leaves and a flowering stalk 1 to 2 ft. high, bearing a pair of opposite bracts about the middle. Flowers tiny, in a long slender inflorescence; petals white, delicately fringed; stamens 10; carpels maturing to a miter-shaped capsule, to which the common name refers. Spring.

RANGE: Over much of our area and adjacent regions.

HABITAT: Deep woods, in rich, often neutral soil.

CULTURE: Readily grown in a shaded wild garden.

Parnassia Family (*Parnassiàceae*)

FEATURES: Plants low, with heart-shaped entire leaves in basal tufts. Flowers solitary, on tall stalks with a round bract about the middle; sepals 5, barely united; petals 5, white with green veins; stamens 5, alternating with groups of sterile stamen-like structures; carpels 4, well united.

Eastern Parnassia (*Parnássia glaúca*)   Pl. 60
FEATURES: As given for the family. Blooming in autumn.
RANGE: Southern Canada and northern parts of our area.
HABITAT: Moist grasslands and thickets, in cool neutral soil.
CULTURE: Can be grown in a cool, moist wild garden, but susceptible to attack by fungi and other garden pests.
NOTES: A common name given in books is GRASS-OF-PARNAS-SUS, but the plant has nothing grass-like about it.

Stonecrop Family (*Crassulàceae*)

FEATURES: Plants small, succulent. Inflorescence flat-topped, with somewhat spiraled branches. Sepals 4 or 5, united at base; petals 4 or 5; stamens 8 or 10; carpels 5, distinct.

Triplet Stonecrop (*Sèdum ternàtum*)   Pl. 60
FEATURES: Plant 3 to 6 in. high. Flowers about ⅓ in. across; petals white. Leaves whorled in threes, roundish. Spring.
RANGE: Appalachians and adjacent parts of our area.
HABITAT: Wooded rocky slopes and sandy flats, in neutral or moderately acid soil.
CULTURE: Desirable for a woodland garden, yielding a sub-evergreen ground cover.
NOTES: Other species occur locally in our area.

Ditch-stonecrop Family (*Penthoràceae*)

FEATURES: Plant 1 to 2 ft. high. Flowers tiny, green; petals rudimentary or obsolete; carpels 5, maturing to a star-like capsule. Leaves elliptic, finely toothed.

Ditch-stonecrop (*Pénthorum sedoìdes*)   Pl. 60
FEATURES: As given for the family. Summer.
RANGE: Over our area and adjacent regions.
HABITAT: Swamps and stream banks, in muddy soil.
CULTURE: Readily cultivated in a swamp garden.

Meadow-beauty Family (*Melastomàceae*)

FEATURES: Small plants with opposite leaves. Flowers showy; sepals 4, united to an urn-shaped structure; petals 4, delicate, somewhat oblique; stamens 8, conspicuous; carpels 4, well united, maturing to a 4-valved capsule.

Meadow-beauty (*Rhéxia virgínica*)   Pl. 62
FEATURES: Plant 1 to 2 ft. high. Flowers 1 in. across; petals bright purple, falling at midday. Summer.
RANGE: Southern, Northeastern, and adjacent Midland states.
HABITAT: Moist open woods and bog margins, in strongly acid soil.
CULTURE: While best adapted to damp, peaty situations, will grow in a fairly dry rock garden if the soil is acid enough.

Loosestrife Family (*Lythràceae*)

FEATURES: Leafy-stemmed herbs. Sepals 4 to 6, united to a tube; petals 4 to 6; stamens 4 to 12; carpels 2, united.

Wand Loosestrife (*Lýthrum alàtum*)   Pl. 63
FEATURES: Plant 2 or 3 ft. high. Flowers purple, in bract axils, ⅓ in. across. Leaves oblong, up to 1 in. long. Summer.
RANGE: Over our area except far northeastward.
HABITAT: Damp thickets in neutral to moderately acid soil.
CULTURE: Readily grown in a swamp garden.
NOTES: The coarser and showier WILLOW LOOSESTRIFE of Europe (*L. salicària*) has escaped from cultivation and become a pernicious weed along many northeastern streams and lakes.

Cactus Family (*Cactàceae*)

FEATURES: Stems much enlarged and fleshy; leaves minute, spine-like. Flowers showy, their parts numerous; sepals united with the ovary, maturing to a pear-shaped, fleshy, edible fruit.

Prickly-pear (*Opúntia humifùsa*)   Pl. 62
FEATURES: Stem joints flat. Petals yellow. Early summer.
RANGE: Midland states and adjacent regions.
HABITAT: Open rocky or sandy barrens, in often neutral soil.
CULTURE: Suitable for the rock or sand garden.
NOTES: Other, closely related, species occur in our area.

Wild-ginger Family (*Aristolochiàceae*)

FEATURES: Plants with heart-shaped entire leaves and aromatic sap. Flowers bronzy; sepals 3, united below to the fleshy ovary; petals obsolete; stamens 6 or 12; carpels 6, united.

Pipe-vine (*Aristolòchia sìpho*)　　　　　Pl. 62

FEATURES: Plant a high-twining vine. Flowers on bracted stalks in leaf axils; calyx tube 1 in. long, strongly curved, tipped by an upturned, flat, triangular limb; stamens 6; capsule 2 in. long, 6-ridged. Leaves large. Early summer.
RANGE: Midland states and Appalachians.
HABITAT: Wooded rocky slopes in moderately acid soil.
CULTURE: Well known in cultivation, and often called DUTCH-MANS-PIPE in reference to the shape of the calyx.

Wild-ginger (*Ásarum canadénsè*)　　　　Pl. 62

FEATURES: Plant low, hairy, with paired large leaves at branch tips of fleshy underground stems. Flowers solitary in the forks between leaf stalks. Stamens 12. Early spring.
RANGE: Over our area and down the Appalachians.
HABITAT: Woods on rocky or loamy slopes, often in neutral soil.
CULTURE: Readily cultivated in a woodland garden.
NOTES: Divisible into several subspecies on the basis of the shape and position of the conspicuous free sepal tips.

Sandalwood Family (*Santalàceae*)

FEATURES: A chiefly tropical family of root parasites. Flowers dull-colored; sepals 5, united below into a cup adherent to the ovary; petals obsolete; stamens 5; carpel 1, maturing to a small fleshy fruit with central stone.

Star-toadflax (*Comándra umbellàta*)　　　Pl. 61

FEATURES: Plant 1 to 2 ft. high. Flowers small, whitish, in compact groups. Leaves small, alternate. Early summer.
RANGE: Over our area and adjacent regions.
HABITAT: In woods, parasitic on roots of trees and shrubs.
CULTURE: Difficult, but will sometimes grow from seed.
NOTES: The plant resembles TOADFLAX, but the flowers are starry, suggesting the common name here used. A less apt book name is BASTARD-TOADFLAX.

Evening-primrose Family (*Onagràceae*)

FEATURES: Flower parts mostly in fours, or stamens 8; sepals united into a long tube, coherent with the ovary; carpels well united, maturing to a capsule.

Fireweed (*Epilòbium angustifòlium*)   Pl. 63

FEATURES: Plant 3 to 5 ft. high. Flowers about 1 in. across, in a long slender inflorescence; petals bright purple; seeds bearing long white hairs. Summer.

RANGE: In all lands bordering on the Arctic.

HABITAT: Open woods and thickets, becoming abundant after fires, to which the common name refers.

CULTURE: Can be grown in a wild garden, but spreads rapidly.

NOTES: Other species, with smaller flowers, occur in our area.

Bastard Evening-primrose (*Oenothèra biénnis*)   Pl. 63

FEATURES: Plant biennial, 2 to 4 ft. high. Flowers about 1 in. across and 2 in. long, opening in late afternoon; petals broad, blunt, light yellow; capsule narrow-cylindric, about 1 in. long. Leaves elliptic with wavy and sparsely-toothed margins. Summer and early autumn.

RANGE: Eastern half of North America.

HABITAT: Thickets and barrens, invading old fields and roadsides as a weed.

CULTURE: Readily grown in any barren spot.

NOTES: This plant is a complex hybrid. Various species, differing in details of leaves and fruit, occur in our area also.

Tall Gaura (*Gaúra biénnis*)   Pl. 61

FEATURES: Plant 2 to 4 ft. high, biennial. Flowers in slender spikes, bilateral, about ⅓ in. across; petals white, turning pink as they wither toward afternoon; fruit ellipsoidal, strongly 4-ribbed. Summer.

RANGE: Over our area except far northeastward.

HABITAT: Thickets and grasslands, in dry, moderately acid soil.

CULTURE: Suitable for a dry wild garden.

NOTES: Other species, some showier, occur in the west Midlands. In damp woods of our area there grow members of the related genus *Circàea*, called in the books ENCHANTERS-NIGHTSHADE; the small bur fruits stick to one's clothing in abundance.

Carrot Family (*Umbellíferae*)

FEATURES: Flowers small, in umbels, i.e., inflorescences with the flower stalks arising from 1 point on a stem; sepals 5, united with the ovary; petals and stamens 5; carpels 2, maturing to separate small 1-seeded dry fruits.

Pepper-and-salt (*Erigenìa bulbòsa*) Pl. 64

FEATURES: Plant a few inches high, arising from a small tuber. Flowers few; petals white and anthers blackish red, their color contrast suggesting the common name. Leaves twice divided in threes, the ultimate divisions oblong. Early spring.
RANGE: Midland and adjacent parts of Northeastern states.
HABITAT: Wooded slopes and flats in rich neutral soil.
CULTURE: Desirable for the shaded rock garden, in view of its early blooming.

American Poison-hemlock (*Cicùta maculàta*) Pl. 64

FEATURES: Plant coarse, several feet high, arising from a cluster of fleshy roots containing a deadly poisonous principle. Flowers white, numerous in a compound umbel. Leaves large, doubly pinnate, the divisions to 3 in. long, coarse-toothed. Summer.
RANGE: Eastern half of the United States and adjacent Canada.
HABITAT: Swamps and wet thickets, in muddy soil.
CULTURE: Will spread rapidly by seed in a moist wild garden.
NOTES: Wholly unrelated to the non-poisonous HEMLOCK tree.

Golden-alexander (*Zízia aúrea*) Pl. 63

FEATURES: Plant 1 to 2 ft. high. Flowers yellow, in compound umbels. Leaves twice divided in threes, the ultimate segments 1 to 2 in. long, toothed. Late spring.
RANGE: Eastern half of the United States and adjacent Canada.
HABITAT: Moist meadows and thickets; soil acidity various.
CULTURE: Readily grown in a wild garden.
NOTES: There are other species of this and closely related genera in our area. Many other members of the family are also present, some large, showy-flowered plants, others humble weeds. They are distinguished by details of leaves and especially of the tiny fruits, but mostly require a specialist to even assign them to the correct genus.

Ginseng Family (*Araliàceae*)

FEATURES: Flowers small, in umbels, their organs mostly in fives; sepals united with the ovary, which bears a disk on top; petals greenish or whitish; fruit a berry.

Dwarf Ginseng (*Pànax trifòlium*)   Pl. 64

FEATURES: Plant a few inches high, arising from a deep-seated globular root ½ in. thick. Flowers tiny, white, in a stalked umbel arising from a whorl of 3 compound leaves; fruit a small yellow berry. Leaflets 3 or 5, about 1 in. long, oval, blunt, toothed. Early spring.

RANGE: Over our area except far northwest, and adjacent Canada.

HABITAT: Moist woods, in neutral or somewhat acid soil.

CULTURE: Readily grown in a woodland garden.

NOTES: The true GINSENG (*P. quinquefòlium*) is a taller plant with a fleshy taproot possessing alleged medicinal qualities, which commands a high price in the drug trade, especially in China. Its leaflets are much coarser, up to 4 in. long, and are broadened above the middle and then abruptly pointed; the flowers are greenish and the berries red. While occurring nearly throughout our area, it has been exterminated locally.

Dogwood Family (*Cornàceae*)

FEATURES: A group comprising mostly shrubs and trees. Flowers small, in umbels; sepals 4 or 5, united with the ovary; petals 4 or 5; stamens usually 4; carpels 2, well united, maturing to a juicy fruit with central stone.

Bunchberry (*Córnus canadénsis*)   Pl. 64

FEATURES: Plant a few inches high, with slender running stems sending up stalks bearing a whorl of oval leaves and the yellow flower umbel subtended by a whorl of 4 to 6 conspicuous white bracts; fruit red, in a compact cluster to which the name refers.

RANGE: Northern North America and northeastern Asia, extending down across our area in cool situations.

HABITAT: Damp woods and hummocks in swamps, in cold, moist, strongly acid, humus-rich soil.

CULTURE: Difficult to cultivate far from its native haunts, unless the garden can be kept strongly acid and cool.

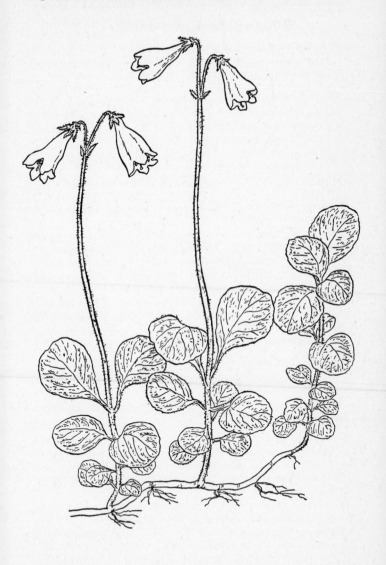

Key to Families

UNION OF PETALS very slight; petals 4 to 5, stamens 8 to 10.

    PLANT having green pigment . . . . . . **Pyrola** F.

    PLANT lacking green pigment, saprophytic . **Indian-pipe** F.

UNION OF PETALS considerable.

    STAMEN NUMBER twice petal number . . . . **Heath** F.

    STAMEN NUMBER equal or less than petal number.

      STAMEN POSITION above petals . . . . **Primrose** F.

      STAMEN POSITION otherwise.

     OVARY free from bases of other flower parts.

       FLORAL SYMMETRY radial or essentially so.

        CARPELS 2, separate at least in fruit; juice milky.

         STAMENS separate . . . . . **Dogbane** F.

         STAMENS partly united . . . **Milkweed** F.

        CARPELS otherwise.

         PARTITIONS IN OVARY obsolete; stigmas 2.

          LEAVES opposite, entire . . . . **Gentian** F.

          LEAVES otherwise.

           PLANT aquatic; leaves either heart-shaped or divided into 3 leaflets . **Bogbean** F.

           PLANT not aquatic; leaves toothed, lobed, or pinnately divided . . **Waterleaf** F.

         PARTITIONS IN OVARY present.

          CARPEL NUMBER, ovary cavities, and stigmas 3 . . . . **Phlox** F.

         CARPEL NUMBER 2 or 4.

          STAMEN NUMBER 4; flowers not quite radial.

           FRUIT a group of 4 nut-like structures.

                part of **Verbena** F.

           FRUIT a capsule with 2 cavities.

                Acanthus F.

          STAMEN NUMBER 5.

          OVARY 4-lobed, maturing to a group of 4 nut-like structures . . **Borage** F.

          OVARY scarcely if at all lobed, maturing to a capsule or berry.

           FRUIT a capsule containing a few large seeds . . . **Morning-glory** F.

           FRUIT a berry containing numerous small seeds . . . . . **Potato** F.

FLORAL SYMMETRY definitely bilateral.
  SEEDS becoming surrounded by nut-like structures.
    CARPELS 4.
      OVARY not lobed; herbage not aromatic.
                  part of **Verbena F.**
      OVARY deeply lobed; herbage often aromatic.
                         Mint F.
    CARPEL solitary . . . . . **Lopseed F.**
  SEEDS not surrounded by nut-like structures.
    CARPEL NUMBER 2.
      SEEDS borne on flat surfaces **Snapdragon F.**
      SEEDS borne on projections . **Acanthus F.**
    CARPEL NUMBER apparently 1.
      FRUIT horned . . . . **Unicorn-plant F.**
      FRUIT not horned.
        PLANT aquatic, insectivorous. **Bladderwort F.**
        PLANT parasitic . . . . **Broomrape F.**
OVARY united with bases of other flower parts.
  STAMENS separate upward.
    FILAMENTS partly fused with corolla tube.
      LEAVES opposite, with stipules, or whorled.
                        Madder F.
      LEAVES opposite, lacking stipules. **Honeysuckle F.**
    FILAMENTS free from corolla tube . **Bellflower F.**
  STAMENS united upward.
    FLOWERS separate, strongly bilateral . **Lobelia F.**
    FLOWERS densely clustered in a head.
      JUICE milky; flowers short-lived, all alike, the
        petals united upward into a strap-shaped
        ray . . . . **Chicory F.**
      JUICE not milky; flowers long-lived; rays developed
        only on marginal flowers, or not at all.
                        Daisy F.

Pyrola Family (*Pyrolàceae*)

FEATURES: Low evergreen plants with slender, running, underground stems. Flowers radial or somewhat bilateral; sepals 5, united below; petals 5, barely united; stamens 10; carpels 5, united, maturing to a capsule with numerous minute seeds.

Mottled Pipsissewa (*Chimáphila maculàta*)   Pl. 65

FEATURES: Shoots a few inches high. Flowers pinkish white, fragrant, about ¾ in. across, 2 or 3 nodding at stalk tip. Leaves dark green with pale mottling along veins, up to 2½ in. long and ¾ in. wide, sparsely toothed. Summer.

RANGE: Over our area and adjacent Southern states.

HABITAT: Woods, in moderately acid, humus-rich soil.

CULTURE: Difficult to transplant; may grow in an acid garden.

NOTES: GREEN PIPSISSEWA (*C. umbellàta*) differs in that the leaves are solid green, broadened upward, and finely toothed. It ranges across northern North America, Europe, and Asia.

Thin-leaf Pyrola (*Pýrola ellíptica*)   Pl. 65

FEATURES: Plant tufted, sending up a stalk with slender inflorescence a few inches high. Flowers bilateral, nodding, ⅔ in. across; petals white; style conspicuous, curved. Leaves basal, short-stalked, elliptic, up to 3 in. long. Summer.

RANGE: Northern North America, down in cool parts of our area.

HABITAT: Woods, in moderately acid, humus-rich soil.

CULTURE: Can be grown in an acid woodland garden.

NOTES: Other species differ in details of leaves and flowers.

Indian-pipe Family (*Monotropàceae*)

FEATURES: Plants without chlorophyl, absorbing their nourishment saprophytically from decaying humus. Stalks scaly, a few inches high. Sepals and petals 4 or 5, more or less united; stamens 8 or 10; carpels about 5, united; capsule erect.

Indian-pipe (*Monótropa uniflòra*)   Pl. 65

FEATURES: Stalks white or pink. Flowers solitary, nodding, about ¾ in. long, white or pinkish. Summer.

RANGE: Over North America, except far north; also eastern Asia.

HABITAT: Woods, in more or less acid humus.

CULTURE: Like all saprophytes, next to impossible to cultivate.

Indian-pipe Family, concluded

Pine-sap (*Monótropa hypópitys*)   **Pl. 65**

FEATURES: Stalks and flowers buff to red. Flowers several, nodding, about ¾ in. long. Summer and autumn.

RANGE: Eastern North America, but rare in the Midland states.

HABITAT: Woods, in moderately acid humus.

CULTURE: Not practicable.

NOTES: This entity is separable into several subspecies; we have two summer-blooming buff ones differing in hairiness, and an autumn-blooming deep red one.

Heath Family (*Ericàceae*)

FEATURES: Chiefly shrubs, as AZALEAS, KALMIAS, RHODODENDRONS, not covered in this book; two low evergreen members here described. Flowers radial or somewhat bilateral; sepals 4 or 5, united below; petals 4 or 5, well united; stamens 8 or 10; carpels 5 or 10, united.

Trailing-arbutus (*Epigaèa rèpens*)   **Pl. 68**

FEATURES: Plant a prostrate undershrub. Flowers fragrant, ⅔ in. long, clustered in leaf axils; petals 5, white to pink, forming a funnel-shaped tube with starry limb; capsule splitting into 5 valves, exposing a fleshy white pulp sprinkled with minute seeds. Leaves evergreen. Early spring.

RANGE: Eastern half of North America.

HABITAT: Wooded slopes and sandy flats, in strongly acid soil.

CULTURE: Difficult to cultivate, except in an area which can be kept strongly acid and free from garden earthworms.

Wintergreen (*Gaulthèria procúmbens*)   **Pl. 68**

FEATURES: Stems slender, creeping underground, sending up shoots a few inches high. Flowers solitary in leaf axils, nodding; petals 5, white, united to an urn-shaped tube; ovary and calyx together enlarging into a fleshy red berry. Leaves at shoot tips, evergreen, elliptic, 1 to 2 in. long. Whole plant aromatic with "oil of wintergreen." Summer.

RANGE: Northeastern North America and Appalachians.

HABITAT: Woods and bog margins, in acid, humus-rich soil.

CULTURE: Can be grown in an acid woodland garden.

Primrose Family (*Primulàceae*)

FEATURES: Flowers radially symmetrical; sepals 5 to 8, united into a cup at base; petals 5 to 8 or rarely obsolete, somewhat united basally; stamens attached to petals; carpel 1.

Swampcandles (*Lysimàchia terréstris*)   Pl. 66

FEATURES: Plant a foot or so high, with narrow opposite leaves. Flowers in a long terminal inflorescence, $\frac{1}{3}$ in. across; petals 5, yellow with purple streaks. Summer.

RANGE: Eastern half of North America, except far south.

HABITAT: Marshes and moist thickets, in moderately acid soil.

CULTURE: In a garden spreads rapidly by underground stems.

NOTES: Often attacked by a virus which produces distorted flowers and bulb-like outgrowths on the stalk. Linnaeus, receiving an infected plant, thought it to be a ground-dwelling MISTLETOE, so named it *Viscum terréstre*, one of the most curious cases of misinterpretation on record.

Fringed Loosestrife (*Steironèma ciliàtum*)   Pl. 66

FEATURES: Plant 2 or 3 ft. high, with broadish opposite leaves on conspicuously hairy stalks. Flowers stalked in leaf axils, about $\frac{3}{4}$ in. across; petals 5, yellow, somewhat toothed at tip. Summer.

RANGE: Northern North America.

HABITAT: Damp thickets, in various kinds of soil.

CULTURE: Will soon form large patches in a moist wild garden.

NOTES: Sometimes placed in the genus *Lysimàchia*. Several other species occur in our area; especially common is WHORLED LOOSESTRIFE (*L. quadrifòlia*), with leaves in whorls of 3 to 6, and flowers in their axils.

Maystar (*Trientàlis americàna*)   Pl. 68

FEATURES: Stem slender, creeping underground, sending up stalks a few inches high tipped with a whorl of 6 to 8 taper-pointed leaves. Flowers few, on long stalks from the leaf star, about $\frac{1}{2}$ in. across; petals about 7, white, pointed. Spring.

RANGE: Northeastern half of North America.

HABITAT: Damp woods and hummocks in swamps, in acid soil.

CULTURE: Can be grown in a wild garden which is kept acid and cool in summer.

Primrose Family, concluded

Midland Shootingstar (*Dodecàtheon meàdia*)   Pl. 66

FEATURES: Plant a rosette of somewhat spoon-shaped basal leaves, sending up a stalk a foot or so high, with a terminal umbel. Flowers showy; petals 5, pink to white, the free part turned back, stamens extending forward in a cone; capsule ½ in. long, firm. Late spring.

RANGE: Midland and adjacent Northeastern and Southern states.

HABITAT: Open woods and grasslands, on rocks, slopes, and flats, in neutral to moderately acid soil.

CULTURE: Readily grown in a wild or rock garden.

NOTES: Called by the early settlers of the Midlands PRAIRIE-POINTERS, being far more abundant then than it is now.

Jewel Shootingstar (*D. amethystìnum*)   Pl. 66

FEATURES: Plant similar to the preceding but only about half as large; petals deep purple-pink; capsule ⅓ in. long, frail. Early spring.

RANGE: In two isolated regions: Mississippi and tributary valleys, Wisconsin to Missouri; and Susquehanna and neighboring valleys, Pennsylvania.

HABITAT: Shaded cliffs, in neutral or slightly acid soil.

CULTURE: One of the loveliest native plants for the cool, shady rock garden; the foliage vanishes by midsummer.

NOTES: This species has been confused with the next preceding, but they differ so markedly in blooming time, petal, capsule, and leaf characters that they seem very distinct. The curious disjunct range is evidently the result of ice advances of the glacial period.

Salt-primrose (*Glaúx marítima*)   Pl. 68

FEATURES: Plant low, with branching stems bearing small, narrow, gray-green opposite fleshy leaves. Flowers in leaf axils, about ⅛ in. across; sepals 5, pink, united to a tube; petals obsolete. Summer.

RANGE: Widely scattered over the Northern Hemisphere; in our area chiefly northern, though extending to Maryland.

HABITAT: Sea beaches, salt-spring runs, and brackish marshes.

CULTURE: May grow in a moist, limy swamp garden.

Gentian Family (*Gentianàceae*)

FEATURES: Leaves opposite, entire. Sepals united to a tube; petals 4, 5, or 10–12, variously united; stamens alternating with the petals; carpels 2, united.

Upland Pinkstar (*Sabàtia angulàris*)   Pl. 67

FEATURES: Plant biennial, 1 to 2 ft. high, usually branched, the stem 4-angled. Flowers starry; sepals 5, small; petals 5, pink with yellow basal spot; carpels united up to middle of style. Leaves sessile, up to 1 in. long; first year's growth a rosette of roundish leaves. Summer.

RANGE: Southern states and lower half of our area.

HABITAT: Thickets and meadows, in damp or summer-dry neutral to moderately acid soil.

CULTURE: First-year rosettes moved to a wild garden may produce flowering stalks the following season.

NOTES: Several other species of *Sabàtia* grow in our area, chiefly in brackish marshes toward the coast. They differ in details of foliage and flowers; one has 10 to 12 petals.

Yellow Midland Gentian (*Gentiàna flávida*)   Pl. 67

FEATURES: Plant perennial, 1 to 2 ft. high. Flowers bell-shaped; sepals 5, well united; petals 5, pale yellow, their free tips alternating with short white fringes. Leaves broad toward base, sessile, 3 to 4 in. long. Autumn.

RANGE: Midland and adjacent parts of Northeastern states.

HABITAT: Damp thickets and grasslands, in neutral to moderately acid soil.

CULTURE: Delicate and difficult to cultivate, especially in gardens where fungi are active.

Narrow-leaf Gentian (*G. lineàris*)   Pl. 67

FEATURES: Plant perennial, 10 to 20 in. high. Flowers narrowly funnel-shaped; sepals 5, narrow; petals 5, light blue with greenish tip, their short, rounded, free tips alternating with a pale few-toothed membrane. Summer.

RANGE: Southern Canada and cool parts of our area.

HABITAT: Bogs and stream banks in strongly acid, peaty soil.

CULTURE: Can be grown in a bog garden maintained in strongly acid condition and kept cool in summer.

Gentian Family, continued

Short-leaf Midland Gentian (*Gentiàna pubérula*) **Pl. 70**

FEATURES: Plant perennial, a foot or so high. Flowers few, funnel-shaped, 1½ in. long, in upper leaf axils; sepals narrow; petals violet-blue, their triangular free tips alternating with short pale fringes. Leaves oblong, up to 1 or 2 in. long. Autumn.

RANGE: Midland and adjacent Northeastern and Southern states.

HABITAT: Damp grassland in neutral or moderately acid soil.

CULTURE: Difficult to cultivate, since readily injured by fungi, insects, slugs, and garden pests generally.

Fringe-tip Closed Gentian (*G. andréwsii*)   **Pl. 70**

FEATURES: Plant perennial, 1 to 1½ ft. high. Flowers clustered in upper axils, club-shaped, 1½ in. long; sepals 5, somewhat unequal; petals 5, dark violet-blue, united throughout, alternating with pale fringes which extend beyond them, to which the common name refers. Leaves sessile, up to 3 in. long. Autumn; one of the latest native plants to bloom.

RANGE: Over our area, adjacent Southern states, and Canada.

HABITAT: Moist thickets, in neutral to moderately acid soil.

CULTURE: The easiest of the GENTIANS to grow, in a moist wild garden, though not immune to pest attack.

NOTES: A closely related species is frequent in our area also, SHORT-FRINGE CLOSED GENTIAN (*G. claúsa*), in which the free petal tips equal the alternating fringes in length.

Pine Gentian (*G. porphýrio*)   **Pl. 70**

FEATURES: Plant perennial, about 1 ft. high. Flowers funnel-shaped, at tips of the stem or branches; sepals 5, narrow; petals dark violet-blue, pale and green-dotted in the throat, united two thirds their length, the tips much exceeding the alternating short fringes. Leaves narrow, up to 2 in. long. Late summer and autumn.

RANGE: Atlantic lowlands, New Jersey to Florida.

HABITAT: Damp, grassy pinelands, in strongly acid soil.

CULTURE: Can be grown in a sandy wild garden well supplied at depth with acid water.

NOTES: One of the most beautiful of late-season flowers.

Gentian Family, continued

Fringed Gentian (*Gentiàna crinìta*)   Pl. 70

FEATURES: Plant biennial, 1 to 2 ft. high, branched upward. Flowers 2 in. long, on long stalks; sepals 4, unequal; petals 4, lavender-blue, united below to a bell-shaped tube, the rounded blades fringed. Leaves moderately broad. Autumn.

RANGE: Northern parts of our area and Southern uplands.

HABITAT: Cool, damp, grassy thickets, in neutral to moderately acid soil.

CULTURE: Difficult to grow. The seed must be kept moist, injury to roots avoided when transplanting, and the garden kept free of slugs and fungi; then it may bloom the second season.

NOTES: One of the most famous of American wild flowers.

Stiff Gentian (*G. quinquefòlia*)   Pl. 67

FEATURES: Plant annual, 6 in. to 2 ft. high, often branched. Flowers in terminal and axillary clusters, ¾ in. long; sepals 5, small; petals 5, violet-blue, united to a funnel, with free triangular blades. Leaves broadened at base. Late summer and autumn.

RANGE: Northeastern and adjacent Midland and Southern states.

HABITAT: Grassy thickets on thinly wooded slopes, in neutral to moderately acid soil.

CULTURE: Seed sown in a wild garden may yield blooming plants the following year if pests are not too active.

Midland Monument-plant (*Frasèra caroliniénsis*)   Pl. 69

FEATURES: Plant triennial, 3 to 5 ft. high. Flowers in a large compound inflorescence, about 1 in. across; sepals 4, narrow; petals 4, greenish white with purple dots and a fringed basal gland. Leaves numerous, lily-like, mostly whorled in fours, those of the first- and second-year rosettes broadened toward tip. Summer.

RANGE: Midland and adjacent Northeastern states.

HABITAT: Thickets and open woods in dry neutral to moderately acid soil.

CULTURE: Well-developed rosettes transplanted to a wild garden may yield flowering stalks the following year, if pests are not too active.

Gentian Family, concluded

Penny-leaf (*Obolària virgínica*)   Pl. 69

FEATURES: Plant perennial, a few inches high, bearing grayish scales in place of leaves, obtaining much of its nourishment from decaying humus. Flowers small, clustered toward stalk tip in axils of roundish bronzy-green bracts, to which the name refers; sepals 2, spoon-shaped; petals 4, white, shaded lilac, united about half their length. Spring.

RANGE: Southern parts of our area and adjacent Southern states.

HABITAT: Woods, in humus-rich, moderately acid soil.

CULTURE: Almost impossible to transplant successfully, being partially saprophytic.

Bogbean Family (*Menyanthàceae*)

FEATURES: Aquatic or bog plants. Flowers starry; sepals and petals 5, united at base; stamens 5, adjoining petals; carpels 2, united, maturing to a firm egg-shaped capsule.

Bogbean (*Menyánthes trifoliàta*)   Pl. 69

FEATURES: Plant low, its thick, scaly stem creeping in wet peat. Flowers ⅜ in. across, in a cylindric inflorescence at the tip of a stalk 6 in. high; sepals small; petals white, with glistening hairs on their upper surface. Leaves basal, their stalks several inches long, the blade divided into 3 elliptic leaflets somewhat resembling those of beans, as the name indicates. Summer.

RANGE: Northern North America, down into cooler parts of our area; close relatives occur in Europe and Asia.

HABITAT: Peat bogs and stream margins, in acid to neutral soil.

CULTURE: Can be grown in a cool bog garden.

Northern Floating-heart (*Nymphoìdes lacunòsum*) Pl. 69

FEATURES: Plant aquatic, rooted in mud, sending up long slender stalks to the water surface. Flowers small, in a dense cluster adjacent to a heart-shaped floating leaf and a group of tubers; sepals very small; petals white. Summer.

RANGE: Eastern half of the United States and adjacent Canada.

HABITAT: Ponds and sluggish streams.

CULTURE: Desirable for a water garden.

Dogbane Family (*Apocynàceae*)

FEATURES: Plants with milky juice. Flowers small but numerous, funnel-shaped. Sepals and petals 5, united below; stamens alternating with petals; carpels 2, maturing to long tubular fruits; seeds often bearing long hairs.

Rosy Dogbane (*Apócynum androsaemifòlium*)   Pl. 71
FEATURES: Plant 2 or 3 ft. high, with opposite elliptic leaves. Flowers about ⅓ in. across, fragrant, in a compound inflorescence; sepals short; petals pink. Summer.
RANGE: Northern North America and cooler parts of our area.
HABITAT: Open woods and thickets in moderately acid soil.
CULTURE: Will spread rapidly in a garden by underground stems.

Milkweed Family (*Asclepiadàceae*)

FEATURES: Plants with milky juice. Flowers small but numerous, in umbel inflorescences; sepals 5, barely united; petals 5, united at base and bearing upstanding appendages; stamens 5, united at base; carpels 2, maturing to erect spindle-shaped fruits; seeds bearing tufts of hair.

Four-leaf Milkweed (*Asclèpias quadrifòlia*)   Pl. 71
FEATURES: Plant a foot or so high, with small opposite leaves toward stalk base, a whorl of 4 at middle, and another opposite pair toward stalk tip. Flowers pale pink; fruits slender, about 4 in. long. Late spring.
RANGE: Over our area and cooler parts of Southern states.
HABITAT: Open woods and thickets in moderately acid soil.
CULTURE: Difficult to cultivate successfully, the fleshy roots attracting destructive pests.

Purple Milkweed (*A. purpuráscens*)   Pl. 71
FEATURES: Plant coarse, 2 to 3 ft. high, with large thick opposite leaves. Flowers red-purple; fruits thick, about 4 in. long, fine-hairy. Early summer.
RANGE: Over much of our area except far eastward.
HABITAT: Thickets, in more or less acid soil.
CULTURE: Readily cultivated in a wild garden.

Milkweed Family, concluded

Butterflyweed (*Asclèpias tuberòsa*) **Pl. 71**

FEATURES: Plant a foot or so high, coarse-hairy, unusual in having chiefly watery juice. Flowers bright orange-yellow, varying from pale to deep; fruits about 4 in. long. Leaves oblong, alternate. Summer.

RANGE: Eastern half of the United States and adjacent Canada.

HABITAT: Sandy or rocky slopes, in various types of soil.

CULTURE: Highly desirable for the rock or sand garden.

NOTES: This species is also known as PLEURISY-ROOT. Many additional MILKWEEDS occur in our area; commonest is the COTTON MILKWEED (*A. syrìaca*), a coarse plant spreading rapidly by underground stems.

Morning-glory Family (*Convolvulàceae*)

FEATURES: Plants with mostly creeping or twining stalks, and somewhat milky sap. Flowers rather large; sepals 5, united at base; petals 5, wholly united to a funnel-shaped corolla; stamens 5; carpels well united, maturing to a capsule.

Big-root Morning-glory (*Ipomoèa panduràta*) **Pl. 72**

FEATURES: Stalk several feet long, twining over bushes. Flowers 2 or 3 in. long, on short stalks in leaf axils; sepals somewhat leafy; corolla white with purple throat; carpels 2, united, with a single knob-shaped stigma. Leaves heart-shaped; underground system a huge "sweet-potato." Summer.

RANGE: Eastern half of the United States, except far northeast.

HABITAT: Thickets on dry, moderately acid soil.

CULTURE: Can be grown from a small piece of the root.

Hedge Bindweed (*Convólvulus sèpium*) **Pl. 72**

FEATURES: Stalk elongate, twining. Flowers 2 in. long, on long stalks in leaf axils; calyx covered by a pair of heart-shaped bracts; corolla white to pink; stigmas 2. Leaves between heart- and spearhead-shaped; underground system slender running stems. Summer.

RANGE: Northern North America and Eurasia.

HABITAT: Thickets, in various kinds of soil.

CULTURE: Spreads too rapidly for the small garden.

Morning-glory Family, concluded

Upright Bindweed (*Convólvulus spithamaèus*) **Pl. 72**

FEATURES: Stalk a few inches high, twining only at tip. Flowers
1½ in. long, in axils of lower leaves; corolla white; calyx
covered by a pair of elliptic bracts; stigmas 2, rod-shaped.
Leaves oval; underground system a mass of branched creeping stems, a sort of underground vine. Summer.

RANGE: Eastern half of North America.

HABITAT: Sterile sandy, gravelly, or rocky slopes, in soil of
varying degrees of acidity.

CULTURE: Best kept out of the rock garden.

NOTES: Several other kinds of MORNING-GLORIES grow in our
area, some of them escaped from gardens. The flowers mostly
open in the evening and close during the following day.

Phlox Family (*Polemoniàceae*)

FEATURES: Small plants with showy flowers. Sepals 5, about
half united; petals 5, united below, their blades spreading to
a starry limb; stamens 5, unequal in length; carpels 3, united
up to the slender stigmas; fruit a capsule.

Spring Polemonium (*Polemònium réptans*) **Pl. 75**

FEATURES: Plant about 1 ft. high. Flowers light violet, open
bell-shaped, ½ in. across. Leaves alternate, pinnate with
elliptic leaflets. Spring.

RANGE: Over our area except far northeast.

HABITAT: Open woods, thickets, and margins of meadows, in
neutral to moderately acid soil.

CULTURE: Readily grown and highly desirable in the wild
garden.

NOTES: Also called GREEK-VALERIAN and JACOBS-LADDER.

Woodland Phlox (*Phlóx divaricàta*) **Pl. 74**

FEATURES: Plant 1 to 2 ft. high. Flowers with smooth, narrow
tube and flat limb, lilac to lavender; petal blades rounded
(Midland) or notched (Northeastern states). Leaves opposite, the lower elliptic and evergreen. Spring.

RANGE: Over our area and adjacent regions; rare eastward.

HABITAT: Open woods and shaded slopes, in rich neutral soil.

CULTURE: Thrives in the wild garden and border alike.

Phlox Family, continued

Downy Phlox (*Phlóx pilòsa*)   **Pl. 74**

FEATURES: Plant about 1 ft. high, soft-hairy. Calyx covered with viscid hairs (Northeast and east Midland) or with smooth shining hairs (west Midland states); petals 5, united below to a hairy narrow tube, their blades purple, pink, or white, rounded, spreading to a flat limb ¾ in. across. Leaves narrow, opposite. Late spring.

RANGE: Over our area and adjacent regions, except northeast.

HABITAT: Open thickets and grasslands, in moderately acid soil.

CULTURE: Difficult to cultivate, being susceptible to attack by garden pests.

Meadow Phlox (*P. maculàta*)   **Pl. 74**

FEATURES: Plant 2 to 3 ft. high. Flowers in a cylindric inflorescence, about ½ in. across; petals purple to white, their blades rounded; style elongate. Leaves opposite, broad toward base; stalk often purple-mottled. Summer.

RANGE: Over much of our area except far northeastward.

HABITAT: Wet meadows and thickets along streams, in moderately acid soil.

CULTURE: Readily grown in a moist wild garden.

NOTES: A northern subspecies with well-spaced leaf pairs begins to bloom in early summer, a southern one with narrower and closer leaves in late summer. The well-known SUMMER PHLOX (*P. paniculàta*) is native along streams in the middle parts of our area and the Appalachians. It differs in having larger, often subopposite leaves with the veins conspicuous.

Moss Phlox (*P. subulàta*)   **Pl. 74**

FEATURES: Plant low, forming mossy tufts. Flowers about ½ in. across; petals purple to white, their blades often notched at tip. Leaves needle-like, mostly evergreen. Early spring.

RANGE: Appalachian uplands and adjacent parts of our area, up to Michigan and Ontario.

HABITAT: Rocky, gravelly, or sandy slopes, in dry, neutral to moderately acid soil.

CULTURE: Various color forms are widely grown in rock gardens.

NOTES: Sometimes rather inaptly termed MOUNTAIN-PINK.

Phlox Family, concluded

Midland Phlox (*Phlóx bífida*)   **Pl. 72**

FEATURES: Plant forming broad mounds. Flowers about ¾ in. across; petals white to lavender, deeply notched at tip, forming a 10-rayed star. Leaves narrow. Spring.

RANGE: Midland states, except far northward.

HABITAT: Sand dunes, gravel banks, and rocky slopes, in neutral to moderately acid soil.

CULTURE: Can be grown in a well-drained rock garden.

NOTES: Several other species of *Phlóx* are native in the Appalachians and adjacent regions.

Waterleaf Family (*Hydrophyllàceae*)

FEATURES: Delicate plants with alternate, often lobed leaves. Inflorescence somewhat spiraled. Sepals 5, barely united; petals 5, united below to a tube; stamens 5, equal, alternate with the petals; carpels 2, well united; fruit a capsule.

Lavender Waterleaf (*Hydrophýllum appendiculàtum*)
    Pl. 75

FEATURES: Plant biennial, 1 to 2 ft. high, hairy. Flowers funnel-shaped, ½ in. long; sepals alternating with spurred appendages to which the species name refers; petals lavender-blue; stamens short. Leaves pinnately divided and lobed. Spring.

RANGE: Midland and adjacent Northeastern states.

HABITAT: Open woods on slopes or flats, in neutral soil.

CULTURE: Seeds sown in a shady wild garden will yield rosettes the first year and blooming plants the second.

Virginia Waterleaf (*H. virginiànum*)   **Pl. 73**

FEATURES: Plant perennial, 1 to 2 ft. high, sparsely hairy. Flowers ⅓ in. long; sepals narrow, spreading; petals white to lavender or violet; stamens elongate, their filaments hairy. Leaves pinnately divided into cut-toothed leaflets, mottled as though water-stained, to which the name refers. Late spring.

RANGE: Over our area and adjacent regions.

HABITAT: Open woods in neutral or moderately acid soil.

CULTURE: Readily cultivated in a woodland garden.

Waterleaf Family, concluded

Miami-mist (*Phacèlia púrshii*) **Pl. 75**

FEATURES: Plant annual, 8 to 15 in. high, finely hairy. Flowers opening nearly flat, ⅓ in. across; sepals small; petals lavender-blue grading to white at base, their tip delicately fringed. Leaves around 2 in. long, deeply lobed but the lobes little cut. Spring.

RANGE: Midland states and adjacent regions.

HABITAT: Open woods and thickets, also often invading fence rows and old fields, in mostly neutral soil.

CULTURE: Can be grown from seed in a wild garden.

NOTES: An attractive spring flower; the name refers to the effect it produces in the Miami Valley, Ohio.

Fern-leaf Phacelia (*P. bipinnatífida*) **Pl. 75**

FEATURES: Plant biennial, 1 to 2 ft. high, coarse-hairy. Inflorescence only slightly spiral. Flowers open funnel-shaped, ½ in. across; petals lavender, rounded at tip, bearing a fringed appendage toward base. Leaves pinnately divided into toothed lobes. Early summer.

RANGE: Lower parts of Midland and adjacent Southern states.

HABITAT: Open woods and thickets, in rich neutral soil.

CULTURE: Best grown from transplanted first-year rosettes.

NOTES: Several other PHACELIAS occur locally in our area.

Borage Family (*Boraginàceae*)

FEATURES: Plants with mostly spiraled inflorescences. Sepals 5, united at base; petals 5, united below to a tube, their blades spreading widely; stamens 5, short, alternating with the petals; carpels 2, each deeply divided, maturing to a group of 4 firm 1-seeded fruits.

Woodland Hounds-tongue (*Cynoglóssum virginiànum*)
Pl. 73

FEATURES: Plant 2 ft. high, coarse-hairy. Flowers about ⅖ in. across, lavender; fruits ⅜ in. long, bristly. Leaves mostly basal, the name referring to their shape. Spring.

RANGE: Lower parts of our area and adjacent Southern states.

HABITAT: Open woods in neutral or moderately acid soil.

CULTURE: Suitable for a woodland garden.

Borage Family, concluded

Virginia Bluebell (*Merténsia virgínica*)   **Pl. 78**

FEATURES: Plant a foot or so high, smooth, gray-green. Flowers trumpet-shaped, 1 in. long; buds pink and open corolla lavender-blue; fruits roughish. Leaves large, oval or widened above middle. Early spring.

RANGE: Over our area and adjacent regions.

HABITAT: Woods on flats along streams or on rocky slopes, in rich, mostly neutral soil.

CULTURE: Readily grown in a wild garden or border.

NOTES: One of the most beautiful of our spring flowers. The foliage dies away as the seeds mature, a month or so after blooming.

Golden Gromwell (*Lithospérmum canéscens*)   **Pl. 78**

FEATURES: Plant 8 to 15 in. high, hairy. Flowers ½ in. long; sepals short; petals golden yellow, their blades roundish; fruits white. Leaves narrow. Main root elongate, yellow. Spring.

RANGE: Over our area and adjacent regions, except far northeast.

HABITAT: Rocky or gravelly slopes and margins of grasslands, in dry, neutral to somewhat acid soil.

CULTURE: Highly desirable for the rock garden.

NOTES: Several related species also occur in our area, differing in details of flower and leaf characters. The Indian name for these plants was PUCCOON; they used the roots as a source of yellow dye.

Bristly Marble-seed (*Onosmòdium hispidíssimum*)   **Pl. 73**

FEATURES: Plant 2 to 3 ft. high, bristly-hairy. Flowers small, numerous, in the axils of leafy bracts in a long spiraled inflorescence; corolla tubular, yellowish white; fruits of marble-like color and texture, to which the name refers. Leaves elliptic. Late spring to summer.

RANGE: Over our area except northeastward, and Southern states.

HABITAT: Thickets and grassy slopes, in moderately acid soil.

CULTURE: When grown in a rock garden the spiral inflorescences attract attention, although the flowers are inconspicuous.

NOTES: Other species occur here also, but require a specialist to distinguish.

Verbena Family (*Verbenàceae*)

FEATURES: Plants with opposite leaves and rather small but often showy flowers. Sepals 4 or 5, unequal, united to a tube; petals 4 or 5, united below, their blades spreading to a flat limb; stamens 4, one pair longer than the other; carpels 2 or 4, united but maturing to separate 1-seeded fruits.

Blue Vervain (*Verbèna hastàta*)   Pl. 78

FEATURES: Plant 4 to 5 ft. high. Inflorescence a compound group of spikes; flowers small; petals 5, violet-blue. Leaves rather large, coarsely toothed. Summer.

RANGE: United States and adjacent Canada, except far west.

HABITAT: Moist meadows and thickets along streams, in moderately acid soil.

CULTURE: Readily grown in a wild garden.

Midland Vervain (*V. canadénsis*)   Pl. 78

FEATURES: Plant much branched, about 1 ft. high. Flowers in short spikes, about ½ in. across; petals dull purple, notched at tip. Leaves broad, cut into 3 lobed and coarsely toothed divisions. Late spring and summer.

RANGE: Southern states and adjacent parts of our area.

HABITAT: Thickets and margins of grasslands, in dry, neutral to moderately acid soil.

CULTURE: Desirable for the rock garden, being hardy well north of its native range, and blooming over a long season.

NOTES: The species epithet *canadénsis* is a misnomer, Linnaeus having been misinformed as to the source of the specimen he named (under another genus) in 1767. Other species of *Verbèna,* mostly with rather inconspicuous flowers, grow in our area also.

Fog-fruit (*Líppia lanceolàta*)   Pl. 73

FEATURES: Plant sprawly. Flowers tiny, in knob-shaped groups on long stalks from leaf axils; petals 4, lavender; carpels 2. Leaves elliptic, coarsely toothed, above the tapering base. Late summer and autumn.

RANGE: Southern, Midland, and adjacent Northeastern states.

HABITAT: Moist thickets along streams, in often neutral soil.

CULTURE: Can be grown in a damp wild garden; spreads rapidly.

Mint Family (*Labiàtae*)

FEATURES: Plants with 4-angled stems and opposite leaves, often aromatic. Flowers bilateral; sepals 4 or 5, united; petals 4 or 5, united to form an upper and a lower lip; stamens 4, one pair longer than the other, or only 2; carpels 4, maturing to nearly separate 1-seeded fruits.

Blue-curls (*Trichostèma dichótomum*)   Pl. 76

FEATURES: Plant annual, covered with rank-scented sticky wax. Flowers in a lax compound inflorescence, about ⅓ in. long; sepals very unequal; petals violet-blue, united only at base; stamens violet, their filaments long and curled, to which the name refers. Leaves oblong. Autumn.

RANGE: Southern states and eastern parts of our area.

HABITAT: Open sandy or gravelly slopes, in somewhat acid soil.

CULTURE: Readily grown from seed.

Synandra (*Synándra hispídula*)   Pl. 76

FEATURES: Plant a hairy biennial 1 to 2 ft. high, with large white flowers in axils of leafy bracts in a terminal spike. Petals 4, the upper one concave, the 3 lower well united to form a broad, flat lower lip; stamens 4. Leaves long-stalked, heart-shaped with roundish teeth. Late spring.

RANGE: Southern parts of our area, west of the Blue Ridge.

HABITAT: Damp wooded slopes, in mostly neutral soil.

CULTURE: Desirable for the wild garden.

Frost-mint (*Cunìla origanoìdes*)   Pl. 77

FEATURES: Plant sprawly, its stems somewhat woody. Flowers lavender, small but numerous, in clusters at branch tips; sepals 5, equal, well united; petals 5, the upper 2 forming a short, shallowly notched, erect lip, the lower 3 partly united to a flat spreading lip; stamens 2, exserted. Leaves about 1 in. long, sessile. Autumn.

RANGE: Southern states and adjacent parts of our area.

HABITAT: Shaded rocky or gravelly slopes, in acid soil.

CULTURE: Can be grown in an acid rock garden.

NOTES: The herbage is thyme-scented. The common name refers to conspicuous curly ribbons of ice which develop at the bases of old stems on frosty mornings.

Mint Family, continued

American Mint (*Méntha canadénsis*)   Pl. 77

FEATURES: Plant about 1 ft. high, spreading into a clump by underground stems. Flowers tiny, in dense clusters in leaf axils; corolla tubular, pale lavender. Leaves elliptic, short-stalked, sharply toothed. Late summer and autumn.

RANGE: Northern North America and over our area.

HABITAT: Moist thickets and stream banks, in often neutral soil.

CULTURE: Spreads rapidly in the wild garden.

NOTES: The herbage has a pennyroyal-like odor. This is one of the few sorts of MINT native to North America, the familiar PEPPERMINT, SPEARMINT, etc., being introductions from Europe.

Horse-balm (*Collinsònia canadénsis*)   Pl. 77

FEATURES: Plant 2 to 4 ft. high, branched into a large open inflorescence. Flowers pale yellow, ¼ in. long; petals 5, the upper 4 united nearly to their pointed tips, the lower one with a relatively large fringed blade; normal stamens 2, elongate. Leaves large, coarsely toothed, yielding when crushed a rank citronella-like odor. Main root a thick woody mass. Autumn.

RANGE: Eastern half of the United States and adjacent Canada.

HABITAT: Damp woods in often neutral, humus-rich soil.

CULTURE: Readily grown in a woodland garden.

NOTES: Also known as KNOB-ROOT or STONE-ROOT.

Bristly Woundwort (*Stàchys áspera*)   Pl. 77

FEATURES: Plant coarse-hairy, 2 to 3 ft. high. Flowers ⅓ in. long, clustered in the axils of leafy bracts at several nodes; petals 5, light purple, 2 united to a concave hairy upper lip, and 3 partly united to a flat lower lip; stamens within the upper lip. Leaves rather large, coarse-toothed. Summer.

RANGE: Over our area except far northeast, also Southern states.

HABITAT: Moist thickets, in neutral or moderately acid soil.

CULTURE: Will form clumps in the wild garden.

NOTES: There are several related species here, differing in minor details of pubescence, leaves, and flowers, and requiring close study to distinguish. An alternative common name for members of the genus is HEDGE-NETTLE.

Mint Family, continued

Rosette Sage (*Sálvia lyràta*)   Pl. 76

FEATURES: Plant a hairy perennial, with a rosette of leaves and
a slender 1- to 2-ft. stalk. Flowers about 1 in. long, lavender,
clustered in axils of tiny bracts at a few distant nodes; petals
5, the upper 2 forming a small concave lip, the lower 3 a
broad flat one; stamens 2. Lower leaves large, coarsely lobed;
upper ones smaller, wavy-margined. Summer.

RANGE: Southeastern states and lower parts of our area.

HABITAT: Open woods and thickets in dry and moderately acid
sandy soil.

CULTURE: Desirable in the wild garden, although spreading
rather rapidly by seeds.

NOTES: Other species of SAGE occur in our area, those toward
the western side having especially showy blue flowers.

Scarlet Wild-bergamot (*Monárda dídyma*)   Pl. 79

FEATURES: Plant 2 to 3 ft. high, bearing a terminal flower
cluster above red-based bracts. Flowers about 1½ in. long;
petals 5, bright red, 2 united to a narrow upper lip and 3 to
a broad flat lower one; normal stamens 2, elongate. Leaves
broad, thin, coarse-toothed. Summer.

RANGE: Appalachians and adjacent parts of our area.

HABITAT: Moist woods in often moderately acid soil.

CULTURE: Well known in gardens, spreading by underground
stems into large clumps.

NOTES: The red tubular flowers attract hummingbirds.

Lavender Wild-bergamot (*M. fistulòsa*)   Pl. 79

FEATURES: Plant 2 to 3 ft. high, with flower clusters above
pale-based bracts at branch tips. Flowers 1 in. long; petals
5, lilac, 2 forming a narrow upper lip and 3 a broad lower
one. Leaves broad, coarse-toothed. Summer.

RANGE: Over much of our area and Southern states.

HABITAT: Thickets, margins of woods, and grasslands, in rather
dry, neutral to moderately acid soil.

CULTURE: Can be grown in a dry wild garden.

NOTES: Hybrids with the preceding have violet-purple flowers.
These plants are sometimes called OSWEGO-TEA, BEE-BALM,
etc.

Mint Family, continued

Spotted Wild-bergamot (*Monárda punctàta*)   Pl. 80

FEATURES: Plant 2 or 3 ft. high, branched upward, the upper leaves and bracts pink. Flowers 1 in. long; petals 5, yellow with purple spots, 2 united to an upper lip and 3 to a flat lower one. Leaves shallowly toothed. Summer–autumn.

RANGE: Over our area except northeast, and Southern states.

HABITAT: Open woods and thickets, also invading wastelands, in dry, sandy, rather acid soil.

CULTURE: Desirable for a sand garden.

NOTES: An alternative common name is HORSE-MINT. The herbage has a thyme-like scent, and the plant has been grown commercially as a source of drugs.

Slender Mountain-mint (*Pycnánthemum flexuòsum*) Pl. 76

FEATURES: Plant about 2 ft. high, bearing dense flower clusters at branch tips. Flowers tiny; sepals 5, well united; petals 5, white or lavender, forming 2 lips; stamens 2 long and 2 short. Leaves numerous, narrow, smooth. Summer.

RANGE: Over our area and Southern states.

HABITAT: Thickets and grasslands, in dry, moderately acid soil.

CULTURE: Can be grown in the wild garden.

NOTES: The herbage is pleasantly aromatic. A number of other species also occur here; they differ in details of flowers and foliage.

Obedient-plant (*Physostègia virginiàna*)   Pl. 79

FEATURES: Plant 1 to 3 ft. high. Flowers in an elongate spike, about 1 in. long; sepals 5, well united; petals 5, purple, 2 united to a domed upper lip and 3 to a flat lower one; stamens 4, under the upper lip. Leaves rather narrow, sharply toothed. Summer.

RANGE: Over our area except northeast, and Southern states.

HABITAT: Grassy thickets in neutral to moderately acid soil.

CULTURE: Several color forms, ranging from magenta to white, are grown in garden borders.

NOTES: The common name refers to the way in which the flowers will stay put when pushed into various positions. Some smaller-flowered species also occur in our area.

Mint Family, concluded

Showy Skullcap (*Scutellària serràta*)   Pl. 79

FEATURES: Plant 1 to 2 ft. high. Flowers in pairs toward branch tips, 1 in. long; sepals 2, the upper bearing a hump shaped like a "skullcap"; petals 5, violet-blue, 2 united to a domed upper lip, 2 forming flaps marginal to this, and one flat and extending forward; stamens 4. Late spring.

RANGE: Lower parts of our area and adjacent Southern states.

HABITAT: Open woods in neutral to moderately acid soil.

CULTURE: Desirable for cultivation in the woodland garden.

NOTES: There are many other species here.

Potato Family (*Solanàceae*)

FEATURES: Plants with alternate leaves and often showy flowers. Sepals 5, united; petals 5, united to a starry or funnel-shaped corolla; stamens 5; carpels united.

Horse-nettle (*Solànum carolinénsè*)   Pl. 80

FEATURES: Plant 1 to 2 ft. high, prickly. Flowers 1 in. across, starry, white or lilac; anthers forming a conspicuous yellow central cone; fruit a ¾-in. orange berry. Leaves coarsely lobed. Late spring and summer.

RANGE: Southern states and adjacent parts of our area.

HABITAT: Thickets, grasslands, and waste places.

CULTURE: Spreads too rapidly by underground stems.

Snapdragon Family (*Scrophulariàceae*)

FEATURES: Flowers bilateral. Sepals 5 or 4, united; petals 5 or 4, forming a mostly 2-lipped corolla; stamens 5, 4, or 2; carpels 2, well united.

Oldfield Toadflax (*Linària canadénsis*)   Pl. 82

FEATURES: Plant a 1- to 2-ft. annual. Flowers in a long slender group, ⅓ in. long, lavender, the lower lip bearing a whitish "palate" and a tiny spur at base. Leaves alternate, narrow, numerous. Late spring and summer.

RANGE: Scattered widely over the United States.

HABITAT: Sandy open woods and margins of grassland.

CULTURE: Can be grown in a sand or rock garden.

Snapdragon Family, continued

White Turtle-head (*Chelònè glàbra*)   **Pl. 81**

FEATURES: Plant 2 to 3 ft. high, with a dense flower spike. Flowers 1 in. long, white with dull purplish tip, resembling a turtle's head; lower lip with a hairy "palate"; 4 stamens normal, 1 short and sterile. Leaves opposite, sharply toothed. Autumn.

RANGE: Eastern half of North America.

HABITAT: Swamps and stream banks, in neutral to moderately acid soil.

CULTURE: Desirable for the moist wild garden.

Pink Turtle-head (*C. oblìqua*)   **Pl. 82**

FEATURES: Plant 1½ to 2 ft. high, the flower spike dense. Flowers 1 in. long, deep pink, the palate on the lower lip bearing yellow hairs; 4 stamens normal, 1 short and sterile. Leaves opposite, broad, coarsely toothed. Late summer.

RANGE: Lower parts of our area and adjacent Southern states.

HABITAT: Moist woods and thickets, in fairly acid soil.

CULTURE: Readily grown in the wild garden; some forms spread into colonies by underground stems.

NOTES: The curiously shaped flowers are adapted to pollination by bumblebees, the weight of which depresses the lower lip.

Eastern Penstemon (*Penstèmon hirsùtus*)   **Pl. 80**

FEATURES: Plant 1 to 2 ft. high, the flowers in a somewhat compound group. Flowers 1 in. long, tubular-funnel form, flattened toward tip so that the palate on the lower lip partly closes the orifice, purple or violet with paler tip; 4 stamens normal and 1 sterile but conspicuously hairy. Leaves opposite, shallowly toothed. Spring.

RANGE: Eastern half of the United States and adjacent Canada.

HABITAT: Rocky, gravelly, or sandy slopes, in neutral to moderately acid soil.

CULTURE: Selected bright-colored forms are desirable for the rock garden; it spreads rapidly by seeds.

NOTES: Some authors spell the genus epithet *Pentstèmon*, but this is now regarded as obsolete. A frequently used common name, BEARD-TONGUE, refers to the beard-like mass of hairs toward the tip of the sterile stamen.

Snapdragon Family, continued

Smooth White Penstemon (*Penstèmon digitàlis*)   Pl. 80

FEATURES: Plant 2 to 3 ft. high with numerous flowers in a compound group. Flowers 1¼ in. long, white with fine purple lines, tubular below, abruptly expanding to a rather open throat, the petal blades spreading to form 2 lips; hairy sterile stamen conspicuous. Leaves large, sharply toothed, the upper pairs clasping the stem. Summer.

RANGE: Midland states, and invading the Northeast as a weed.

HABITAT: Margins of woods and grasslands, in various soils.

CULTURE: Can be grown in a wild garden; spreads rapidly.

NOTES: Several other PENSTEMONS occur in our area; they differ widely in stature and details of leaves and flowers. Some are among our most beautiful wild flowers.

Blue-eyed-Mary (*Collínsia vérna*)   Pl. 82

FEATURES: Plant a delicate winter annual 6 to 18 in. high. Flowers ½ in. long, on slender stalks in upper leaf axils; 2 white petals united into an upper lip, and 3 lavender-blue ones into a lower lip; stamens 2 long and 2 short. Leaves opposite, few-toothed. Spring.

RANGE: Midland and adjacent Northeastern states and Canada.

HABITAT: Damp open woods, in often rich, neutral soil.

CULTURE: The seeds should be collected in early summer and sown promptly in a woodland garden; they germinate in autumn, the young plants remain green over winter, and, if not meanwhile destroyed by garden pests, early come into bloom.

NOTES: Seeds in the trade represent a different, western species, of coarser habit and less attractive flowers.

Viscid Monkeyflower (*Mímulus moschàtus*)   Pl. 83

FEATURES: Plant low, tufted, the herbage viscid-hairy. Flowers ¾ in. long, yellow; corolla rather flat-faced, moderately 2-lipped. Leaves opposite, shallowly toothed. Summer.

RANGE: Northwestern North America and locally in the northern parts of our area, perhaps mostly as an escape from gardens.

HABITAT: Moist margins of ponds and streams, in often somewhat acid soil.

CULTURE: Suitable for the margins of a water garden.

Snapdragon Family, continued

Wing-stem Monkeyflower (*Mimulus alàtus*)· Pl. 82

FEATURES: Plant 2 to 3 ft. high, with short-stalked flowers in upper leaf axils. Flowers 1 in. long, lavender; 2 petals forming an upper and 3 a lower lip, the combination remotely suggesting a monkey's face, to which the common name refers; stamens 2 long and 2 short. Leaves opposite, short-stalked, coarsely toothed. Summer.

RANGE: Southern states and lower parts of our area.

HABITAT: Wet thickets, in neutral or slightly acid soil.

CULTURE: Readily grown in a swamp garden.

NOTES: SQUARE-STEM MONKEYFLOWER (*M. ríngens*), a similar plant with sessile leaves and longer-stalked flowers, is more wide-ranging.

Culvers-root (*Veronicástrum virgínicum*) Pl. 81

FEATURES: Plant 3 to 5 ft. high, tipped by a compound inflorescence of dense narrow-cylindric groups of tiny white flowers. Sepals 4, united to a tube; petals 4, well united, their triangular free tips nearly equal in size; stamens 2, extending beyond the corolla. Leaves whorled in groups of 4 to 8, sharp-toothed, up to 6 in. long and 1 in. wide, taper-pointed. Summer and early autumn.

RANGE: Eastern North America, except far north and south.

HABITAT: Moist thickets and margins of grassland, in moderately acid soil.

CULTURE: Desirable for the wild garden.

Brooklime Speedwell (*Verónica americàna*) Pl. 83

FEATURES: Plant with widely spreading succulent stems. Flowers small, in loose clusters in upper leaf axils; petals 4, bright blue, the upper one rather broad and the lower narrow, forming a flattish bilateral corolla; stamens 2, spreading. Leaves opposite, short-stalked, smooth. Summer.

RANGE: Widespread over North America.

HABITAT: Marshes and sluggish streams, rooted in mud.

CULTURE: Can be grown in a water garden.

NOTES: Many other species of SPEEDWELL occur in our area, some closely resembling the above, others less conspicuous plants of woodland or grassland.

Snapdragon Family, continued

Lace-leaf Oak-leech (*Aureolària pediculària*)   Pl. 83

FEATURES: Plant 2 to 3 ft. high, covered with sticky hairs. Flowers in sparse clusters in upper axils, about 1¼ in. long; corolla funnel-form, yellow with bronzy shadings; petals 5, their free tips rounded; stamens 2 long and 2 short. Leaves lobed and toothed in fern-like pattern. Late summer.

RANGE: Over our area, Southern states, and adjacent Canada.

HABITAT: Sandy thickets and acid open woods, near oak trees. The common name refers to the fact that the plant sends down stalks which suck sap from the oak roots.

CULTURE: Will sometimes grow from seed planted near oaks.

NOTES: Also known as FERN-LEAF GOLDEN-FOXGLOVE.

Smooth Oak-leech (*A. flàva*)   Pl. 83

FEATURES: Plant 3 to 4 ft. high, the herbage smooth. Flowers in axils of upper leaves and bracts, about 1½ in. long, funnel-form, yellow; petals 5, their free tips rounded, spreading to form a flattish, barely 2-lipped limb; stamens 2 long and 2 short. Leaves opposite, the lower cut-lobed, the upper merely toothed. Summer.

RANGE: Over our area and Southern states.

HABITAT: Open oak woods, sucking sap from the tree roots.

CULTURE: As with the preceding.

NOTES: VIRGINIA OAK-LEECH (*A. virgínica*) has hairy herbage. A few other species occur in our area; they differ in details, and in part parasitize trees other than oaks.

Woodland Gerardia (*Gerárdia tenuifòlia*)   Pl. 86

FEATURES: Plant a foot or so high, annual, smooth. Flowers long-stalked in axils of bracts, about ⅔ in. long, lilac; blades of 2 petals forming a short erect upper lip and of 3 a spreading lower one. Leaves narrow, opposite. Autumn.

RANGE: Over our area and adjacent regions.

HABITAT: Thickets and woods, in usually rather acid soil; it absorbs sap from the roots of trees or shrubs.

CULTURE: Seeds sown in a woodland garden may yield blooming plants some years later.

NOTES: This and related species are sometimes called WILD-FOXGLOVES. The others differ in details of flowers and leaves.

Snapdragon Family, concluded

Eastern Paintbrush (*Castillèja coccínea*)   **Pl. 86**

FEATURES: Plant biennial, 8 to 15 in. high, its herbage viscid-hairy. Flowers spiked in axils of fan-like bracts which have bright red tips as though dipped in paint; corolla tubular with a long narrow upper lip, dull yellow, up to 1 in. long, obscured by the bracts. Leaves alternate, the upper sparsely toothed. Spring.

RANGE: Over our area and adjacent regions.

HABITAT: Grassy thickets, in often slightly acid soil; it sucks sap from grass roots.

CULTURE: May grow from seed sown while fresh in a grassy plot.

Early Wood-betony (*Pediculàris canadénsis*)   **Pl. 81**

FEATURES: Plant a foot or so high, the herbage hairy. Flowers in a short terminal spike, ¾ in. long; petals yellow to bronzy, 2 united into a long arching upper lip, and 3 to a shorter spreading lower one; stamens 2 short and 2 long, within the upper lip. Leaves alternate, pinnately cut into toothed lobes, thus somewhat fern-like. Spring.

RANGE: Eastern half of North America, except far north.

HABITAT: Open woods and damp grasslands, in moderately acid soil; sometimes absorbing sap from nearby roots.

CULTURE: Desirable for the woodland garden.

NOTES: Although a charming wild flower, this is assigned in some books the unlovely name of FERN-LEAF LOUSEWORT.

Cow-wheat (*Melampỳrum lineàre*)   **Pl. 81**

FEATURES: Plant annual, 6 to 12 in. high, branched upward. Flowers in axils of basally-toothed bracts, ½ in. long, tubular, bilateral; 2 petals forming an arched, white upper lip, and 3 a short, flat, yellow lower one; stamens 2 long and 2 short, under the upper lip. Leaves opposite, small, entire. Summer.

RANGE: Eastern half of North America.

HABITAT: Open woods in rather acid soils; absorbing more or less sap from shrub or tree roots.

CULTURE: Seeds planted in an acid woodland garden may grow.

NOTES: The common name is difficult to explain; the seeds are large and white, but not much like wheat.

Lopseed Family (*Phrymàceae*)

FEATURES: Plant about 2 ft. high, with broad, coarse-toothed
opposite leaves and a compound inflorescence of slender
spikes of small, paired, lavender, 2-lipped bilateral flowers.
Carpel solitary, forming a 1-seeded fruit enclosed in the
tubular calyx, which lops down against the stalk and so
suggests the name.

Lopseed (*Phrỳma leptostàchya*)   **Pl. 84**
FEATURES: As given for the family.
RANGE: Eastern half of North America; also eastern Asia.
HABITAT: Open woods in neutral to moderately acid soil.
CULTURE: Suitable for the woodland garden.

Bladderwort Family (*Lentibulariàceae*)

FEATURES: Plants aquatic or growing in wet soil, getting part
of their nourishment from entrapped insects or other animals.
Roots and leaves minute or obsolete; stem forking below and
bearing bladders which entrap the prey. Flowers bilateral,
2-lipped. Stamens 2; carpel solitary.

Lake Bladderwort (*Utriculària vulgàris*)   **Pl. 86**
FEATURES: Aquatic, forming large masses beneath the water,
and sending above the surface a stout stalk several inches
high, bearing spaced ¾-in. yellow flowers. Summer.
RANGE: Widespread over North America; represented by a
similar if not identical species in Europe.
HABITAT: Lakes and slowly moving waters generally.
CULTURE: Can be grown in a water garden.

Purple Bladderwort (*U. purpùrea*)   **Pl. 86**
FEATURES: Aquatic, sending above the water surface a 4- or
5-in. stalk bearing several ½-in. lavender-purple flowers.
Summer.
RANGE: Scattered over our area and the Southern states.
HABITAT: Ponds and sluggish streams.
CULTURE: Will sometimes grow in a garden pool.
NOTES: A number of other species of BLADDERWORT occur in our
area, differing in details of flower shape and plant form. Some
grow in water, others in moist, sterile, acid peat.

Broomrape Family (*Orobancháceae*)

FEATURES: Parasitic plants, lacking green tissue. Flowers resembling those of the 3 preceding families, but differing in details of fruits and seeds.

Ghost-pipe (*Orobánchè uniflòra*)   Pl. 84

FEATURES: Stem scaly, creeping in litter around a parasitized root, sending up stalks a few inches high, bearing solitary lavender 2-lipped flowers ½ in. long. Spring.

RANGE: Southern, Northeastern, and adjacent Midland states.

HABITAT: Open woods, absorbing nourishment from roots of nearby plants; soil neutral to moderately acid.

CULTURE: Difficult to get started in a garden.

Squaw-root (*Conópholis americàna*)   Pl. 84

FEATURES: Plant consisting of a mass of fleshy tissue, from which ascend multiple thick scaly stalks several inches high, bearing a spike of numerous small yellow flowers in axils of scaly bracts. Spring and early summer.

RANGE: Northeastern and adjacent Midland and Southern states.

HABITAT: Near the bases of oak or rarely other trees, from the roots of which nourishment is absorbed. Soil acid.

CULTURE: May grow from seed planted in an oak woods.

Unicorn-plant Family (*Martyniàceae*)

FEATURES: Mostly tropical plants related to the preceding family, but having normal foliage, and not parasitic.

Unicorn-plant (*Martýnia louisiàna*)   Pl. 87

FEATURES: Plant a coarse, sprawling annual, the herbage bearing sticky hairs. Flowers bronzy pink, long-stalked in sparse terminal clusters, 1½ in. across; petals 5, united below to a funnel-form tube, the blades spreading into a flat, somewhat bilateral limb; stamens 4, exserted; carpels 2, enlarging in fruit to a horn-shaped structure to which the name refers. Late summer.

RANGE: Midland states and adjacent regions, eastward as an escape from gardens.

HABITAT: Thickets and margins of grassland, in neutral soil.

CULTURE: Sometimes grown in the garden border.

Acanthus Family (*Acanthàceae*)

FEATURES: Mild-climate plants with opposite leaves. Flowers resembling those of several preceding families, but capsule having 2 cavities with seeds centrally attached.

Northern Wild-petunia (*Ruéllia strèpens*) Pl. 87

FEATURES: Plant about 2 ft. high. Flowers in the axils of upper leaves, lavender-blue, about 2 in. long; petals 5, united below to a slender tube, the blades spreading to an open funnel-form limb. Summer.
RANGE: Southern states and adjacent parts of our area.
HABITAT: Open woods and thickets, in often neutral soil.
CULTURE: Desirable for the wild garden.

Madder Family (*Rubiàceae*)

FEATURES: Small plants with opposite or whorled leaves. Flower parts mostly in fours, their bases united so that the ovary appears to support the others.

Bluets (*Houstònia caerùlea*) Pl. 85

FEATURES: Low plants with small opposite leaves and solitary flowers on long stalks in upper axils. Flowers 1/3 in. across, lavender to whitish with yellow eye; petals united below to a short tube, their blades spreading to a flat limb; fruit a smooth 2-lobed capsule. Early spring.
RANGE: Northeastern states and adjacent regions.
HABITAT: Open woods and grasslands, often invading old fields, in moderately to decidedly acid soil.
CULTURE: Readily cultivated in an acid wild garden.
NOTES: Also known as QUAKER-LADIES, ANGEL-EYES, etc.

Fringed Summer-bluets (*H. ciliolàta*) Pl. 85

FEATURES: Plant 4 to 8 in. high, tufted. Flowers in groups of 2 or 3 in axils of bracts at branchlet tips, lilac, 1/4 in. long; petals united two thirds their length to a funnel-form corolla. Fruit a round, barely lobed capsule. Summer.
RANGE: Midland states and adjacent regions.
HABITAT: Open rocky or gravelly slopes, in moderately acid soil.
CULTURE: Can be grown in the rock garden.
NOTES: Other species differing in minor details also grow here.

Madder Family, concluded

Snow Bedstraw (*Gàlium boreàlè*) Pl. 84

FEATURES: Plant 1 to 2 ft. high, with a compound inflorescence at top. Flowers tiny, white; carpels 2, partly separating and becoming prickly at maturity. Leaves smooth, in whorls of 4. Summer.

RANGE: Northern North America; also Eurasia.

HABITAT: Open woods on rocky slopes or along streams, in neutral to moderately acid soils.

CULTURE: Suitable for the wild garden.

NOTES: Many other species of BEDSTRAW occur in our area, differing in details of flowers and foliage. The common name refers to the use of these plants to stuff mattresses, etc.

Partridge-berry (*Mitchélla rèpens*) Pl. 85

FEATURES: Plant an evergreen creeper with small, round, shiny opposite leaves. Flowers partly united in pairs in upper axils, ⅓ in. long; petals white or pinkish, united below to a tube, the blades spreading to a hairy limb; fruit a red berry-like structure with 2 "eyes" and 2 large seeds. Spring.

RANGE: Over our area and adjacent Canada.

HABITAT: Woods, in rather acid, humus-rich soil.

CULTURE: Desirable for the woodland garden and as a ground cover under acid-soil shrubs such as AZALEAS.

Honeysuckle Family (*Caprifoliàceae*)

FEATURES: Plants mostly shrubs, except for a few members such as the following; like the preceding family in many respects although the petals often number 5 and may be bilateral.

Twinflower (*Linnaèa boreàlis*) Pl. 87

FEATURES: Plant a somewhat woody creeper with small round-ish leaves, sending up from branch tips stalks bearing a pair of nodding, pink, fragrant, bell-shaped flowers ⅓ in. long. Fruit containing a solitary seed. Summer.

RANGE: Northern North America, southward at high altitudes.

HABITAT: Cold woods and swamps, in strongly acid humus soil.

CULTURE: Difficult to grow beyond its native haunts, requiring especially cool, acid, and pest-free situations.

Honeysuckle Family, concluded

Orange Horse-gentian (*Triósteum aurantìacum*) **Pl. 85**

FEATURES: Plant 2 to 3 ft. high, with large opposite sessile leaves. Flowers in upper axils, about ⅔ in. long; sepals united below with the ovary, their free blades narrow but conspicuous; petals bronzy, united to a funnel-shaped tube; fruit a conspicuous oval, orange-red, berry-like structure containing about 3 stones. Early summer.

RANGE: Over our area and adjacent regions.

HABITAT: Thickets in neutral or moderately acid soil.

CULTURE: Readily grown in a wild garden.

Bellflower Family (*Campanulàceae*)

FEATURES: Delicate plants with milky juice; leaves alternate. Flowers radial, their outer parts in fives; carpels 3 or 2; fruit a capsule with as many cavities, and small centrally attached seeds.

Varied-leaf Bluebell (*Campánula rotundifòlia*) **Pl. 87**

FEATURES: Plant 6 to 18 in. high. Flowers violet-blue, bell-shaped, ¾ in. long, drooping on long stalks from axils of minute bracts. Stem leaves narrow but basal ones roundish, to which the species epithet refers. Summer.

RANGE: Northern North America and upper parts of our area; also in Eurasia.

HABITAT: Cliffs and rocky or sandy slopes, in neutral or moderately acid soil.

CULTURE: In the rock garden spreads rapidly by slender underground stems.

NOTES: Also known as SCOTCH BLUEBELL or HAIRBELL. Cultivated sorts of BELLFLOWER sometimes escape from gardens.

Star Bellflower (*C. americàna*) **Pl. 90**

FEATURES: Plant biennial, 2 to 5 ft. high. Flowers violet-blue, star-shaped, about 1 in. across, in axils of leafy bracts. Leaves fairly narrow, finely toothed. Summer.

RANGE: Eastern half of the United States and adjacent Canada.

HABITAT: Rocky woods, often in rich neutral soil.

CULTURE: Can be grown from seed in a shady rock garden.

Plate 65

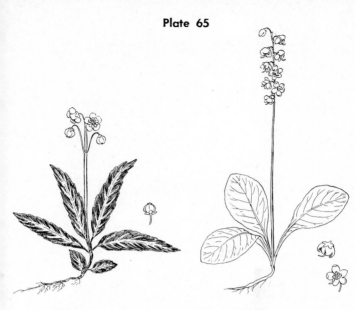

MOTTLED PIPSISSEWA

THIN-LEAF PYROLA

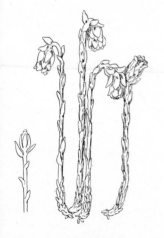

INDIAN-PIPE

PINE-SAP

Plate 66

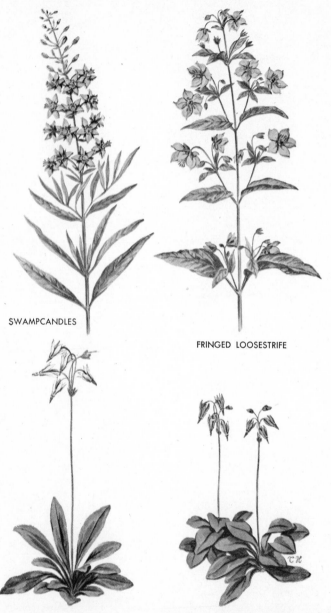

SWAMPCANDLES

FRINGED LOOSESTRIFE

MIDLAND SHOOTINGSTAR

JEWEL SHOOTINGSTAR

Plate 67

UPLAND PINKSTAR

YELLOW MIDLAND GENTIAN

NARROW-LEAF GENTIAN

STIFF GENTIAN

Plate 68

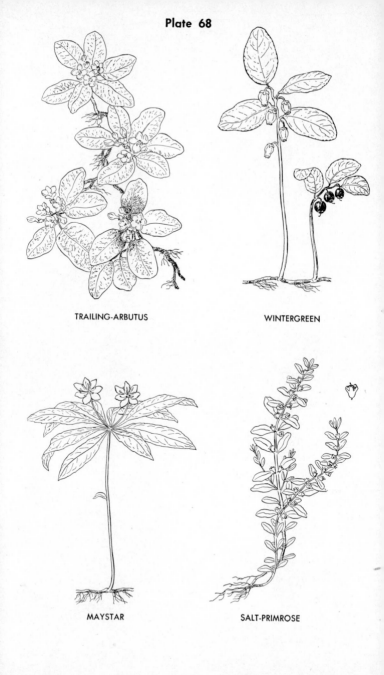

TRAILING-ARBUTUS

WINTERGREEN

MAYSTAR

SALT-PRIMROSE

Plate 69

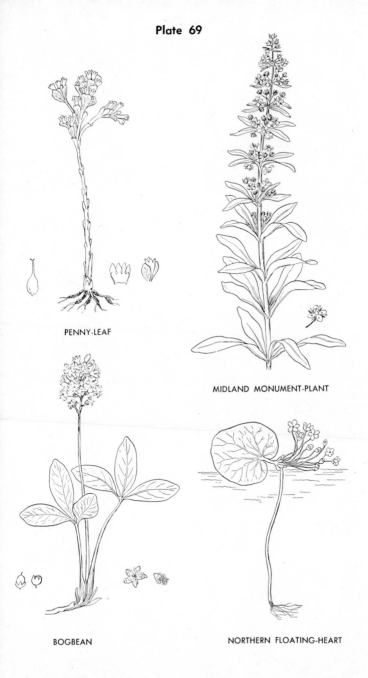

PENNY-LEAF

MIDLAND MONUMENT-PLANT

BOGBEAN

NORTHERN FLOATING-HEART

Plate 70

FRINGE-TIP CLOSED GENTIAN

SHORT-LEAF MIDLAND GENTIAN

FRINGED GENTIAN

PINE GENTIAN

Plate 71

ROSY DOGBANE

FOUR-LEAF MILKWEED

PURPLE MILKWEED

BUTTERFLYWEED

Plate 72

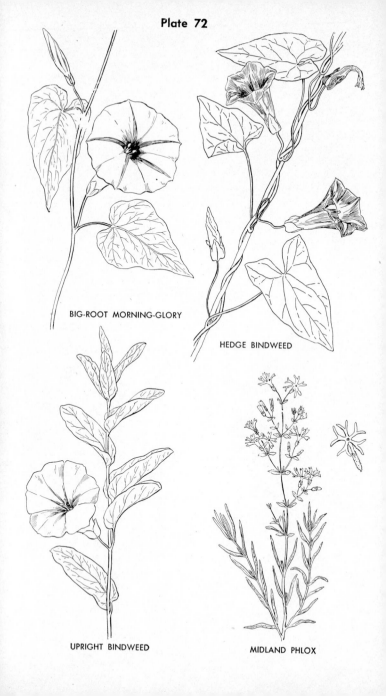

BIG-ROOT MORNING-GLORY

HEDGE BINDWEED

UPRIGHT BINDWEED

MIDLAND PHLOX

Plate 73

VIRGINIA WATERLEAF

WOODLAND HOUNDS-TONGUE

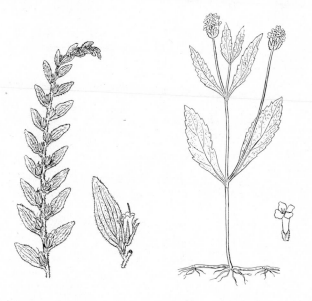

BRISTLY MARBLE-SEED

FOG-FRUIT

Plate 74

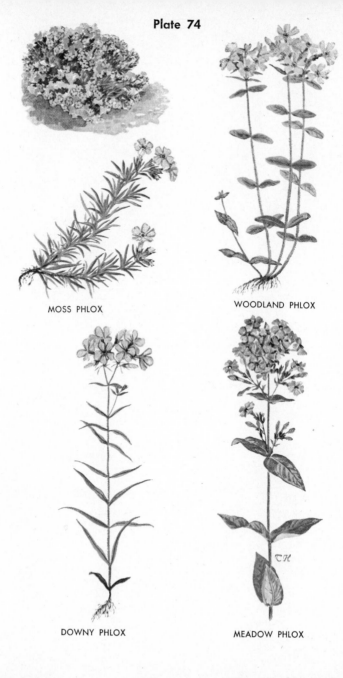

MOSS PHLOX

WOODLAND PHLOX

DOWNY PHLOX

MEADOW PHLOX

Plate 75

SPRING POLEMONIUM

LAVENDER WATERLEAF

MIAMI-MIST

FERN-LEAF PHACELIA

Plate 76

BLUE-CURLS

SYNANDRA

ROSETTE SAGE

SLENDER MOUNTAIN-MINT

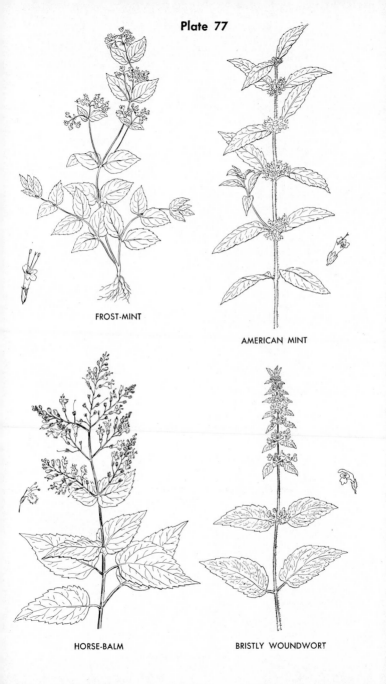

Plate 77

FROST-MINT

AMERICAN MINT

HORSE-BALM

BRISTLY WOUNDWORT

Plate 78

VIRGINIA BLUEBELL

GOLDEN GROMWELL

BLUE VERVAIN

MIDLAND VERVAIN

Plate 79

LAVENDER WILD-BERGAMOT

SCARLET WILD-BERGAMOT

SHOWY SKULLCAP

OBEDIENT-PLANT

Plate 80

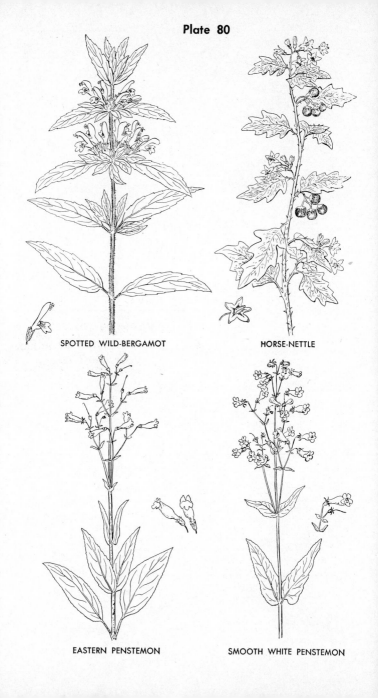

SPOTTED WILD-BERGAMOT

HORSE-NETTLE

EASTERN PENSTEMON

SMOOTH WHITE PENSTEMON

Plate 81

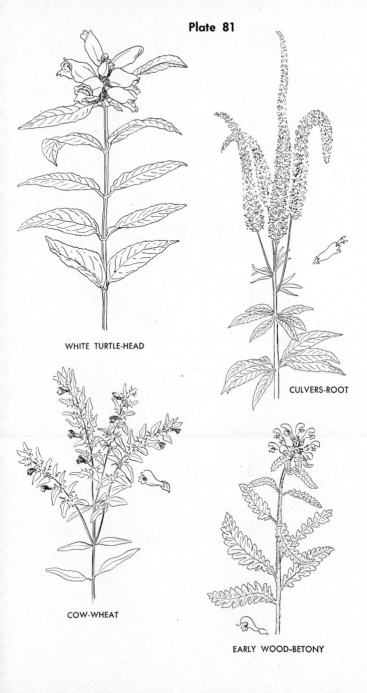

WHITE TURTLE-HEAD

CULVERS-ROOT

COW-WHEAT

EARLY WOOD-BETONY

Plate 82

OLDFIELD TOADFLAX

BLUE-EYED-MARY

PINK TURTLE-HEAD

WING-STEM MONKEYFLOWER

Plate 83

VISCID MONKEYFLOWER

BROOKLIME SPEEDWELL

LACE-LEAF OAK-LEECH

SMOOTH OAK-LEECH

Plate 84

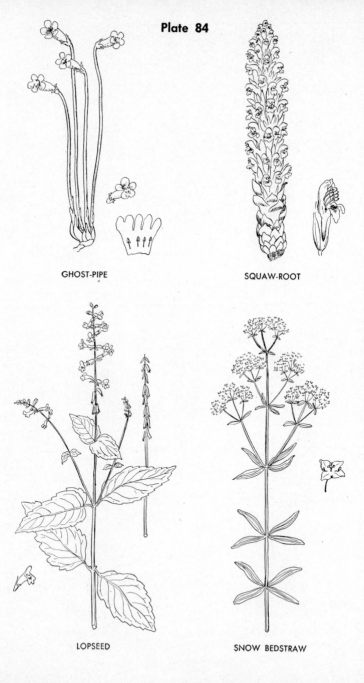

GHOST-PIPE

SQUAW-ROOT

LOPSEED

SNOW BEDSTRAW

Plate 85

PARTRIDGE-BERRY

BLUETS

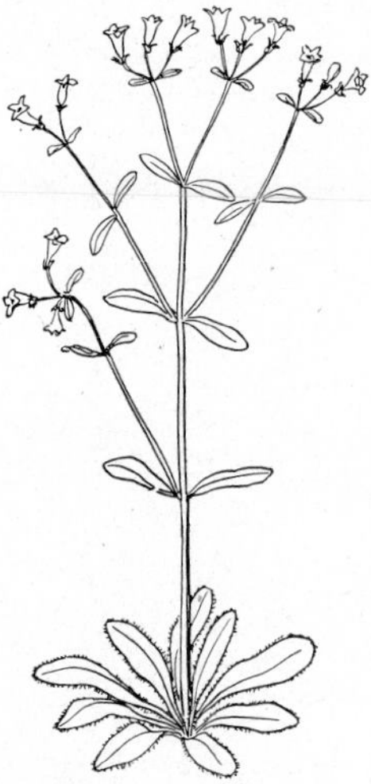

FRINGED SUMMER-BLUETS

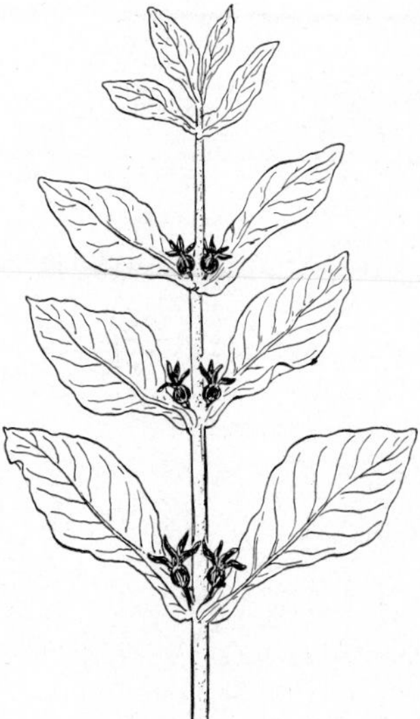

ORANGE HORSE-GENTIAN

Plate 86

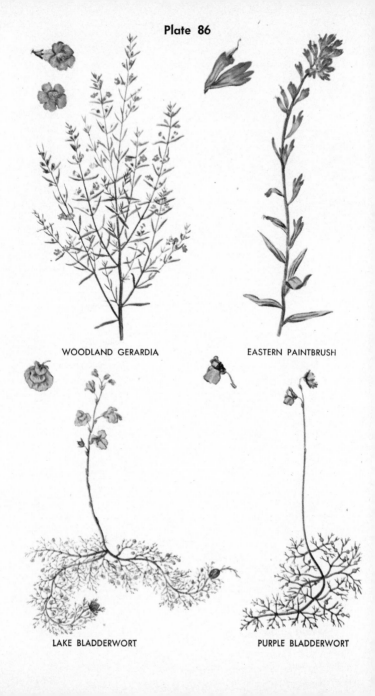

WOODLAND GERARDIA

EASTERN PAINTBRUSH

LAKE BLADDERWORT

PURPLE BLADDERWORT

Plate 89

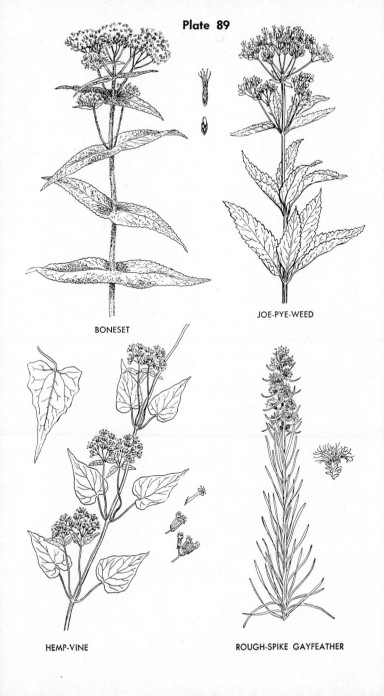

BONESET

JOE-PYE-WEED

HEMP-VINE

ROUGH-SPIKE GAYFEATHER

Plate 90

STAR BELLFLOWER

GREAT BLUE LOBELIA

CARDINAL LOBELIA

GOAT-DANDELION

Plate 91

VEIN-LEAF HAWKWEED

PRAIRIE GAYFEATHER

TALL IRONWEED

PLUME GOLDENROD

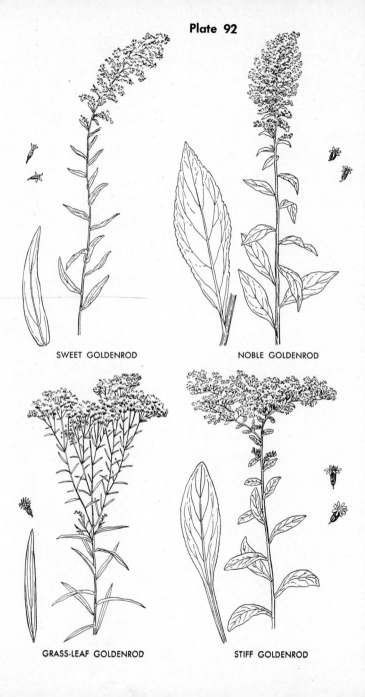

Plate 92

SWEET GOLDENROD

NOBLE GOLDENROD

GRASS-LEAF GOLDENROD

STIFF GOLDENROD

Plate 93

CREAM GOLDENROD

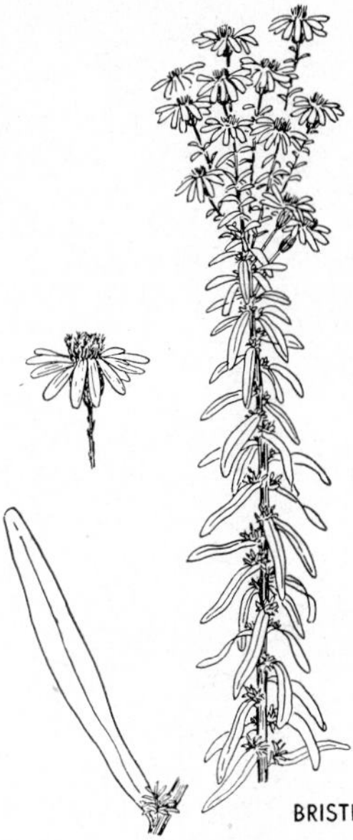

BRISTLY ASTER

WHITE WOOD ASTER

SUMMER-ASTER

Plate 94

NEW ENGLAND ASTER

BROAD-LEAF GOLDEN-ASTER

BLACK-EYED-SUSAN

PURPLE CONEFLOWER

Plate 95

THIN-LEAF SUNFLOWER

SMOOTH COREOPSIS

SWAMP SNEEZE-WEED

GOLDEN GROUNDSEL

Plate 96

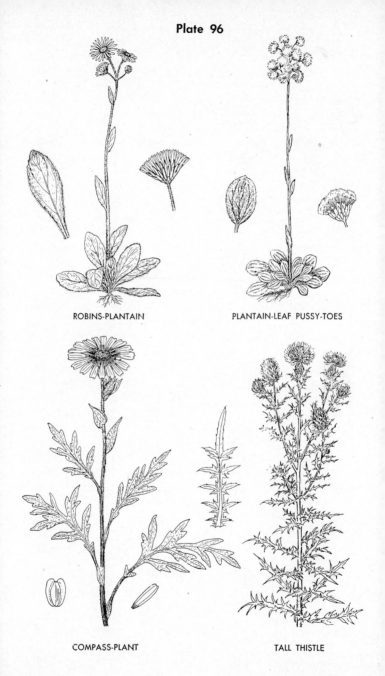

ROBINS-PLANTAIN

PLANTAIN-LEAF PUSSY-TOES

COMPASS-PLANT

TALL THISTLE

Bellflower Family, concluded

Mirror-weed (*Speculària perfoliàta*)   Pl. 88

FEATURES: Plant annual, 6 to 15 in. high. Flowers violet, star-shaped, ½ in. across, in axils of collar-like leafy bracts. Leaves round, clasping the stalk. Summer.

RANGE: Widespread over North America.

HABITAT: Open woods, in sterile soil, and invading wasteland.

CULTURE: Grows readily from seed and may become a weed.

NOTES: The names refer to the leaves of a European species having the shape of the mirrors of antiquity.

Lobelia Family (*Lobeliàceae*)

FEATURES: Delicate plants with milky juice and alternate leaves. Flowers strongly bilateral; sepals 5, united below with the ovary; petals 5, united into a tube below, their free blades forming 2 lips; stamens 5, in a cylinder around the style; carpels 2, well united; fruit a many-seeded capsule.

Cardinal Lobelia (*Lobèlia cardinàlis*)   Pl. 90

FEATURES: Plant 2 or 3 ft. high. Flowers bright red, 1½ in. long, in the axils of small bracts in a long narrow inflorescence. Leaves up to 5 in. long and 1½ in. wide, shallowly toothed, often bronzy. Late summer.

RANGE: Eastern half of the United States and adjacent Canada.

HABITAT: Moist thickets and stream banks, in usually moderately acid soil.

CULTURE: Can be grown in the moist wild garden, though tends to die after blooming; if the stalks are cut back before the seeds mature, will produce perennial, leafy, basal shoots.

Great Blue Lobelia (*L. siphilítica*)   Pl. 90

FEATURES: Plant 1 to 2 ft. high. Flowers blue, 1 in. long, in axils of leafy bracts in a dense terminal inflorescence. Leaves up to 5 in. long and 2 in. wide, obscurely toothed. Late summer.

RANGE: Over our area and adjacent regions.

HABITAT: Moist grassland and margins of woods, in neutral or somewhat acid soil.

CULTURE: Desirable for the wild garden.

Lobelia Family, concluded

Lime Lobelia (*Lobèlia kálmii*)   Pl. 88

FEATURES: Plant slender, branching, 6 to 12 in. high. Flowers lavender-blue, ⅓ in. long, on long stalks in bract axils. Leaves narrow, obscurely toothed. Late summer.

RANGE: Canada and upper parts of our area.

HABITAT: Moist rocky slopes, stream banks, and marshes, in neutral, lime-rich soil.

CULTURE: Can be grown in a cool, moist, limy garden.

NOTES: Several other species of LOBELIA occur in our area, mostly having small lavender-blue flowers; notable are WATER LOBELIA (*L. dortmánna*) in northern ponds, and MEADOW LOBELIA (*L. spicàta*), widespread in thickets and grasslands.

Chicory Family (*Cichoriàceae*)

FEATURES: Plants with milky juice and alternate leaves. Flowers minute, numerous, densely clustered in a flat-topped inflorescence surrounded by sepal-like bracts (and so readily mistaken for one flower), known as a "head." Individual florets consisting of an ovary with which the bases of other floral organs are united; free parts of sepals reduced to pale scales or bristles; 5 petals united to a tube below, and to a strap-shaped "ray" above; anthers of 5 stamens united to a tube around the style, which has 2 slender stigmas at tip. Head opening for a day, closing until the seeds mature, then opening again, enabling the wind to blow the fruits around. The family includes many weeds like CHICORY, DANDELION, and WILD LETTUCE, and a few food plants, notably LETTUCE and SALSIFY.

Goat-dandelion (*Krígia biflòra*)   Pl. 90

FEATURES: Plant smooth, grayish green, a foot or so high. Rays bright orange; heads long-stalked, 2 or 3 together in bract axils. Leaves mostly basal, 1 in. or so across, shallowly few-toothed. Spring and early summer.

RANGE: Over our area except far northeast.

HABITAT: Damp grassland and open thickets, in somewhat acid soil.

CULTURE: Readily grown in a grassy wild garden.

NOTES: Also sometimes classed as *Cýnthia virgínica*.

Chicory Family, concluded

Vein-leaf Hawkweed (*Hieràcium venòsum*)   Pl. 91

FEATURES: Plant a foot or so high. Heads several in an openly branched group at tip of a nearly leafless stalk, ½ in. across; rays orange-yellow. Leaves mostly basal, often hairy, up to 4 in. long and 1½ in. wide, green with bronze veins. Summer.

RANGE: Over our area and adjacent Southern states.

HABITAT: Open woods and thickets in rather acid soil.

CULTURE: Desirable for the shady rock garden.

NOTES: There are many other species of HAWKWEEDS here, some introduced from Europe becoming serious weeds.

White Rattlesnake-root (*Prenánthes álba*)   Pl. 88

FEATURES: Plant 2 to 4 ft. high, smooth, gray-green. Heads about ¼ in. across, nodding in a compound group; rays greenish white; bristles on fruit brown. Leaves large, rhombic or triangular, somewhat lobed. Autumn.

RANGE: Over our area and adjacent regions.

HABITAT: Open woods, in often moderately acid soil.

CULTURE: Readily grown in a woodland garden.

NOTES: Several other species occur in our area, differing in details as to pubescence, leaf shape, and fruit characters.

Daisy Family (*Compósitae*)

FEATURES: Similar to the CHICORY FAMILY, except that the juice is watery, the heads are longer-lived, and some or all of the florets lack "rays."

Tall Ironweed (*Vernònia altíssima*)   Pl. 91

FEATURES: Plant 4 to 8 ft. high, branched above so as to bring the heads to the same level. Florets all rayless, dark purple; fruit tipped with purplish bristles. Leaves rather narrow, finely toothed, smooth. Late summer.

RANGE: Southern states and adjacent parts of our area.

HABITAT: Damp thickets, in neutral or somewhat acid soil.

CULTURE: Suitable for a large-scale wild garden.

NOTES: There are several other sorts of IRONWEED here.

Daisy Family, continued

White Snake-root (*Eupatòrium urticaefòlium*)   **Pl. 88**

FEATURES: Plant 1 to 3 ft. high, branched upward. Heads rather small but numerous in a flattish group; florets all rayless, white; fruits tipped with gray bristles. Leaves opposite, broad, coarsely toothed. Late summer and autumn.

RANGE: Eastern half of the United States, extending a short distance into southeastern Canada.

HABITAT: Woods, in rich, usually neutral soil.

CULTURE: Spreads rapidly by seed in the woodland garden or shaded border.

NOTES: The foliage contains a poisonous principle which, if eaten by cows, gets into the milk and may cause a serious, sometimes fatal, human illness.

Boneset (*E. perfoliàtum*)   **Pl. 89**

FEATURES: Plant 2 to 4 ft. high, branching. Heads tiny but numerous in a flat-topped group; florets all rayless, grayish white; fruits tipped with short gray bristles. Leaves opposite and basally united so that the stems seem to pierce them. Summer.

RANGE: Eastern half of the United States and adjacent Canada.

HABITAT: Swamps and wet thickets, in various soils.

CULTURE: Sometimes cultivated because of its peculiar leaf arrangement, but rather weedy.

NOTES: The common name refers to the inference by "herb doctors" that a plant with united leaves should heal fractured bones. Another name is THOROUGHWORT.

Joe-pye-weed (*E. purpùreum*)   **Pl. 89**

FEATURES: Plant 4 to 8 ft. high. Heads tiny but very numerous in a vast terminal plume; florets all rayless, dull pink; fruits tipped by short gray bristles. Leaves whorled in threes to sixes, coarsely toothed. Autumn.

RANGE: Eastern half of the United States and adjacent Canada.

HABITAT: Moist thickets in neutral or somewhat acid soils.

CULTURE: Suitable for the large-scale wild garden.

NOTES: Many other species of *Eupatòrium* occur in our area; they differ in details of florets and leaves, but require close study to distinguish.

Daisy Family, continued

Hemp-vine (*Mikània scándens*) Pl. 89

FEATURES: Plant a twining vine, reaching heights of 10 to 12 ft. Heads in small groups at branchlet tips; florets pink, rayless, 4 to the head; fruit tipped by numerous fine gray bristles. Leaves opposite, heart-shaped, smooth, 2 to 4 in. long. Late summer.

RANGE: South and Central America, and extending well over the Northeastern states.

HABITAT: Wet thickets, in usually moderately acid soils.

CULTURE: Highly desirable for the swampy wild garden.

NOTES: Also known as CLIMBING BONESET.

Prairie Gayfeather (*Liàtris pycnostàchya*) Pl. 91

FEATURES: Plant consisting of a tuber an inch or so in diameter, from which arise a few simple stalks 2 to 4 ft. high. Heads short-cylindric, crowded in a spike, their bracts with thin bronzy margins; florets few, all rayless, purple; fruit tipped by tawny bristles. Leaves numerous, alternate, narrow. Late summer.

RANGE: Midland states and adjacent regions; locally escaping from gardens well to the east.

HABITAT: Grasslands, in neutral or slightly acid soil.

CULTURE: Well known as a garden plant, thriving in the border.

Rough-spike Gayfeather (*L. squarròsa*) Pl. 89

FEATURES: Plant consisting of a tuber from which arise 1 or 2 simple stalks 9 to 18 in. high. Flower heads short and broad, few on short stalks in axils of small leaves toward stalk tip; their bracts with firm, green, pointed tips; florets numerous, rayless, purple; fruit tipped by fine, buff, feathery plumes. Leaves few, narrow, alternate. Summer.

RANGE: Midland states and adjacent regions.

HABITAT: Gravelly slopes, in moderately acid soil.

CULTURE: Suitable for the sunny wild garden.

NOTES: These plants are inaptly termed in some books BLAZING-STAR, although there is nothing fiery or starry about them. There are several other species in our region, all similar in habit and requiring detailed study to identify; they do well in wild gardens, if rodents do not find the tubers.

Daisy Family, continued

Cream Goldenrod (*Solidàgo bìcolor*)   Pl. 93

FEATURES: Plant 1 to 2 ft. high. Heads ¼ in. long, in narrow cylindric groups at branchlet tips; 6 or 8 outer florets bearing short creamy-white rays; rayless florets yellow; fruits tipped with whitish bristles. Leaves alternate, hairy, the lower stalked and upper sessile, sparsely and shallowly toothed. Late summer.

RANGE: Over our area and adjacent regions.

HABITAT: Open woods and thickets on gravelly slopes, in rather acid soil.

CULTURE: Suitable for the large-scale rock garden.

NOTES: Unusual among GOLDENRODS in its pale ray color, and sometimes called for contrast SILVER-ROD.

Plume Goldenrod (*S. júncea*)   Pl. 91

FEATURES: Plant 1½ to 3 ft. high. Heads ⅛ in. long, in a large plumy group with outcurved branches; 7 to 10 florets bearing small bright yellow rays; fruits tipped with white bristles. Lower leaves stalked and toothed, upper sessile and entire. Early summer.

RANGE: Over our area and well north into Canada.

HABITAT: Open woods and grasslands on rocky slopes, also invading old fields, in somewhat sterile acid soil.

CULTURE: Readily grown in any garden.

NOTES: One of the earliest GOLDENRODS to bloom.

Sweet Goldenrod (*S. odòra*)   Pl. 92

FEATURES: Plant slender, 2 to 3 ft. high. Heads ⅙ in. long, in a small one-sided group; inner bracts elongate, yellowish; 3 or 4 florets bearing rather large yellow rays. Leaves narrow, entire, obscurely veined, shining, dotted with minute glands yielding a pleasing anise fragrance. Summer.

RANGE: Southern states and adjacent parts of our area, extending up to central New England.

HABITAT: Open woods and thickets, in sterile sandy or gravelly, moderately to strongly acid soil.

CULTURE: Will grow in an acid wild garden.

NOTES: The dried foliage when steeped in hot water gives an agreeably flavored tea.

Daisy Family, continued

Noble Goldenrod (*Solidàgo speciòsa*) **Pl. 92**

FEATURES: Plant 3 to 5 ft. high. Heads ⅓ in. long, in a large, leafy, conical group with ascending branches; 5 or 6 florets bearing showy yellow rays; fruits tipped with white bristles. Leaves large, the lower stalked and obscurely toothed, the upper entire and sessile. Late summer.

RANGE: Over our area except far northeast.

HABITAT: Open woods, in rather rich neutral soil.

CULTURE: Desirable for the large-scale wild garden.

NOTES: This and 2 additional GOLDENRODS had to be illustrated in black and white, but their coloring is like that of the PLUME GOLDENROD, shown on colored plate 91.

Grass-leaf Goldenrod (*S. graminifòlia*) **Pl. 92**

FEATURES: Plant 2 to 3 ft. high, branched above. Heads tiny but numerous in a flat-topped group; florets about 25, more than half of them bearing yellow rays; fruits tipped with fine bristles. Leaves narrow, entire. Late summer.

RANGE: Eastern half of the United States and adjacent Canada.

HABITAT: Damp thickets and margins of grassland, also invading waste places, in moderately acid soil.

CULTURE: Can be grown in the wild garden, but may become weedy.

Stiff Goldenrod (*S. rígida*) **Pl. 92**

FEATURES: Plant 2 to 4 ft. high, stout, rough-hairy. Heads bell-shaped, in a large, somewhat leafy convex-topped group; florets ⅓ in. long, 8 or 10 of them bearing rather large rays; fruits tipped by short bristles. Leaves large, thick, rigid, the upper entire and sessile. Late summer.

RANGE: Over our area, except northeast, and adjacent regions.

HABITAT: Dry rocky or gravelly slopes, in neutral soil.

CULTURE: Suitable for a dry, open wild garden, or for the large-scale rock garden.

NOTES: Numerous other GOLDENRODS occur here, but can be distinguished only by close study. The tradition that these plants cause "hay fever" has been found by botanists to be wholly unfounded, the illness being due to the pollen of RAGWEED, which blooms at the same time.

Daisy Family, continued

Broad-leaf Golden-aster (*Chrysópsis mariàna*)   Pl. 94

FEATURES: Plant 1 to 2 ft. high, soft-hairy. Heads hemispherical, both rayless and rayed florets bright yellow, nearly 1 in. across, long-stalked in upper leaf axils; fruit tipped with both long and short bristles. Leaves alternate, obtusish, the upper sessile. Late summer.

RANGE: Southern states and adjacent parts of our area.

HABITAT: Open woods and grassy thickets, in rather acid soil.

CULTURE: Desirable for the large-scale rock garden.

NOTES: MIDLAND GOLDEN-ASTER (*C. villòsa*), which differs in being lower and thriving in neutral soils, is especially desirable as a rock-garden subject.

New England Aster (*Áster nòvae-ángliae*)   Pl. 94

FEATURES: Plant 2 to 5 ft. high, rough-hairy, branched upward. Heads 1½ in. across, their viscid-hairy bracts with spreading tips, the 40 to 50 narrow rays violet to pink; fruits tipped with pinkish bristles. Leaves oblong, clasping the stalk. Late summer.

RANGE: Over our area and adjacent regions; in spite of the name, rare in New England except as a garden escape.

HABITAT: Thickets and grasslands, in neutral soil; also invading wasteland.

CULTURE: A well-known garden border subject.

White Wood Aster (*A. divaricàtus*)   Pl. 93

FEATURES: Plant 1 to 2 ft. high, the slender stalk somewhat zigzag. Heads in a flat-topped group, 1 in. across, the 6 or 8 narrow rays white, the rayless florets bronzy; fruits tipped with whitish bristles. Leaves thin, long-stalked, heart-shaped, long-tapering, coarsely toothed. Late summer.

RANGE: Over our area and adjacent regions.

HABITAT: Open woods, in moderately acid soil.

CULTURE: Spreads rapidly into colonies in the woodland garden and may have to be restrained.

NOTES: Closely related is the BIG-LEAF ASTER (*A. macrophýllus*), which produces numerous large, thickish, rough, heart-shaped basal leaves, and tall stalks bearing rather small lavender flower heads.

Daisy Family, continued

Bristly Aster (*Áster linariifòlius*)   Pl. 93

FEATURES: Plant 6 to 18 in. high, the stiff stalks somewhat branched upward. Heads solitary at branchlet tips, ¾ in. across, their bracts numerous, brownish and dry; rays 10 to 15, lavender; rayless florets yellow, becoming bronzy; fruits silky, tipped by a dense crown of short bristles and a tuft of somewhat longer tawny ones. Late summer and autumn.

RANGE: Eastern half of the United States.

HABITAT: Rocky or sandy slopes, in rather acid soil.

CULTURE: Desirable for the rock garden, although it becomes floppy unless planted in an especially dry, sterile spot.

NOTES: This is also known as SANDPAPER ASTER, in reference to the rough herbage. There are many other species of ASTER in our area, but they differ in such minor details of heads and foliage as to require close study for identification.

Robins-plantain (*Erígeron pulchéllus*)   Pl. 96

FEATURES: Plant 10 to 20 in. high. Heads few, slender-stalked, about 1 in. across; rays numerous, lavender; rayless florets yellow; fruit smooth, tipped with long whitish bristles. Leaves chiefly basal, blunt, sparsely toothed, the few on the stalk pointed. Spring.

RANGE: Eastern half of the United States and adjacent Canada.

HABITAT: Thinly wooded slopes, in neutral or somewhat acid soil.

CULTURE: Desirable for the wild garden.

NOTES: There are several other species of this genus here; they differ from ASTERS in the fewer bracts on the heads.

Summer-aster (*Sericocárpus asteroìdes*)   Pl. 93

FEATURES: Plant 9 to 18 in. high, branched upward. Heads in a flat-topped group, cylindric, about ½ in. long; rays few, white; rayless florets bronzy; fruits silky-hairy, tipped with tawny bristles. Leaves rather small, finely toothed, the upper sessile. Summer.

RANGE: Northeastern states and adjacent regions.

HABITAT: Open woods on sandy slopes, in moderately acid soil.

CULTURE: Suitable for the partly shaded rock garden.

NOTES: Also classed as *Áster patérnus;* blooms earlier than the commoner ASTERS.

Daisy Family, continued

Black-eyed-Susan (*Rudbéckia hírta*)   Pl. 94

FEATURES: Plant biennial, 1 to 2 ft. high, the stalks tufted.
Heads large, long-stalked at branch tips; rays 10 to 15,
orange-yellow; rayless florets blackish brown, forming a
rounded conical mass; fruits lacking bristles. Leaves thick,
obscurely toothed, the upper sessile. Summer.

RANGE: Midland states and adjacent regions; also spreading as
a weed eastwardly.

HABITAT: Thickets and grasslands, in rather sterile and somewhat acid soil.

CULTURE: Readily grown in the wild garden.

NOTES: There are several other members of this genus here;
they are often termed CONEFLOWERS in allusion to the shape
of the group of rayless florets.

Purple Coneflower (*Echinàcea purpùrea*)   Pl. 94

FEATURES: Plant perennial, 2 to 4 ft. high. Heads large, on
long stalks at branch tips; rays about 15, lilac-purple, up to
3 in. long, tending to droop; rayless florets bronzy, in a globular group; fruits tipped with a crown of small scales. Leaves
large, coarsely toothed. Summer.

RANGE: Midland states and adjacent regions.

HABITAT: Moist thickets, in neutral or somewhat acid soil.

CULTURE: Occasionally grown in the border.

NOTES: Other species of this and related genera occur toward
the western side of our area.

Plantain-leaf Pussy-toes (*Antennària plantaginifòlia*)
                                                           Pl. 96

FEATURES: Plant creeping, sending up stalks 8 to 15 in. high.
Heads clustered at stalk tips, their bracts papery; florets
bronze, all rayless, the staminate and carpellate on separate
plants; fruits tipped with long bristles. Leaves bluntish, dull
green with webby hairs above, silvery beneath. Spring.

RANGE: Eastern half of the United States and adjacent Canada.

HABITAT: Open woods and margins of grassland, on sterile
slopes, in moderately acid soil.

CULTURE: This and related species deserve a place in the rock
garden or a steep bank in the wild garden.

NOTES: There are numerous sorts of PUSSY-TOES, but they
mostly differ in only minor details.

Daisy Family, continued

Compass-plant (*Sílphium laciniàtum*)   Pl. 96

FEATURES: Plant 5 to 10 ft. high, rough-hairy and resinous. Heads short-stalked at branch tips, 3 to 4 in. across; rays yellow, notched at tip; rayless florets also yellow; fruits laterally winged. Leaves alternate, large, deeply and openly cut into narrow lobes, tending to stand on edge and point northward and southward, to which the name refers. Late summer.

RANGE: Midland and adjacent Southern states.

HABITAT: Grasslands, in neutral to slightly acid soil.

CULTURE: Adapted to the large-scale wild garden.

NOTES: Other members of the genus have less-divided leaves.

Thin-leaf Sunflower (*Heliánthus decapétalus*)   Pl. 95

FEATURES: Plant 1 to 3 ft. high, branched upwards. Heads numerous at branch tips, 2½ in. across; rays 10 or 12, yellow; rayless florets also yellow; fruits lacking scales. Leaves broad and thin, stalked, toothed, the lower opposite and upper alternate. Late summer.

RANGE: Over our area except far northwest.

HABITAT: Moist thickets, in neutral or somewhat acid soils.

CULTURE: Suitable for the shaded wild garden.

NOTES: There are many other SUNFLOWERS in our region. One, *H. tuberòsus,* produces, on its creeping underground stems, edible tubers known as JERUSALEM ARTICHOKES.

Smooth Coreopsis (*Coreópsis lanceolàta*)   Pl. 95

FEATURES: Plant 1 to 2 ft. high, smooth. Heads few, on long stalks, 2 in. across; rays about 8, bright yellow, lobed at tip; rayless florets also yellow; outer bracts of heads different in shape from inner; fruits with lateral wings and 2 small terminal scales. Leaves narrow, blunt, entire or divided into few long lobes. Summer.

RANGE: Midland states and adjacent regions; extensively escaping from gardens northeastward.

HABITAT: Dry gravelly slopes and grassy thickets, in moderately acid soil.

CULTURE: A well-known garden plant.

NOTES: About a dozen other sorts of COREOPSIS occur here.

Daisy Family, concluded

Swamp Sneeze-weed (*Helènium autumnàle*) **Pl. 95**

FEATURES: Plant 2 to 4 ft. high, branched upward. Heads numerous on long stalks from leaf axils, 1½ in. across; rays about 15, yellow, round-lobed at tip, drooping; rayless florets in a hemispherical group, bronzy; fruit sparse-hairy, tipped with bristle-pointed scales. Leaves alternate, narrow, shallowly toothed. Autumn.

RANGE: Eastern half of the United States and adjacent Canada.

HABITAT: Wet thickets and grassy marshes, in neutral or moderately acid soils.

CULTURE: Grown to some extent in garden borders, some striking bronzy-rayed forms having been developed by horticulturists.

Golden Groundsel (*Senècio aùreus*) **Pl. 95**

FEATURES: Plant 1 to 2 ft. high, smooth. Heads long-stalked, ¾ in. across; rays about 10, golden yellow, narrow; rayless florets dull yellow; fruit tipped by conspicuous soft white bristles. Basal leaves large (or in one variant small), heart-shaped, with rounded teeth; stem leaves oblong, toothed or lobed. Spring.

RANGE: Southern states and lower parts of our area.

HABITAT: Wet thickets along streams and grassy marshes, in neutral or slightly acid soil.

CULTURE: Desirable for the wild garden, increasing by seeds.

NOTES: Also known as GOLDEN RAGWORT, in reference to the irregularly cut lower stem leaves. Several other species occur in our area, most in drier habitats.

Tall Thistle (*Cìrsium altìssimum*) **Pl. 96**

FEATURES: Plant 3 to 6 ft. high. Heads at tips of branchlets, about 2 in. across; florets all rayless, lilac-purple; outer bracts short-prickly; fruits tipped with grayish bristles. Leaves large, their margins prickly-toothed, woolly beneath. Late summer.

RANGE: Over our area and Southern states, except northeastward.

HABITAT: Grassy thickets, in somewhat acid soils.

CULTURE: Can be grown in the large-scale wild garden.

NOTES: Many other THISTLES grow here, but are not easy to tell apart.

APPENDIX 1

Lists of Flowers According to Color

1. RED OR PINK

2. YELLOW OR ORANGE

3. BRONZY OR GREENISH

4. BLUE, VIOLET, LAVENDER, PURPLE, OR LILAC

4. BLUE, VIOLET, etc., Continued

5. WHITE

5. WHITE, Continued

Iris Family (*Iridàceae*)

Yellow Iris (*Ìris pseudácorus*)

FEATURES: Plant 2 to 3 ft. high. Flowers yellow, about 4 in. across; sepals 3, with large round blade; petals 3, small and narrow. Summer.

SOURCE: Europe.

Blackberry-lily (*Belamcánda chinénsis*)   Pl. 97

FEATURES: Plant 2 to 3 ft. high. Flowers orange with purple spots, 2 in. across, in clusters; sepals and petals similar. Fruit at maturity displaying a blackberry-like group of seeds, to which the name refers. Leaves IRIS-like, to 8 in. long; stem base bare, yellow. Summer.

SOURCE: Asia.

Orchis Family (*Orchidàceae*)

Hellebore Orchid (*Epipáctis helleborìne*)   Pl. 97

FEATURES: Plant 1 to 2 ft. high, with the aspect of a REIN-ORCHID. Flowers bronzy purple, several in a cylindric group; lip sac-shaped at base but not spurred, the tip spreading. Late summer.

SOURCE: Europe.

FREE-PETAL DICOTS

Buttercup Family (*Ranunculàceae*)

Tall Buttercup (*Ranúnculus àcris*)

FEATURES: Plant 2 to 3 ft. high. Flowers bright yellow, about 1 in. across; sepals 5, spreading; petals 5, showy. Leaves about as broad as long, deeply cut-lobed. Late spring through summer.

SOURCE: Europe.

Bulblet Buttercup (*R. bulbòsus*)   Pl. 98

FEATURES: Plant 1 to 1½ ft. high, the stem base bulb-like. Flowers as in the preceding, but sepals bent downward. Leaves longer than broad, less cut. Spring and early summer.

SOURCE: Europe.

Buttercup Family, concluded

Mat Buttercup (*Ranúnculus rèpens*)

FEATURES: Stems creeping, rooting at nodes and forming mats. Otherwise similar to the native SWAMP BUTTERCUP (Pl. 34). Spring.

SOURCE: Europe.

European Columbine (*Aquilègia vulgàris*)

FEATURES: Plant similar to the native species (Pl. 35). Flowers violet-blue, their spurs short. Late spring.

SOURCE: Europe.

Field Larkspur (*Delphínium ajàcis*)

FEATURES: Plant a slender annual. Flowers much as in our native species (Pl. 38), deep violet-blue; carpel solitary. Summer.

SOURCE: Europe.

Poppy Family (*Papaveràceae*)

Celandine (*Chelidònium màjus*)   Pl. 98

FEATURES: Plant 1 to 2 ft. high. Flowers ½ in. across; petals 4, yellow. Leaves divided into roundish lobes. Fruit a slender tube. Juice cloudy yellow. Late spring and summer.

SOURCE: Europe.

Field Poppy (*Papàver rhoèas*)   Pl. 98

FEATURES: Plant 1 to 2 ft. high, hairy. Flowers about 3 in. across; petals 4 to 6, red; fruit top-shaped. Juice milky. Summer.

SOURCE: Europe.

Fume-root Family (*Fumariàceae*)

Fumitory (*Fumària officinàlis*)   Pl. 98

FEATURES: Plant a delicate annual with ferny foliage. Flowers dull pink, ¼ in. long, 1-sided, in a cylindric group. Summer.

SOURCE: Europe.

Cress Family (*Cruciferae*)

Whitlow-grass (*Dràba vérna*)

FEATURES: Plant a tiny annual with basal rosette of small hairy leaves and a 2- to 4-in. stalk bearing a few white flowers with the family feature of 4 petals and 6 stamens. Fruit an ovoid pod ¼ in. long. Earliest spring.

SOURCE: Europe.

Shepherds-purse (*Capsélla búrsa-pastòris*)   Pl. 99

FEATURES: Plant annual, 8 to 15 in. high. Flowers white, small, and numerous. Fruit a triangular, somewhat purse-shaped structure. Leaves chiefly basal, variably lobed. Nearly throughout the growing season.

SOURCE: Europe.

NOTES: This homely grassland weed has proved of great value in research in genetics, enabling Professor George H. Shull of Princeton University to work out the principles on which the development of hybrid corn was based.

Penny-cress (*Thláspi arvénsè*)   Pl. 99

FEATURES: Plant a smooth annual 8 to 15 in. high. Flowers white, minute, numerous in a long slender group. Fruit disk-shaped though with a terminal notch, nearly ½ in. across. Summer.

SOURCE: Europe.

Rocket (*Hésperis matronàlis*)   Pl. 99

FEATURES: Plant a hairy biennial 2 to 3 ft. high. Flowers lilac or white, fragrant, ¾ in. across, numerous in somewhat branched groups. Fruit 2 or 3 in. long, slender, somewhat knobby. Leaves broad, hairy, finely toothed, extending up the stem. Summer.

SOURCE: Europe.

Black Mustard (*Brássica nìgra*)

FEATURES: Plant annual, several feet high, branching. Flowers yellow, ⅓ in. across, numerous. Fruit a 4-sided slender ½-in. pod lying close to the stem. Leaves mostly with a large terminal lobe and smaller lateral ones. Summer.

SOURCE: Europe.

Cress Family, concluded

Yellow-cress (*Rorìpa sylvéstris*)

FEATURES: Plant a low-growing smooth perennial. Flowers yellow, ¼ in. across, in sparse cylindric groups. Fruit tubular, ½ in. long, on a slender ¼-in. stalk. Leaves 3 or 4 in. long, divided in ferny pattern into sharp-toothed lobes. Summer.
SOURCE: Europe.

Garlic-mustard (*Alliària officinàlis*)   Pl. 99

FEATURES: Plant a smooth biennial 2 to 3 ft. high. Flowers white, numerous in long branching groups. Fruit slender, 4-sided, about 1½ in. long on short stout stalks. Leaves large, roundish, wavy-margined, garlic-scented when crushed. Early summer.
SOURCE: Europe.

Mallow Family (*Malvàceae*)

Cheese Mallow (*Málva neglécta*)   Pl. 100

FEATURES: Plant a trailing annual. Flowers pinkish, ½ in. across, clustered in leaf axils; petals 5, notched at tip; stamens in a column. Fruit a ring of small carpels suggesting a tiny cheese. Leaves roundish. Summer.
SOURCE: Europe.
NOTES: Often assigned the epithet *M. rotundifòlia*.

Musk Mallow (*M. moschàta*)

FEATURES: Plant perennial, 1 to 2 ft. high. Flowers pink or white, 1½ in. across, in sparse groups at branch tips. Fruit doughnut-shaped, hairy. Leaves deeply divided in palmate pattern into narrow sharp-toothed lobes. Summer.
SOURCE: Europe. Once widely cultivated.

Oxalis Family (*Oxalidàceae*)

European Oxalis (*Oxális europaèa*)

FEATURES: Plant 8 to 15 in. high, branchy. Flowers yellow, ½ in. across, in sparse clusters. Fruit and leaves much as in native species (Pl. 43). Late spring to autumn.
SOURCE: Europe.

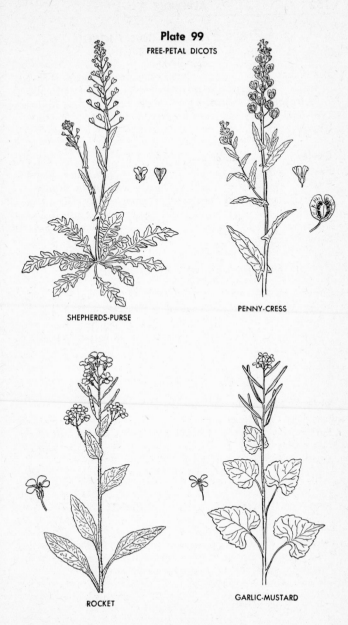

Plate 99
FREE-PETAL DICOTS

SHEPHERDS-PURSE

PENNY-CRESS

ROCKET

GARLIC-MUSTARD

Plate 100
FREE-PETAL DICOTS

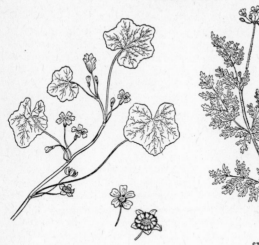

CHEESE MALLOW

STORKS-BILL

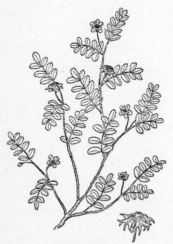

PUNCTURE-WEED

CYPRESS SPURGE

Geranium Family (*Geraniàceae*)

Storks-bill (*Eròdium cicutàrium*)　　　　　**Pl. 100**

FEATURES: Plant biennial, producing the first year a rosette of
fern-like leaves and the second year a branched leafy stalk
5 to 10 in. high. Flowers rose-purple, ⅓ in. across, like other
members of the family (Pl. 42). Fruit a slender rod 1 to 1½
in. long, to which the name refers. Spring.

SOURCE: Europe.

Caltrop Family (*Zygophyllàceae*)

Puncture-weed (*Tríbulus terréstris*)　　　　**Pl. 100**

FEATURES: Plant a sprawling annual forming mats a foot or
more across. Flowers yellow, ½ in. across, borne singly in leaf
axils; sepals and petals 5 each, short-lived; stamens 10; carpels 5, well united. Fruit a burr with 5 segments, each bearing several spines so sharp and stout as to be capable of
puncturing thin rubber. Leaves pinnate with about 12 obliquely oblong leaflets, hairy. Summer.

SOURCE: Southern Europe.

NOTES: Grows in the southern parts of our area.

St. Johnswort Family (*Hypericàceae*)

St. Johns-weed (*Hypéricum perforàtum*)

FEATURES: Plant 1 to 2 ft. high, branchy. Flowers much as in
our native species (Pl. 43), ¾ in. across, yellow; petals
copiously black-dotted, to which the name refers; stamens in
3 clusters; styles 3. Leaves oblong, numerous, less than 1 in.
long. Summer.

SOURCE: Europe.

Spurge Family (*Euphorbiàceae*)

Cypress Spurge (*Euphòrbia cyparíssias*)　　　**Pl. 100**

FEATURES: Plant 1 ft. high, spreading by underground stems
into dense patches. Flowers incomplete as in native species,
greenish yellow, in flat-topped groups. Leaves numerous, very
narrow. Juice milky. Spring.

SOURCE: Europe.

Pink Family *(Caryophyllàceae)*

Grass-leaf Chickweed *(Stellària gramínea)*
FEATURES: Plant slender, sprawly, a foot or so high. Flowers small, white, the 5 petals deeply cleft to yield a 10-rayed star, on long thread-like stalks in an openly branched inflorescence. Leaves opposite (as in most members of the family), narrow, up to 1½ in. long. Spring and summer.
SOURCE: Europe.

Streamside Chickweed *(S. aquática)*
FEATURES: Plant sprawly, a foot or so high. Flowers nearly ½ in. across, white, 10-rayed stars, in compact groups. Leaves short and broad. Spring and summer.
SOURCE: Europe.

Corn-cockle *(Agrostémma githàgo)*   Pl. 101
FEATURES: Plant 2 to 3 ft. high, hairy. Flowers rose-pink, 2 in. across, with 5 broad spreading petals. Leaves narrow, to 4 in. long. Summer.
SOURCE: Europe.
NOTES: Grows chiefly in grain fields.

Mullein-pink *(Lýchnis coronària)*
FEATURES: Plant 1 to 2 ft. high. Flowers deep crimson, 1 in. across, in sparse groups. Leaves moderately large, covered with dense white wool to which the name refers. Summer.
SOURCE: Europe. Often grown in gardens.

White Campion *(L. álba)*   Pl. 101
FEATURES: Plant biennial, 1 to 2 ft. high, branchy, sticky-pubescent. Flowers white, 1 in. across, the staminate and pistillate ones on separate plants; petals 5, notched; styles 5, elongate. Leaves rather broad. Summer.
SOURCE: Europe.

Thrift Catchfly *(Silènè armèria)*
FEATURES: Plant a smooth branchy annual 1 ft. high. Flowers rose-pink, ½ in. across, in flat-topped groups; calyx tubular; styles 3. Leaves to 3 in. long. Summer.
SOURCE: Europe.

Pink Family, concluded

Bouncing-bet (*Saponària officinàlis*)   **Pl. 101**

FEATURES: Plant a smooth perennial 1 to 2 ft. high. Flowers pale pink, 1 in. across, in dense clusters; petals 5, shallowly notched; styles 2. Leaves oval, to 3 in. long. Summer.

SOURCE: Europe.

NOTES: Spreads by underground stems into vast patches in gravelly waste places. Also known as SOAPWORT, the juice making a lather in water.

Deptford Pink (*Diánthus armèria*)   **Pl. 101**

FEATURES: Plant a smooth slender annual 8 to 15 in. high. Flowers small, deep pink with pale dots, in sparse flat-topped groups with pointed bracts; calyx tubular; petals 5, fringy; styles 2. Summer.

SOURCE: Europe.

Buckwheat Family (*Polygonàceae*)

Princes-feather (*Polýgonum orientàlè*)

FEATURES: Plant annual, several feet high. Flowers small, rose-pink, in long, slender, drooping spikes. Leaves hairy, heart-shaped, with dry sheaths at base. Summer.

SOURCE: Asia. Often cultivated.

Rose Family (*Rosàceae*)

Indian-strawberry (*Duchésnea índica*)

FEATURES: Plant creeping, forming vast mats. Flowers in leaf axils, yellow, ¾ in. across; receptacle at maturity becoming red and fleshy, dotted with tiny 1-seeded fruits, resembling a STRAWBERRY but tasteless. Spring and summer.

SOURCE: India, to which the name refers.

Sulfur Cinquefoil (*Potentílla récta*)

FEATURES: Plant 1 to 2 ft. high, hairy. Flowers light yellow, ¾ in. across, in sparse groups; petals 5, short-lived. Leaves divided into 5 toothed leaflets. Summer.

SOURCE: Europe.

Pea Family (*Leguminòsae*)

Red Clover (*Trifòlium praténsè*)

FEATURES: Plant perennial, 10 to 20 in. high, branchy, hairy. Flowers deep pink, about ⅓ in. long, crowded in an egg-shaped cluster to 1 in. in diameter; petals arranged as in most members of the family (Pl. 58), rather long and narrow. Leaves as in CLOVERS in general divided into 3 leaflets, in this species all alike, broadly oval, blunt, 1 to 1½ in. long. Blooming nearly throughout the growing season.

SOURCE: Europe.

Alsike Clover (*T. hýbridum*)

FEATURES: Plant similar to the next preceding, smooth. Flowers pale pink, ¼ in. long, short-stalked, in a globular group. Leaflets smaller and broader than in the preceding. Summer.

SOURCE: Europe.

White Clover (*T. rèpens*)

FEATURES: Plant creeping, forming mats, smooth. Flowers white or slightly pinkish, ¼ in. long, short-stalked, in a globular group. Leaflets much as in the next preceding, though rather smaller. Nearly throughout the season.

SOURCE: Europe.

NOTES: The number of leaflets sometimes increases to 4 or more.

Rabbit-foot Clover (*T. arvénsè*)

FEATURES: Plant annual, 8 to 15 in. high, branchy, hairy. Flowers whitish, tiny, in a dense cylindric group ¾ in. long; sepals with long narrow tips surpassing the petals, producing a fuzzy effect to which the name refers. Leaflets narrow, ½ to ¾ in. long. Summer.

SOURCE: Europe.

Hop Clover (*T. agràrium*)

FEATURES: Plant annual, 8 to 15 in. high, smooth. Flowers yellow, ⅓ in. long, in a dense rounded group. Leaflets rather narrow, ½ to ¾ in. long. Summer.

SOURCE: Europe.

NOTES: There are two other yellow-flowered CLOVERS introduced in our area; they are lower and have smaller parts.

Plate 101
FREE-PETAL DICOTS

CORN-COCKLE

WHITE CAMPION

BOUNCING-BET

DEPTFORD PINK

Plate 102
FREE-PETAL DICOTS

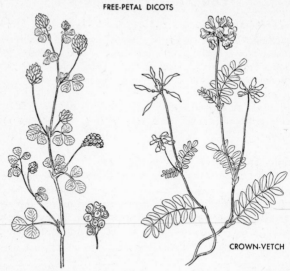

BLACK MEDICK

CROWN-VETCH

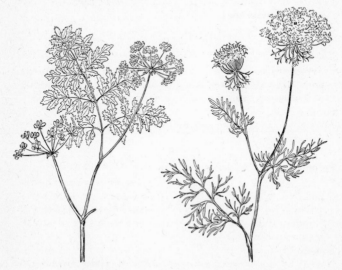

POISON-HEMLOCK

QUEEN ANNES-LACE

Pea Family, concluded

Black Medick (*Medicàgo lupulìna*)   **Pl. 102**

FEATURES: Plant CLOVER-like, annual, creeping and forming mats. Flowers yellow, tiny, in a dense cylindric cluster ½ in. long. Fruit a small, black, spirally, coiled, 1-seeded structure. Blooming throughout the growing season.

SOURCE: Europe.

NOTES: Distinguished from the CLOVERS by the peculiar fruits. The important forage plant ALFALFA is another species of this genus.

White Sweet-clover (*Melilòtus álba*)

FEATURES: Plant annual, 3 to 6 ft. high, branchy, with CLOVER-like leaves, yielding when crushed an intense fragrance suggesting vanilla or new-mown hay, to which the name refers. Flowers white, small but numerous in long-cylindric groups. Leaflets narrow, to ¾ in. long. Summer and autumn.

SOURCE: Europe.

Yellow Sweet-clover (*M. officinàlis*)

FEATURES: Similar to the preceding in most respects, except that the flowers are yellow.

SOURCE: Europe.

Crown-vetch (*Coronílla vària*)   **Pl. 102**

FEATURES: Plant a perennial with sprawling stems. Flowers pink, about ½ in. long, in a globular cluster. Leaves pinnate, with about 15 narrow leaflets. Summer.

SOURCE: Europe.

NOTES: A garden plant, spreading by underground stems into vast patches.

Perennial-pea (*Láthyrus latifòlius*)

FEATURES: Plant a large, sprawling, perennial vine. Flowers pink, ¾ in. across, borne in sparse groups on long stalks arising from leaf axils. Leaves consisting of a pair of narrowly elliptic leaflets and a terminal branched tendril by which the plant may climb. Summer.

SOURCE: Europe.

NOTES: Often cultivated under the name of HARDY SWEET-PEA.

Stonecrop Family (*Crassulàceae*)

Mossy Stonecrop (*Sèdum àcrè*)

FEATURES: Stems tufted, 2 to 3 in. high, thickly covered with tiny fleshy leaves. Flowers yellow, in flat-topped groups at stem tips; petals 5, pointed, forming a star; carpels 5, separate. Early summer.

SOURCE: Europe.

Live-forever (*S. purpùreum*)

FEATURES: Stems 1 ft. high, with alternate smooth, succulent, gray-green toothed leaves to 2 in. long. Flowers dull purple stars, developing only in the northern parts of our area where stimulated by the long summer days. Late summer.

SOURCE: Northern Asia.

NOTES: In spite of the usual failure of seeds to mature, this species has spread widely over our area, clumps being started by mere fragments of leafy shoots.

Loosestrife Family (*Lythràceae*)

Willow Loosestrife (*Lýthrum salicària*)

FEATURES: Plant 3 to 5 ft. high. Flowers purple, numerous, clustered in bract axils toward stem tip; petals 5, somewhat unequal; stamens and carpels variable. Leaves willow-like, as the name suggests. Summer.

SOURCE: Europe.

NOTES: This species resembles the native *L. alàtum,* illustrated on Pl. 63, but has larger and more numerous flowers. It is spreading rapidly along river and pond shores and in marshes in our area, destroying many native plants.

Carrot Family (*Umbellíferae*)

Goat-weed (*Aegopòdium podagrària*)

FEATURES: Plant 1 to 2 ft. high. Flowers tiny, white, in umbels. Leaves twice divided in threes, the leaflets broad, about 2 in. long, toothed, sometimes mottled with white. Summer.

SOURCE: Europe.

NOTES: Used as an edging in some gardens, but spreads aggressively by slender underground stems.

Plate 103
UNITED-PETAL DICOTS

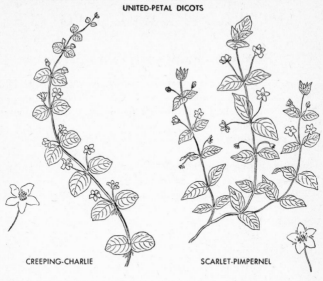

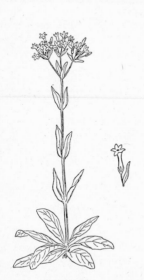

CREEPING-CHARLIE

SCARLET-PIMPERNEL

CENTAUR-PINK

VIPERS-BUGLOSS

Plate 104
UNITED-PETAL DICOTS

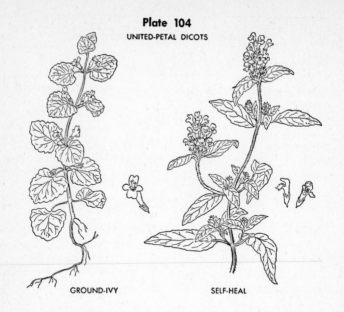

GROUND-IVY

SELF-HEAL

FIELD-MARJORAM

BITTERSWEET NIGHTSHADE

Borage Family, concluded

Comfrey (*Sýmphytum officinàlè*)

FEATURES: Plant a coarse perennial 1½ to 2½ ft. high. Flowers yellowish with bronze shading, tubular, ¾ in. long. Leaves large, hairy, pointed. Summer.

SOURCE: Europe.

Forget-me-not (*Myosòtis scorpioìdes*)

FEATURES: Plant a sprawling perennial. Flowers blue with yellow eye, ⅓ in. across, in a long spiraled group. Leaves oblong, blunt, hairy. Summer.

SOURCE: Europe. Extensively cultivated.

Vipers-bugloss (*Èchium vulgàrè*)   Pl. 103

FEATURES: Plant a coarse, bristly biennial 1 to 2 ft. high. Buds pink and open flowers blue, obliquely funnel-shaped, ¾ in. long, numerous. Summer.

SOURCE: Europe.

Mint Family (*Labiàtae*)

Catnip (*Népeta catària*)

FEATURES: Plant a gray-hairy aromatic perennial 1½ to 2½ ft. high. Flowers pale lilac, strongly 2-lipped, ½ in. long, in dense clusters. Leaves heart-shaped, coarsely toothed. Summer and autumn.

SOURCE: Europe.

Ground-ivy (*N. hederàcea*)   Pl. 104

FEATURES: Plant creeping, forming mats. Flowers lavender, 2-lipped, ⅔ in. long, borne in axils of roundish blunt-toothed leaves. Spring.

SOURCE: Europe.

Self-heal (*Prunélla vulgàris*)   Pl. 104

FEATURES: Plant a low perennial. Flowers lilac, 2-lipped, ½ in. long, in dense terminal short-cylindric spikes. Leaves 1 to 2 in. long, sparsely toothed. Summer.

SOURCE: Europe.

Mint Family, concluded

Motherwort (*Leonùrus cardìaca*)

FEATURES: Plant an erect perennial 2 to 4 ft. high. Flowers lilac, ⅓ in. long, in dense whorls at upper stem nodes. Leaves mostly 3-lobed. Summer.

SOURCE: Europe.

Field-marjoram (*Orìganum vulgàrè*)　　　**Pl. 104**

FEATURES: Plant a hairy perennial 1 to 2 ft. high. Flowers lilac, small, numerous, in flat-topped clusters. Leaves broad at base, tapering to a blunt point. Late summer.

SOURCE: Europe.

Round-leaf Mint (*Méntha rotundifòlia*)

FEATURES: Plant a hairy perennial with rank minty odor, 1 to 2 ft. high. Flowers minute, pinkish, in dense interrupted terminal spikes. Leaves elliptic, sessile, blunt, shallowly toothed. Late summer.

SOURCE: Europe.

Spearmint (*M. spicàta*)

FEATURES: Plant a smooth perennial 8 to 15 in. high. Flowers pinkish, tiny, in a slender interrupted spike. Leaves narrow, sharply toothed, pointed. Late summer.

SOURCE: Europe.

Peppermint (*M. piperìta*)

FEATURES: Plant a smooth perennial 1 to 2 ft. high. Flowers pinkish, tiny, in a dense thickish spike. Leaves narrow, short-stalked, sharply toothed, pointed. Late summer.

SOURCE: Europe.

Beefsteak-leaf (*Perìlla frutéscens*)

FEATURES: Plant a stout, branchy, bronzy-green annual. Flowers white, ⅛ in. long, spaced in branched groups. Leaves broad, to 5 in. long, tapering to a sharp point, coarsely toothed. Late summer and autumn.

SOURCE: India.

NOTES: The name of this old-fashioned garden plant refers to the resemblance of the leaf color to raw beefsteak.

Potato Family (*Solanàceae*)

Bittersweet Nightshade (*Solànum dulcamàra*)   **Pl. 104**
FEATURES: Plant a high-climbing vine. Flowers ½-in. stars of
violet petals with cone of yellow stamens. Leaves up to 3 in.
long, often lobed at base. Summer.
SOURCE: Europe. Often cultivated.

Jimson-weed (*Datùra stramònium*)
FEATURES: Plant a smooth annual 2 to 4 ft. high. Flowers
lavender, funnel-shaped, about 4 in. long, in upper leaf axils.
Fruit egg-shaped, 2 in. long, spiny. Leaves tapering to both
ends, wavy-lobed. Summer.
SOURCE: Tropical America.

Snapdragon Family (*Scrophulariàceae*)

Mullein (*Verbáscum thápsus*)
FEATURES: Plant a coarse, woolly biennial several feet high.
Flowers yellow, ¾ in. across, in a long spike; petals 5. Leaves
large and thick. Summer.
SOURCE: Europe.

Moth-mullein (*V. blattària*)   **Pl. 105**
FEATURES: Plant a somewhat viscid biennial 2 to 4 ft. high.
Flowers yellow or white, 1 in. across, spaced in a long slender
group. Leaves long-triangular, the upper 1 to 2 in. long.
Summer and autumn.
SOURCE: Europe.

Butter-and-eggs (*Linària vulgàris*)   **Pl. 105**
FEATURES: Plant a pale smooth perennial 1 to 2 ft. high.
Flowers yellow with orange palate, bilateral, 1 in. long.
Leaves narrow. Summer and autumn.
SOURCE: Europe.

Birds-eye Speedwell (*Verónica chamaèdrys*)
FEATURES: Plant a sprawly perennial. Flowers lavender-blue,
¼ in. across; petals 4, unequal; stamens 2. Leaves broad,
hairy, with coarse rounded teeth. Late spring.
SOURCE: Europe.

Madder Family (*Rubiàceae*)

Yellow Bedstraw (*Gàlium vèrum*)
FEATURES: Plant a bushy perennial 6 to 18 in. high. Flowers yellow, tiny, numerous in compound clusters; petals 4. Leaves narrow, in whorls of 6 at stem nodes. Summer.
SOURCE: Europe.

Teasel Family (*Dipsacàceae*)

Teasel (*Dipsacus sylvéstris*)   **Pl. 105**
FEATURES: Plant a stout, prickly biennial 3 to 5 ft. high. Flowers lilac, tiny, numerous in a short-cylindric mass with intermingled bristles. Leaves large, the upper clasping the stem. Late summer.
SOURCE: Europe.

Bellflower Family (*Campanulàceae*)

Roving Bellflower (*Campánula rapunculoìdes*)   **Pl. 105**
FEATURES: Plant a slender perennial 1 to 3 ft. high, spreading by underground stems into patches. Flowers violet, bell-shaped with the 5 petal tips spreading, 1 in. long, nodding in a long 1-sided group. Leaves heart-shaped. Summer.
SOURCE: Europe. Often grown in gardens.

Chicory Family (*Cichoriàceae*)

Chicory (*Cichòrium íntybus*)   **Pl. 106**
FEATURES: Plant a branchy perennial 1 to 3 ft. high. Flower heads 1½ in. across, the numerous rays blue or white. Leaves narrow, wavy-margined. Summer and autumn.
SOURCE: Europe.

Dandelion (*Taráxacum officinàlè*)
FEATURES: Plant a stemless perennial with long fleshy tap-root. Flower heads 1½ in. across, with 100 or more yellow-rayed florets. Leaves several inches long, irregularly lobed and toothed. Nearly throughout the year.
SOURCE: Europe.

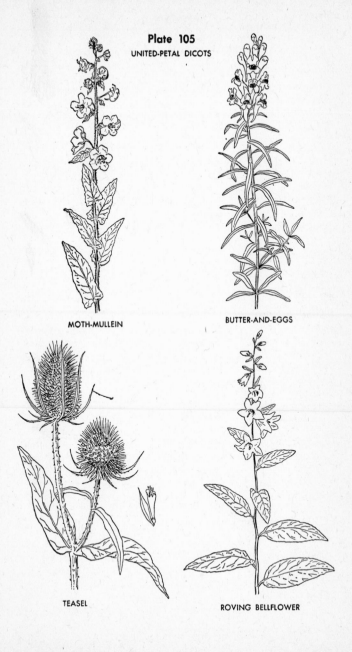

Plate 105
UNITED-PETAL DICOTS

MOTH-MULLEIN

BUTTER-AND-EGGS

TEASEL

ROVING BELLFLOWER

Plate 106

UNITED-PETAL DICOTS

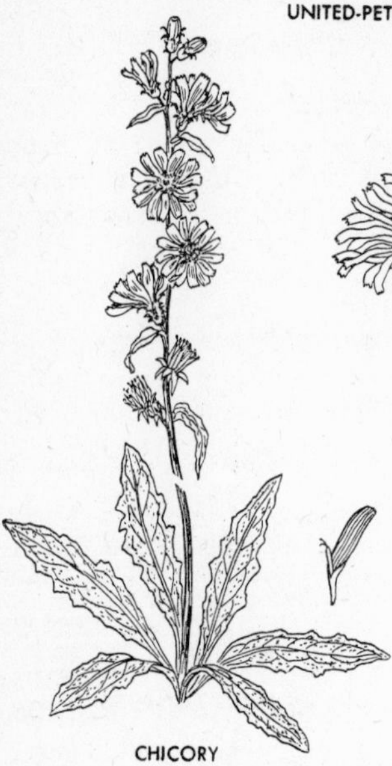

CHICORY

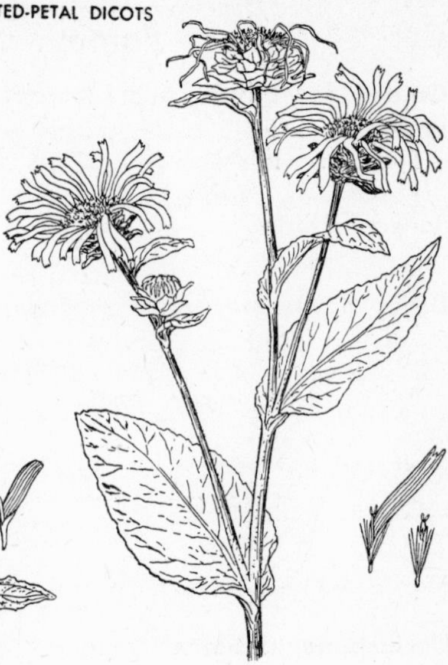

ELECAMPANE

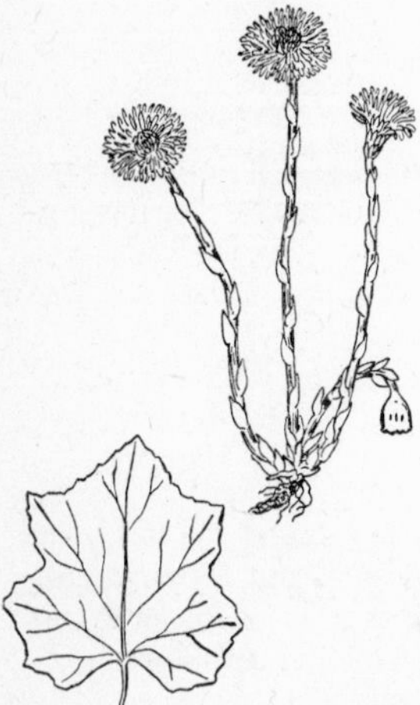

COLTS-FOOT

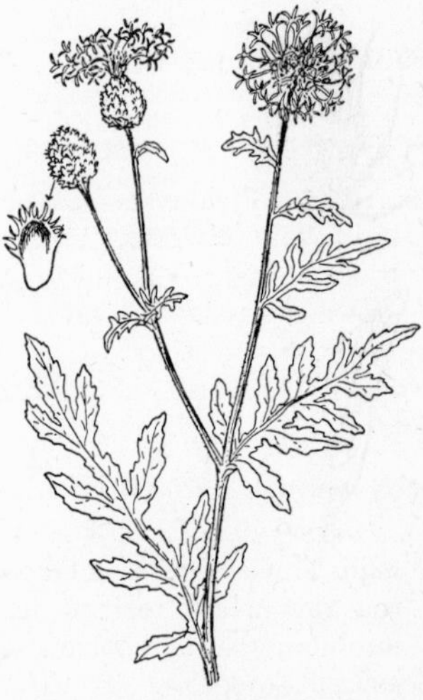

BLACK KNAPWEED

Chicory Family, concluded

Golden Sow-thistle (*Sónchus arvénsis*)

FEATURES: Plant a coarse prickly perennial 2 to 4 ft. high. Flower heads 1½ in. across, the floret rays golden yellow. Leaves long, narrow, coarsely lobed. Summer and autumn.

SOURCE: Europe.

Devils Hawkweed (*Hieràcium aurantìacum*)

FEATURES: Plant low, spreading by runners into patches. Flower heads ¾ in. across, the floret rays bright orange-red. Leaves coarsely hairy, elliptic, up to 5 in. long. Summer.

SOURCE: Europe.

NOTES: A bad weed in the northern parts of our area. There are also several weedy species with yellow flowers.

Daisy Family (*Compósitae*)

Elecampane (*Ínula helènium*)   Pl. 106

FEATURES: Plant a coarse hairy perennial 2 to 4 ft. high. Flower heads 3 in. across, the numerous narrow rays bright yellow. Leaves large, broadly elliptic, finely toothed. Summer.

SOURCE: Europe.

Quick-weed (*Galinsòga ciliàta*)

FEATURES: Plant a small, rapidly growing, hairy annual. Flower heads tiny, numerous, the rays white, few, short. Leaves opposite, broad, thin, few-toothed, pointed. Over most of the growing season.

SOURCE: South America.

NOTES: The name refers to this weed's rapid propagation.

May-weed (*Ánthemis cótula*)

FEATURES: Plant a rank-scented branchy annual 10 to 20 in. high. Flower heads numerous, 1 in. across, the 10 to 12 narrow rays white, toothed at tip. Leaves 1 to 2 in. long, cut into numerous fine narrow segments. Summer and autumn.

SOURCE: Europe.

NOTES: Also known as DOG-FENNEL and STINKING DAISY.

Daisy Family, concluded

Field Daisy (*Chrysánthemum leucánthemum*)

FEATURES: Plant a smooth perennial 1½ to 2½ ft. high. Flower heads 1½ in. across, the 20 or more rays white. Leaves narrow, coarsely toothed. Summer.

SOURCE: Europe.

Tansy (*Tanacètum vulgàrè*)

FEATURES: Plant a smooth perennial 1½ to 2½ ft. high. Flower heads numerous in a flat-topped group, ⅓ in. across, the florets yellow, barely rayed. Leaves large, divided in fern-like pattern into numerous sharp segments. Summer.

SOURCE: Europe. A common old-fashioned garden plant.

Colts-foot (*Tussilàgo fárfara*)   **Pl. 106**

FEATURES: Plant a low perennial. Flower heads solitary, on scaly stalks a few inches high, 1 in. across, with numerous narrow yellow rays, while in bud resembling a small horse hoof, to which the name refers. Leaves broad. Spring.

SOURCE: Europe.

Burdock (*Árctium mìnus*)

FEATURES: Plant a coarse biennial several feet high. Flower heads numerous, globular, the tubular florets lavender, and bracts bearing hooked prickles. Leaves broad, the lower heart-shaped. Summer and autumn.

SOURCE: Europe.

Bull Thistle (*Círsium lanceolàtum*)

FEATURES: Plant a coarse, prickly biennial 3 to 5 ft. high. Flower heads 2 in. high, the tubular florets lilac, and bracts all spine-tipped. Summer and autumn.

SOURCE: Europe.

Black Knapweed (*Centaúrea nìgra*)   **Pl. 106**

FEATURES: Plant a rough perennial 1 to 2 ft. high. Flower heads ¾ in. across, the tubular florets purple, and bracts dark-fringed. Leaves narrow. Summer.

SOURCE: Europe.

NOTES: There are other KNAPWEEDS differing in bract features.

APPENDIX 3

An Outline of Plant Ecology

The ascertainment of the name of a wild flower, to which the text of this book is directed, need not be the end of a trail. It may well be the beginning of consideration of the place of the plant in nature's scheme of things—the field of Plant Ecology.

Ecology is derived from the same root as the more familiar word "colony." It is not, as might appear from a glance at the more technical literature, a plan for telling us what we already know in words we cannot understand; nor is it, as held in some circles, a scheme of grouping plants into imaginary "associations." It consists in the scientific study of plants, and of animals as well, in relation to their environment—how they adapt themselves to the physical conditions they encounter on the earth, and how they get along with one another.

In many fields of endeavor man tends to oppose the processes of nature, and in striving for immediate results fails to look ahead and envisage future developments. The ecologist, on the other hand, ever tries to work along with nature and to consider the ultimate effects of present-day activities. An ecological viewpoint is, then, essential for success in such fields as forestry, grazing-range management, and progressive agriculture in general. The control of soil erosion, that serious threat to the future well-being of our country, is largely based on the principles of ecology. The attractive wild flowers described in this book are fast disappearing, but by the establishment and maintenance of nature preserves, ecologists hope to save many of them for the enjoyment of future generations.

From time to time, as a result of volcanic eruptions, landslides, dust storms, fires, floods, etc., portions of the earth's surface become devoid of life. In general, however, they do not remain so very long. One of the most characteristic attributes of normal living organisms consists in their ability to reproduce themselves. As the number of individuals of any species increases, more territory is required for their support. Ultimately, then, in the course of their expansion, plants of various sorts will reach life-free areas and, whenever the environmental conditions are otherwise favorable, will proceed to colonize them.

The means by which organisms get around are accordingly of interest to the ecologist. In the case of bacteria and the lesser algae the whole plant is so minute as to be capable of transport by the wind far and wide. Many larger plants produce spores which get carried around in the same manner and ultimately give rise to full-sized plants again. Sticky plates taken to high altitudes in airplanes catch various kinds of spores, some of them, alas, capable of producing plant diseases when carried down in the rain.

Then there are seeds. Some of these, notably of the orchids, are so minute as to be transported by the wind. Others are larger and heavier, but by one means or another succeed in getting around. Running water may carry them from higher to lower ground, but uphill movement is also possible.

Some seeds, such as those of the milkweeds, bear tufts of hair which enable them to float on the breeze. Others, which we might term "hitchhikers," have their surfaces covered with viscid substances, bristles, etc., and so adhere to the feet, feathers, or fur of birds or various animals, and may get carried long distances before they fall off. In many cases these features are shown, not by the seeds themselves, but by the structure in which they are enclosed, termed by botanists the fruit, irrespective of edibility. Fruits that do have sweet pulp may be carried afar by animals before being consumed; the seeds may then be discarded, or, if swallowed, excreted, remote from the plant which produced them. Edible seeds and nuts may be buried by rodents and then forgotten. How some weed seeds get around is something of a mystery, although there can be no question as to their success.

Plants require for their growth the elements hydrogen, oxygen, carbon, and nitrogen, along with lesser amounts of other elements. The first two are supplied by water, which is always present where life exists. Under the stimulating effect of light, green plants obtain carbon from the carbon dioxide gas in the air. Yet even though the element nitrogen makes up over three fourths of the earth's atmosphere, plants in general are unable to assimilate it from this source; they must absorb it, along with the minor nutrient elements, from the substratum.

Through electrical activity in the upper atmosphere, small amounts of nitrogen become united with other elements and are brought down in the rain. Some of the microscopic algae, when blown or washed into a life-free area, can obtain sufficient nitrogen from the rain water permeating the mineral substratum to grow, reproduce, and spread there. The same is true of the curious structures known as lichens. These are combinations of two sorts of plants—a fungus which makes up the bulk of the mass, and an alga whose microscopic cells are enmeshed in the filamentous fungus tissue. They thrive in a variety of habitats, the only requisite seeming to be that mineral nutrients be especially small in amount; and they can withstand the blistering heat of tropical deserts as well as the congealing cold of arctic and antarctic regions.

A few sorts of micro-organisms, belonging to the group known as slime- or blue-green-algae, are able to assimilate gaseous nitrogen, and if they reach a life-free area they can grow there especially rapidly. When individuals of any of these groups of organisms die, the compounds into which they have built the absorbed nutrients accumulate; and then another group of micro-organisms comes into the picture, namely the bacteria. Unlike the algae, these obtain their carbon and energy from preformed compounds, so can grow in the absence of light, utilizing the algal residues. Some of them get their nitrogen from the same source, others can assimilate it from the air. They build up, among the mineral particles, brown to black carbon-nitrogen compounds known collectively as humus, thereby developing a soil. The organisms taking part in this process are classed as pioneer plants. Though individually minute, they multiply so rapidly and in such prodigious numbers that their aggregate effect is large.

Newly developed bodies of water may be as devoid of life as the land areas thus far considered. In them, too, pioneer algae and bacteria will proceed to build up complex carbon-nitrogen compounds, the humus formed mingling with sand or mud on the bottom of the pond or lake.

Spores and seeds of more highly organized and massive plants will of course be reaching life-free areas all the time, but until an adequate supply of nitrogen is available they are unable to get started growing there. Once the pioneer micro-organisms have supplied this lack, the larger plants can proceed to colonize these areas. The earliest of the invaders are often mosses or liverworts, since they can get along with minimal supplies of nutrients. They are the higher-plant pioneers.

Colonization by new plants begins as soon as an area is barely able to support their life. As their individuals die, more and more plant-tissue constituents become available for the ever active bacteria and fungi to turn into humus. The first result may be improvement of the site, until the maximum luxuriance of any one sort of plant is attained. Ultimately, however, the accumulation of residues may lead to diminution in vigor and falling off of growth activity.

Grasses and forbs (i.e., herbs other than grasses) may next colonize the area, suppressing if not destroying the earlier established mosses. They too at first improve conditions for their growth, later decrease in vigor. Shrubs are likely to come in next, repeating the process of replacement of previous occupants. And finally, if the climate is suitable, a stately forest may come to occupy what was originally a lifeless wasteland.

The process just described is termed succession. If it starts on dry land, the series of stages is classed as a xerosere; if on a body of water, a hydrosere. In either case a stage is reached sooner or later in which no further change of plant cover occurs; this is called the climax. What types of plants will make up this final vegetation cover depends on the soil and climate of a given area. In working out plans for the best utilization of tracts of land, it is essential for the ecologist to ascertain what stage in the succession has been attained, and what nature's climax there is likely to be.

There are innumerable variations in the details of succession from one place to another. All the stages may telescope into one, as in semideserts, where climax shrubbery comes in as soon as the pioneer micro-organisms have furnished a minimum of nitrogen. Or the process may not go beyond the grass stage, as in prairie lands. Again, the climax plants may be destroyed by parasites, by fire, or by some of the activities of man, who is so eminently successful in disturbing natural processes. Then the succession has to start over again from some earlier stage. In any case, so important is the ascertainment of what nature tends to do in any given area that ecologists are continually observing and placing on record the successional details in many parts of the earth.

How long a time is required for climax vegetation to develop depends on circumstances. In especially favorable situations a hundred years may be enough, in bleak or unstable places a thousand or more. How long a climax, once developed, will persist is somewhat in dispute. Some ecologists hold that, given stable environmental conditions, it will maintain itself indefinitely. Living nature, however, seems to thrive on change, so perhaps degeneration followed by destruction and then by rejuvenation is the fate of what appears to us to be permanent climax vegetation.

In the course of the above discussion various environmental factors have been casually mentioned. Ecologists give much attention to the measurement and evaluation of the significance of these factors. Since life cannot exist without water, studies of the moisture content of both substratum and atmosphere, and the rate at which it evaporates from the one to the other, are highly important. The adaptations to their environment in this respect which are shown by plants are of interest. Waterlilies have canals in their stalks through which air can reach their roots, while cacti have fleshy tissue in which water can be stored during rainless periods of 'months' or years' duration, and so on. What sorts of plants will invade a given life-free area may be determined largely by the moisture available there. Plants vary in their rate of transpiration, that is, the movement of water from the roots where it is absorbed to the surfaces of exposed organs, where it evaporates; and the lower the rate, the drier the habitat they will occupy.

Light is fundamentally important because most plants need its stimulus to build the carbon from atmospheric carbon dioxide into their tissues. Extensive measurements of light intensity in various habitats have accordingly been made by ecologists. Some plants thrive in dim light, as under a dense forest canopy or even in a shallow cave, while others need full sunlight. Forest trees differ widely in the ability of their seedlings to develop in the shade of the parents, a matter of considerable practical importance. In recent years it has also been observed that seasonal changes of day length have a profound influence on the development of flowers and seeds in many species. Light relationships may, then, restrict the migration of plants from one area to another, as well as affect the sequence of successional stages.

Temperature likewise has much to do with plant growth, and gets measured and evaluated by ecologists. While a few sorts of algae and lichens can withstand extreme contrasts, most plants thrive only over more or less restricted ranges. Horticulturists are well aware of the need of protecting plants native to southern climes against winter's cold; and in the discussion of the cultivation of wild flowers in earlier pages of this book, emphasis has been placed on the less familiar fact that those of northern range often need protection against excessive summer heat. The extremes of temperature to which a given area is subject, then, are of importance in restricting the ability of individual species to become established in that area. In addition to the temperature of the air, that of the soil needs consideration, for it affects the biological and chemical processes there.

The character of the substratum is, finally, a highly influential ecological factor, for into it extend the roots and other absorbing organs of plants. As already pointed out, an assemblage of rock fragments becomes suitable for the growth of ordinary plants only after pioneer micro-organisms have developed usable nitrogen compounds there, creating a soil. Many other substances needed by plants are also obtained from the soil, notably calcium, potassium, iron, phosphorus, sulfur, and minute amounts of still more. Absence of any of these in available form will prevent occupancy of an area by incoming species; the development of humus tends, however, to increase the availability of most of them.

One of the most important features of the substratum in connection with availability of nutrients is the reaction—that is, the acidity or alkalinity. The situation in this respect can be ascertained by the use of indicators—dyes which change their colors under the influence of reaction. Some species of plants will not thrive in an area where the acidity of the soil or water is too low, other species if it is too high; the observed preferences of most of the wild flowers treated here are given under the heading Habitat.

Rock fragments are in general neutral in reaction—neither acid nor alkaline. Rain water dissolves bases from them, however, leaving a more or less acid residue. Plant debris is itself somewhat acid, and when it is slowly and incompletely disintegrated by the action of micro-organisms, the humus formed may increase in acidity, becoming peat. When, on the other hand, conditions favor more rapid and thorough decomposition, the product is neutral leafmold or muck.

In regions of ample rainfall, such as those covered in this book, the bases dissolved from mineral and humus materials are dissolved and carried downward, so that soils tend to become acid at the surface and neutral at moderate depth. A partial overturn may occur where there is some peculiarity of circulation of the underground water; but on the whole there is in ordinary soils a definite decrease in acidity downward.

Two corollaries to this acidity-gradient phenomenon deserve attention. First, seeds, which rarely reach any considerable depth, germinate in a medium more acid than that favored by the adult plant into which they develop. Second, when it is desired to ascertain the degree of soil acidity at which a given species is observed to thrive, tests must be made at the roots of the plant itself, not merely of soil from somewhere in the vicinity. The data given in the text for individual wild flowers were obtained with this situation in view. Some species, to be sure, are relatively indifferent to the factor of reaction, but enough of them do show apparent preferences to make such information useful. Thousands of tests with indicators have been made at places throughout our area where the species were observed to be thriving and reproducing, which constitutes the best indication of favorable reaction.

In the discussion of succession on a preceding page, certain sorts of plants were mentioned as though they were growing alone. Actually, however, two or more organisms usually tend to occupy an area simultaneously, and must manage to get along with one another. The phenomenon of living together is termed symbiosis, and the assemblage of different organisms a community. The study of plant and animal communities is one of the major fields of ecological research.

Plant communities can be regarded as separated into layers. Thus in a well-developed forest there will be tall trees and low trees; tall, low, and prostrate shrubs; tall, low, creeping herbs; ground-covering mosses, lichens, algae; and of course the ever present soil-inhabiting micro-organisms. There may also be plants which depend on one another for support; air plants and various lesser sorts grow on the stems or branches of the larger ones, and vines climb on those with firmer tissues. Most communities will of course be simpler in make-up than this, but the general relations are the same.

Whenever two or more organisms invade the same territory, competition will arise between them. If they are of the same species, or members of the same layer, the result will be reduction of the number of individuals to the point where those that remain are able to obtain sufficient nourishment for their existence. Between the occupants of different layers the relations may be more complex.

The members of the higher layers capture most of the light energy, so that those of lower layers have to adapt themselves to lesser amounts of this factor. Also, the more massive a plant the more extensive will be its root system, and the more moisture and nutrients will it absorb from the substratum; smaller plants, accordingly, may have difficulty in obtaining enough of these. Many of the wild flowers treated in this book belong to the low herb layer of forest communities, and may thrive better in cultivation than they do in the wild because of relief from these competitions for light, moisture, and nutrients. On the other hand, some occur in nature in grassland, and may themselves dominate the community. (Instead of competing, the trees may help nourish the wild flowers under them by the falling leaves and other litter.)

The classification of plant communities is discussed in detail in Chapter IV of the standard American work, *Plant Ecology,* by Weaver and Clements (2d edition, 1938). As therein recorded, ecologists term the major unit of climax vegetation a formation. In the region covered by the present book, the principal formation is deciduous forest, with small areas of coniferous forest and grassland, the latter toward the west side, where the climate is relatively dry, and at least in primeval times fires swept over frequently enough to keep trees from getting well started.

A formation comprises two or more major subdivisions known to ecologists as associations. Each of these is designated by the names of two or more plants seemingly characteristic of it, and so conspicuous that they may be considered to be dominants. In the eastern part of our region there are among others chestnut oak-hemlock, pin oak-red maple, and white oak-tulip-tree associations. Around the southern Great Lakes a beech-sugar maple association is highly developed, and further south a series of oak-hickory associations. The grassland formation to the west includes big bluestem-Indian grass, needle grass-wheat grass, and various other associations.

These associations are further divisible into consociations, characterized by a single dominant; on the other hand, they may be separable into societies, made up of subdominant but conspicuous species. Wild flowers such as May-apple, spring-beauty, and woodland phlox often grow in such profusion as to constitute well-marked forest-floor societies.

An association, then, is not as sometimes supposed a list of plants which happen to grow near one another, and attempts to base ecological inferences or horticultural practices on such lists will lead into difficulties. One such published list included, along with a miscellaneous series of wild flowers, water-lilies, cat-tails, and hawthorns in a "pond association." Actually the waterlilies undoubtedly grew in deep water, the cat-tails in shallow water, and the hawthorns on a nearby dry bank. Their ecology and horticultural requirements are widely divergent. Again, it was once inferred that since trailing-arbutus grows in southern New Jersey it belongs in a "salt-marsh association." It doesn't.

Instead of actively competing, plants of different growth forms may actually help one another, at least indirectly. Higher ones shelter the occupants of the forest floor from heat, drought, etc., although the most important interrelationship concerns the matter of nutrition. The wide-ranging root systems of the larger plants gather nutrients from far and wide in the substratum, concentrating these in the individual to which they belong. When debris from the latter falls to the ground, and the ever active micro-organisms proceed to work it over, these nutrients are made available to smaller plants in greater amount than if they had to depend on the foraging ability of their own roots.

A special case of competitive symbiosis, where the organisms are in close and permanent contact, is the phenomenon of parasitism. A few sorts of flowering plants, such as the broom-rapes, dodders, and mistletoes, obtain much or all of their nutrition by direct absorption from a host. The majority of parasites, however, belong to the plant groups of fungi and bacteria.

One widespread representative of this sort of relationship has already been mentioned, namely, the structures known as lichens. In these, micro-organisms, mostly green algae, are parasitized by certain types of fungi unable to exist under any other conditions. The alga assimilates carbon from the air, nitrogen and mineral nutrients from the traces which come down in the rain or dissolve out from the substratum; the fungus absorbs the compounds into which these are built.

Of particular interest are the mycorhizas. Here fungi invest the roots of forest trees, and in a few cases smaller plants, such as the orchids. While the fungus gains nutrients from the host, it also aids the latter in obtaining moisture and nitrogen from the substratum, so the relationship is by no means a one-sided one. Another sort of root parasitism is the root nodule characteristic of the legume family of flowering plants. In this case bacteria occupy swellings on the roots and absorb nutrients there; but as they can assimilate nitrogen from the air, they contribute to the nutrition of their host also. When they die, the nitrogen they have accumulated passes into the soil humus, and not only the legumes which supported them but also other plants which chance to grow near by will benefit.

How animals fit into plant communities remains to be considered. Since all animals depend on plants either directly or indirectly for their food, the relationship is in the broad sense one of parisitism. There are, however, interesting deviations. In the insectivorous plants, insects attracted by color or fragrance may drown in water held in the hollow leaves of pitcher-plants, become entrapped by viscid secretions on the leaves of sundews, get sucked into bladders on the submerged stems of bladderworts, and so on. The softer parts of the insects are then digested and absorbed, nourishing the plant. Such plants are accordingly able to grow in especially sterile soils, low in available nitrogen and phosphorus. In these cases where animals eat plants or plants consume animals, the symbiosis is to be classed as antagonistic, in that one of the organisms concerned is injured or destroyed. On the other hand, just as in the plant communities of which the interrelationships have been discussed on preceding pages, there can be mutual benefit in relations between the two groups of organisms.

Of the greatest interest is the reciprocal relationship concerned in the cross-pollination of flowers by insects or in some cases by birds. Reproduction in many plants is favored by having pollen, which contains male protoplasm, move from one flower to another, and in the latter reach the stigma, the viscid tip of the carpel, permitting fertilization of the ovules containing female protoplasm. In cases where the flowers are inconspicuous the pollen is buoyant, and gets carried by the wind from one flower to another. Such pollen has to be produced in large amounts to have a reasonable chance of reaching the proper spot.

In most showy or fragrant flowers the pollen is heavy and sticky. Insects attracted by the conspicuous features come to feed on the nectar—the sweet liquid secreted in the depths of the flower. All unknowingly they brush against the anthers, and some of the pollen adheres to them. Now, once an insect gets a taste of some agreeable food, it instinctively seeks for more of the same. This results in its visiting a succession of flowers of a given species. Some of the pollen is then likely to get rubbed off upon stigmas, and the sexual reproductive process can proceed. Because of the greater certainty of success in such cases, only relatively small amounts of pollen need be produced.

The adaptations of flowers to visits by definite sorts of insects are remarkable. Flowers with open throat or short tube and of yellow color are visited by certain species of bees; other bees may be attracted by fragrances, irrespective of color. Since bees alight while feeding, the texture of such flowers is usually firm, and the anthers and stigmas are deep-seated. Flowers of similar shapes but of bronzy hues and rank or putrid odors attract flies instead, corresponding to the tendency of these insects to feed on decaying animal matter of similar colors and odors.

Flowers with long slender tubes attract butterflies and moths, which have long probosces capable of reaching the deep-lying nectar. Since these insects hover while feeding, the anthers and stigmas often protrude beyond the flower face, and can thus be contacted by the insects. Colors and odors are significant here also. Butterflies favor pink or lavender, although if the fragrance appeals to them they may visit flowers of other hues. On the other hand moths, which fly chiefly at dusk, can find flowers best if they are white or pale, and if the fragrance is especially powerful. Hummingbirds, which have long bills and also hover while feeding, visit flowers of similar shapes, but they prefer red coloring.

The various shapes and colors of the flowers illustrated in this book can be correlated with insect visitors along the lines of the above discussion. A nature lover can spend many enjoyable hours observing the sorts of insects which visit individual species of flowers, what parts of their bodies collect the pollen, and how it gets onto the stigmas.

A final word may be added as to the bearing of the foregoing observations on flowers in relation to insects upon the problem of pollen allergy or "hay fever." Contrary to widespread popular belief, such studies demonstrate that this illness is caused only by the lightweight, wind-borne pollens of inconspicuous flowers such as those of grasses and ragweeds. Showy flowers—including, it must be emphasized, goldenrods and roses, so often mistakenly blamed—attract insects, which means that their pollen is heavy; it therefore cannot reach human nostrils and so does not cause hay fever.

APPENDIX 4

Wild Flower Literature

A. REFERENCE WORKS

BRITTON, N. L., and BROWN, A. *Illustrated Flora of the Northern United States.* 3 vols. 2d edition, 1913. New York: Charles Scribner's Sons. New edition in preparation, 1947.[1]

ROBINSON, B. L., and FERNALD, M. L. *Gray's New Manual of Botany.* 7th edition, 1908. New York: American Book Co. New edition in preparation, 1947.

B. RECENT REGIONAL FLORAS

DOLE, E. J., et al. *Flora of Vermont.* 3d edition. Burlington: Free Press Printing Co., 1937.

TATNALL, R. R. *Flora of Delaware and the Eastern Shore.* Wilmington: Society of Natural History of Delaware, 1946.

DEAM, C. C. *Flora of Indiana.* Indianapolis: State Department of Conservation, 1940.

JONES, G. N. *Flora of Illinois.* Notre Dame, Indiana: The American Midland Naturalist, 1945.

RYDBERG, P. A. *Flora of the Prairies and Plains of Central North America.* New York: New York Botanical Garden, 1932.

C. FIELD GUIDES

CUTHBERT, M. J. *How to Know the Spring Flowers.* Dubuque, Iowa: William C. Brown Co., 1943.

GATES, F. C. *Wild Flowers in Kansas.* Topeka: State Board of Agriculture, 1934.

GLEASON, H. A. *Plants of the Vicinity of New York.* New York: New York Botanical Garden, 1935.

SCHAFFNER, J. H. *Field Manual of the Flora of Ohio.* Columbus: R. C. Adams Co., 1928.

SCHUYLER-MATHEWS, F. *Field Book of American Wild Flowers.* New York: G. P. Putnam's Sons, 1902; also several subsequent editions.

STEYERMARK, J. A. *Spring Flora of Missouri.* St. Louis: Missouri Botanical Garden, 1940.

---

[1] The nomenclature of this Guide approaches that of the latter.

INDEX